ACRL PUBLICATIONS IN LIBRARIANSHIP NO. 64

Transforming Information Literacy Programs

Intersecting Frontiers of Self, Library Culture, and Campus Community

CARROLL WETZEL WILKINSON AND
COURTNEY BRUCH, EDITORS

W9-CCD-563

Association of College and Research Libraries
A division of the American Library Association
Chicago, 2012

The paper used in this publication meets the minimum requirements of American National Standard for Information Sciences–Permanence of Paper for Printed Library Materials, ANSI Z39.48-1992. ∞

Library of Congress Cataloging-in-Publication Data
Transforming information literacy programs : intersecting frontiers of self, library culture, and campus community / edited by Carroll Wilkinson and Courtney Bruch.

     pages cm. — (ACRL publications in librarianship ; 64)
   Includes bibliographical references and index.
   ISBN 978-0-8389-8603-5 (pbk.) — ISBN 978-0-8389-9412-2 (kindle) — ISBN 978-0-8389-9413-9 (epdf)
   1. Information literacy—Study and teaching (Higher) 2. Wilkinson, Carroll Wetzel, editor of compilation. 3. Bruch, Courtney, editor of compilation.
   ZA3075.T73 2011
   025.5'2777—dc23

                                    2011050153

Printed in the United States of America.

16 15 14 13 12   5 4 3 2 1

Table of Contents

Section IV: Charting Next Steps   179

Preface and Acknowledgment

Information literacy is now an established worldwide movement and one of its prominent advocacy organizations in the United States, the National Forum on Information Literacy, recently celebrated its 20th anniversary. President Barack Obama issued a proclamation in October 2009 declaring Information Literacy Awareness Month. Using a new decade beginning with 2009 as a marker[1], this book aims to broadly analyze current and future issues for information literacy programming development in academic libraries.

This book is based upon two assumptions. First, commitment to new forms of collaboration that bring about a positive evolution of information literacy programming in the decade ahead is imperative. Secondly, information literacy, and the many words and phrases that are used to define its meaning, demands deep and sustainable social reform in academic libraries to address our workplace, campus, and the nation's educational needs. In 2007 Gibson referred to a cultural shift needed for "deep, enterprise-wide level" change.[2] We hope this book will serve as a catalyst for that shift by revealing frontier options and strategies in information literacy program development for transformational change. The progress we envision cannot happen until a critical mass of librarians challenge underlying assumptions about librarian authority and contributions to educational agendas.

Our friendship and working relationship emerged as a product of participation in the 2007 Winnipeg ACRL Immersion Program Track. The seed for this book was a conversation, though we had no idea of its outcome at the time, about unexpected obstacles we encountered in information literacy programming within two different higher education environments. Two years after our invaluable Immersion experience, we returned to the American Library Association Conference to present a poster (http://systems.lib.wvu.edu/files/2FrontierLibrary7-7-09.pdf) about mixed successes in information literacy program development. Program attendees and Immersion faculty urged us to continue exploring the subject of resistance and creation of sustainable change as it relates to information literacy programming. We want to especially thank Craig Gibson of Ohio State University Libraries (and luckily for us, one of our Immersion faculty members) for his determined encouragement throughout the process of proposing and writing this book.

The book raises a broad scope of themes including the intellectual, psychological, cultural, definitional and structural issues that academic instruction librarians face in higher education environments. The chapters in this book represent the voices of eight instruction librarians, including two Immersion faculty members. Other perspectives come from a library dean, a library school faculty member, a library coordinator of school library media certification programs, and a director emerita from a School of Education.

The book is broken into four sections:

SECTION I OUTLINING CURRENT BOUNDARIES

Bruch and Wilkinson review information literacy literature of the past five years and provide an overview and analysis of the complex mixture of issues that information literacy librarians face. Seymour reports on an ethnographic study of nine librarians in two states who are living and working with those issues. This section stresses the need for exploration of the fundamental values and assumptions currently associated with information literacy culture. Additionally, it makes suggestions for strategic action to enrich the evolving culture.

SECTION II FRONTIERS OF SELF

This section provides two frameworks for considering information literacy. Elmborg explores the intellectual meaning of learning while Kopriva examines a historical perspective on educational reform in the field of librarianship. Both chapters analyze issues of authority and power and offer opportunities for conversations surrounding individual professional transformation.

SECTION III FORTIFYING INSTITUTIONAL PARTNERSHIPS

This section explores key institutional issues facing information literacy librarians and the programs they develop. Zald and Millet illustrate leadership challenges instruction librarians face from within the academy and demonstrate the use of assessment as a catalyst for cultural and educational change. Schroeder examines librarian perception of the relationship between critical thinking and information literacy, discussing the implications of shifting vocabulary to fit environments and culture. Carr argues for curricular integration and vertical alignment of information literacy throughout the educational K–20 spectrum, suggesting information literacy and library ecosystems offer a shared pathway to foster lifelong learning.

SECTION IV CHARTING NEXT STEPS

Important strategic actions for library workplaces are discussed in this section. Cunningham and Donovan respond to the current invisibility of librarians in education, encouraging teaching librarians to describe and document their educational efforts. Seamans argues for taking ownership of the important role librarians play in student learning and accentuates the imperative to demonstrate that role to campus leaders.

Armed with new understanding of the frontiers of self, library culture, and campus communities, readers can talk to others and begin vital and exciting initiatives to shape the future of information literacy development. Transformation does not happen without risk, persistence, and courage; yet it can start with something as simple as an open conversation between two librarians who both care about solving a difficult problem. As editors, we offer readers a challenge: do not shy away from this opportunity. Join with us to explore the issues that are holding progress back, solve some of the issues using discussion here as a foundation, and join with colleagues to lead in your educational communities.

Notes

1. The ALA Presidential Committee on Information Literacy initially released a report and recommendations for information literacy in 1989.
2. Gibson, Craig. 2007. "Information Literacy and IT Fluency: Convergences and Divergences." *Reference and Users Services Quarterly* 46(3): 24.

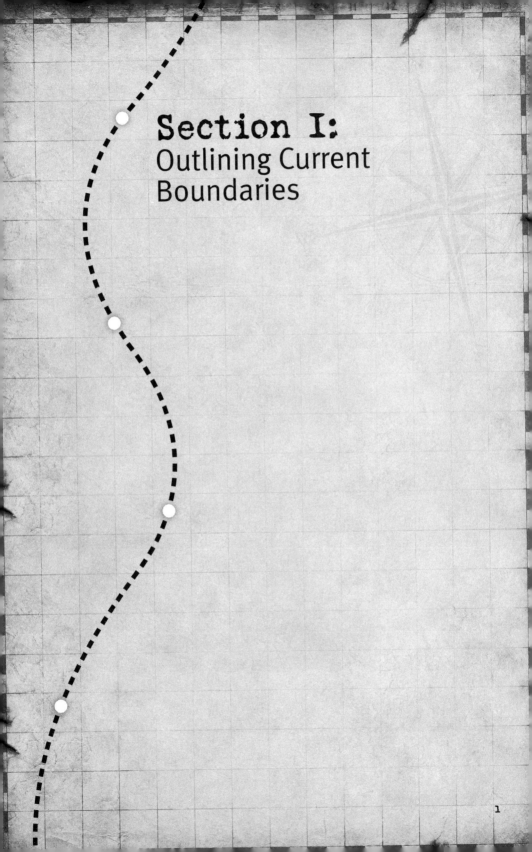

Section I:
Outlining Current Boundaries

1

Surveying Terrain, Clearing Pathways

Courtney Bruch and Carroll Wetzel Wilkinson

OVERVIEW

Over the past two decades, academic librarians have worked to integrate information literacy instruction into their libraries. As a result, the last twenty years have produced a dazzling array of educational achievement in academic librarian practice and research. Yet, despite these accomplishments, many libraries are still struggling to create a comprehensive information literacy culture. The substantial library and institutional transformation it takes to embrace comprehensive information literacy culture is complex and differs according to institution. As a result, some academic libraries are still in the beginning stages of addressing not only the evolved educational role of the academic librarian, but also the disconnects that accompany a profession going through expansion and reform (Ondrusek 2008, 58–61). The authors believe cutting through the thicket of rhetoric, attitudes, and beliefs about information literacy allows for investigation of the remaining frontier issues that, to us, cry out for attention.

This chapter asks readers to consider academic librarian dharma in addition to reviewing the recent library and information science (LIS) literature, acknowledging the accomplishments of librarians working with information literacy. The chapter explores unfinished work including challenges associated with creating information literacy culture. The authors use those challenges and lived experience to identify underlying issues, specifically immunity and resistance to change on the information literacy frontier. The steps necessary to create an information literacy culture differ according to institution; therefore, the "Understanding What is Possible" section offers a variety of change techniques that can be applied by those interested in expanding or experimenting with change in their existing programs. Finally, the authors identify points of action, many of which are explored more deeply in following chapters, to collaboratively transform information literacy programming development. Comprehensive information literacy culture depends upon library leaders' and key campus stakeholders' ability to examine and address issues that create discord surrounding information literacy. Intentionally using interdisciplinary organizational change scholarship and practices offer pathways for sustained vitality of information literacy programming in the upcoming decade.

I. LIBRARIAN DHARMA

Dharma can be defined several ways: "essential quality or character" or "virtue" or "conformity to religious law, custom or duty." Reference to the dharma of any field is made to convey its intrinsic nature or core essence. One immediate, present-day example of dharma is the duty of police officers to "protect and serve" the public. Many professions are guided by professional organizations that express member values and expectations in guiding documents including mission statements or ethical codes. These guiding documents provide a glimpse of the profession's dharma. Most professions have their own unique, collective dharma, often sanctioned by professional associations which oversee and support the affairs of the members. A more formal example of professional dharma is from the National Education Association's (NEA) (2011) Code of Ethics. The Code is a document that serves as a statement of principles to educate, promote high quality work and strengthen public perception of the profession and its dharma.

Academic librarians have a professional association, the Association of College and Research Libraries (ACRL), a division of the American Library Association (ALA), which provides leadership and oversight to the community of librarians served. Like the NEA members, librarians adhere to statements of their principles, such as a Code of Ethics (American Library Association 2008) and Bill of Rights (American Library Association 1996) that reflect *their* dharma. Ultimately, these documents spell professional librarian dharma: the provision and protection of fair and equal access to information, respect for intellectual property, privacy rights, and firm resistance to censorship. Neither ALA's Code of Ethics nor the Bill makes a statement about librarians' responsibility for education. Dole et al (2000) determined the trend amongst librarians was to include information literacy in their values. Information literacy was also highly valued in an ALA Midwinter forum entitled "Enduring Values for the New Millennium". (Branch 1998, 176–7). Although the content of their observations revolve around intellectual freedom and social responsibility, Symons and Stoffle (1998, 56–8) favor identifying and regularly invoking core values of librarianship to gauge individual actions and activities. They claim the lack of clearly established professional values leads to problems when conflicting standards emerge. This revelation, or lack of consensus when defining librarian values and dharma, may explain some of the underlying tension in our field about information literacy program development and librarian roles in classroom instruction.

Despite the absence of references to educational duties in guiding documents, a quick review of library literature indicates a long history of educational imperatives amongst academic librarians. "In the U.S., in the late nineteenth century, public librarians emphasized an educational role for libraries; in the 1870s, for example reference service and its associated teaching function gained recognition as a legitimate purpose of libraries" (Gibson 2008, 14). In their chapter "History of Information Literacy," Grassian and Kaplowitz outline library involvement in activist instructional efforts from the first ALA conference, to the modern library instruction movement of the late 60's and early 70's, to the information literacy movement of the late 20th century, noting Melvil Dewey, "the library is a school, and the librarian in the highest sense is a teacher" (2009, 9). Gibson (2008, 10–23) traces the history of the information literacy movement from the conception of the term in 1974 to the normative definition of information literacy, and the more recent creation of best practices for information literacy programming. Both of these readings indicate increasing librarian involvement in educational endeavors accompanied by a proud history of playing instrumental roles in advocating for library-related instruction, and later, information literacy recognition.

II. INFORMATION LITERACY SCHOLARSHIP LITERATURE REVIEW

In the 1990s, Barr and Tagg identified a paradigm shift in the undergraduate higher education environment. They maintained the traditional and dominant "instruction paradigm", or the creation of complex structures in order to deliver instruction, is shifting to a "learning paradigm", in which the mission evolves from instruction to "that of producing learning with every student by whatever means work best" (Barr and Tagg 1995, 13). Around the same time, academic libraries began to move bibliographic instruction (derived from a teaching paradigm model) to information literacy (derived from a learning paradigm model) instruction. Many librarians agree information literacy is a complementary component to the learning paradigm shift, requiring a restructuring of the academic libraries' involvement in defining the "formation of the intellectual experience of the student" (Owusu-Ansah 2001, 282) Reflective of this trend, recent literature emphasizes the exciting exploration of situating information literacy within research and curricula conversations as well as the imperative for honing teaching, instructional design, and assessment skills.

Situating Information Literacy in Academic Traditions and Intellectual Rigor

Library instruction has been slow "to develop a strong practitioner theory base to inform its work, and the bridge between learning theory and information literacy has yet to be completely built" (Elmborg 2005, 6).[1] The information environment students navigate daily to complete a variety of work, personal, and school-related tasks has changed dramatically over the past decade. As a result, academic librarians have begun a discussion about revisiting the definition of information literacy (discussed both later in this chapter and in subsequent chapters in this book) and ACRL's Information Literacy Standards. Nonetheless, approaches for linking information literacy to academic traditions and sociocultural perspectives continue to mature. Some instructional librarians have accepted the paradigm shift and see themselves as full participants in the educational process (Ondrusek 2008, 58–61) and as a result, librarians have begun to better examine how the profession contributes not only to student learning but also to learning and research applications beyond our field.

Information Seeking Process

This conversation could not be complete without mention of Kuhlthau's early research on the Information Seeking Process, developed in the 1980's and refined in the 1990's. Her findings conclude the Information Search Process occurs in six stages: initiation, selection, exploration, formulation, collection, presentation and the ability of the affective domain to influence student ability to organize information (Kuhlthau 2004). Researchers (Budd 2008, 321; Elmborg 2005, 9–10; and Ondrusek 2008, 63) have argued that the Information Search Process cannot be easily extended to pedagogical methods. Kuhlthau et al (2008) contend that affective, cognitive and physical experience of users comprise a theoretical and explanatory framework for designing user centered information services and systems, and timing interventions in order to support students in the research process.

Phenomenological Cognitive Action

In contrast to Kuhlthau, Budd (2008, 323–4) defines Phenomenological Cognitive Action as "the intentional effort to learn and to know, grounded in the mind's ability to employ logic and reason, within the context of recognizing that one's own perceptions are engaged in a dialogue with those of others," and argues that this approach completes the "pedagogical necessity of locating the intersection between materialism and constructivism." Budd (2009) believes requiring students to reflect on their experiences in the world, through Phenomenological Cognitive Action, can serve as a means to reconfigure both library instruction programs and sessions.

Praxis-based Pedagogy

Jacobs (2008), Elmborg (2005) and others look toward composition and rhetoric's critical literacy and praxis[2]-based pedagogy for inspiration. Because teaching information literacy can never be perfected due to malleable students, content and situations, librarians should turn to creative, reflective dialogue with both librarian and faculty colleagues. A praxis approach, coupled with reflective, critical habits of mind would allow practitioners to successfully explore how information literacy can be infused in the classroom, reference situations, collection development, committee work, and other organizations in order to best address librarians' roles within systemic educational endeavors.

Phenomenography

Meanwhile, librarians from around the world are examining phenomenography and ontology for pedagogy that fosters lifelong learning skills. Australian researcher Bruce introduced phenomenography, or "a methodology that elicits people's conceptions or experiences on a particular phenomenon" (Ondrusek 2008, 65), to librarianship in the late 1990s. She emphasized a "holistic evaluation of people's experience of information literacy as an aspect of learning" (Andretta 2007, 155) as opposed to assessing skills such as those named in the ACRL Standards. More librarians (Maybee 2007; Maybee 2009; Andretta 2007) are beginning to consider phenomenography as a viable framework. Most recently, Bruce (2008) has defined "informed learning" as how we interact with and use information as we learn. She calls for a research agenda to examine informed learning in different, real-life contexts.

Ontology and Practice Theory

In her article, "Framing Information Literacy as an Information Practice: Site Ontology and Practice Theory," Lloyd (2010, 253) argues information literacy should be examined through a sociocultural lens as it "is not constituted by a single way of knowing about information but is a product of the many ways of knowing, that interconnect to form the practice." She highlights four examples, or activities, in which information literacy practices "produce, reproduce and maintain the cultural identities, practices and performances" within a particular social group. (254) Viewing information literacy in this manner allows librarians and researchers an opportunity to understand the complexity and variation of information literacy practices across a range of disciplines and different environments.

These approaches reveal librarians' deeper involvement in educational and research endeavors; particularly as it relates to helping individuals or groups of people make meaning of research and the process it entails. All authors indicate the need for further study to follow up on their work and we will surely see development and application of the ideas in the future.

Developing Teaching and Instructional Design Expertise

Much of the research conducted by practicing librarians explores how academic librarians can hone their teaching and instructional design skills. Walters (2006) reviewed instructional improvement in library programs and linked that notion to instructional improvement in higher education. He encouraged the design of research studies to emphasize best teaching practices. The publication *Communications in Information Literacy* dedicated a column encouraging librarians to develop statements of teaching philosophy designed to foster reflection about teaching while simultaneously serving as a reminder of priorities and values. (Zauha 2008, 64–6) Meanwhile Booth (2011, xvi–xvii) advocates the development of instructional literacy, or "the combination of skills and knowledge that facilitates effective, self-aware, and learner focused educational practice." An informal review of library literature of the past five years reveals a multitude of pilot projects and case studies, all of which indicate 21st century librarians are exploring how to best facilitate information literacy learning in everyday practice.

Everyday practice has delved into a new frontier: offering instruction digitally and combining digital instruction with reference services. For example, Oud (2009) recently linked research in cognitive psychology and education to the effective use of multimedia in learning to create guidelines for tutorials produced by academic librarians. In his article, "A Portal to Student Learning: What Instruction Librarians Can Learn from Video Game Design", Schiller (2008) suggests instruction librarians can benefit from looking at new media, particularly video games, to enhance information literacy instruction. He presents a methodology for analyzing pedagogical techniques used in gaming design in order to potentially link gaming scenarios to learning situations and to relate information literacy instruction to students familiar with gaming.

Meanwhile, Desai and Graves (2006) analyzed instant message (IM) reference transcripts from Morris Library at the Southern Illinois University Carbondale in order to determine how instruction was facilitated during IM reference transactions. They determined it would be difficult to measure acquisition of information literacy standards yet noted commercial virtual reference providers and other communication formats were expanding and offering new features that have the potential to enrich instruction. Librarians will continue to examine these and other techniques as avenues for delivering instruction in the future.

Accountability and Campus Contributions through Assessment

Driven by demands for accountability, assessment has become an important topic amongst institutions of higher learning and the academic librarians that work in them. Through assessment, colleges and universities have a lens to view the effectiveness of individual and collective instruction and are able to provide students an opportunity to demonstrate learning. Of greater importance to information literacy programming, assessment has the potential to provide administrators, librarians and faculty with the evidence needed to modify or expand curriculum. Assessment can be a powerful argument to include information literacy programming as part of the curriculum. Gilchrist (2009) provides a concise review of the development of educational assessment as it pertains to libraries and information literacy. She argues that writing, research and practices in libraries coincided with and responded to assessment trends in higher education. Others (Oakleaf 2009; Oakleaf, and Kaske, 2009) have advocated librarian involvement in writing assessment plans for information literacy in higher education. Meanwhile, Gilchrist and Zald (2008) have presented examples for developing learning outcomes and assessment for a variety of settings ranging from the 50-minute library session to programmatic levels. In the spring of 2009, ACRL created a working group to consider an initiative on the value of libraries. The result is a comprehensive research report (ACRL 2010, 11) with the stated intention of providing "1) a clear view of the current state of the literature on value of libraries within an institutional context, 2) suggestions for immediate "Next Steps" in the demonstration of academic library value, and 3) a "Research Agenda" for articulating academic library value."

III. CHALLENGES ASSOCIATED WITH CREATING INFORMATION LITERACY CULTURE

Despite all of these advancements and achievements, the literature of the past five years also reveals increasing evidence of challenges fueled by cultural conflicts associated with the creation of a comprehensive information literacy culture. A quick appraisal of recent library literature might indicate library leaders have addressed information literacy programming in some way and the challenge of information literacy curricula integration is being met. Yet, this type of integration is not happening in all academic libraries. Ideal curricula integration includes objective measures such as meaningful learning outcomes in many (or most) campus disciplines and programs, or the adoption and completion of program goals at the institutional level, in addition to a group of librarians willing to experiment with pedagogy and assessment in order to evolve and improve their teaching methods. Changing a culture on this frontier requires years of political persuasion both within and outside of the library environment simultaneously by cultivating respect of academic librarian knowledge, integrating librarians into the classroom, compelling departmental ownership of curriculum reform and rewarding innovative and authentic teaching. The stories of success commonly affiliated with information literacy emphasize teaching not "the cultural shift that is required to implement information literacy at a deep, enterprise-wide level". (Gibson 2007, 24) A frontier still exists for information literacy's credibility and resonance in many US higher education institutions. This is evident on a number of levels: national, institutional and professional.

National

Since the ALA Presidential Committee on Information Literacy defined information literacy in 1989, the concept has received much attention. Soon the National Forum on Information Literacy encouraged and supported information literacy development in both the American Association for Higher Education and the National Education Association. (Grassian and Kaplowitz 2009,14) Most recently, President Barack Obama (2009) issued a proclamation in October 2009 declaring Information Literacy Awareness Month. Unfortunately, these endorsements do not currently reflect a national imperative to teach information literacy. "Of the eight regional accrediting organizations, two of them, North Central [now Higher Learning Commission] and Northwest, lack an emphasis on information literacy or library instruction in any of their accrediting criteria" (Rollins et al 2009, 456). Saunders (2009) notes,

> Such widespread attention would seem to give information literacy a place of prominence in college and university curricula. However, lack of agreement on terminology, methods of implementation, and even dispersal of responsibilities often diverts attention from questions of program development. Thus far, institutions of higher education have been left to their own discretion about whether and how to incorporate information literacy into the curricula. (100)

It has become clear that information literacy education will not be pursued by all institutions without a national or accrediting mandate. In the absence of such requirements, librarians and faculty are often left to individual or institution collaboration initiatives. As Ondrusek (2008, 61–72) indicates, some librarians and faculty are collaborating to integrate information literacy into education; others have not been as successful.

Definitions of information literacy and similar concepts complicate matters. Information literacy as a phrase and meaningful concept has been thoroughly questioned, criticized, and revised. In their 2009 article, "Are We There Yet? The Difficult Road to Re-Create Information Literacy", Rollins et al conducted a series of surveys in order to determine roadblocks that prevented a localized group of academic libraries and their institutions from addressing information literacy as a core competency. Their findings included the need for a standard definition of information literacy and that respondents, "largely understood information literacy to be synonymous with antiquated notions of user or bibliographic instruction" (460). The authors additionally noted an "overall lack of effort to produce formal definitions for information literacy, to include information literacy in planning documents, and to firmly plant information literacy within the general education curriculum" (462). Recently Mackey and Jacobson (2011, 76) recognized the need to move beyond a skill based approach, and instead, emphasizing the development and distribution of content in different environments. These authors suggest using the term "metaliteracy" as a conceptual framework to unify all literacy formats. Bruce (2008) states, "In my involvement with the information literacy agenda...I have come to see that the term information literacy is often used to represent many concepts that should be recognized as separate" (4–5). Purdue (2003) mentions information literacy as a problematic hurdle with faculty, "In discussions that I've had with faculty from other disciplines, IL has almost always been treated with suspicion. One reason for this response is that the term "Information Literacy" is jargon, and another discipline's jargon is almost always unfriendly to outsiders." (653) Meanwhile, the Council of Independent Colleges in recent years, which still endorses ALA's definition, is hosting workshops, many involving librarians, that "no longer focus on information "literacy" but instead focus on information "fluency" within specific field of the humanities." (Richard Eckman, pers. comm. 2011)

In response, Budd (2009) has recently provided a perspective on the larger view of information literacy, suggesting librarians stop defining it narrowly and instead substitute a statement focused on central tenets of higher education. He says:

> Libraries' instructional programs are invaluable to facilitating learn-
> ing, knowledge growth, and communication. Librarians can enable
> understanding of the nature and purposes of communication, help
> students engage in dialogue with what others say, write, and show,
> and foster, through phenomenological cognitive action, student
> learning. (67)

Institutional validation cannot happen until all groups: librarians, faculty and institutional administrators see the importance of information literacy. The lack of commonly understood definitions dilutes librarian ability to communicate this importance. Furthermore, recurring issues surrounding common definitions and lack of support behind large endorse-ments trickle down to institutional challenges. If individual librarians are to create cultural and educational shifts on their respective campuses, broad definitions need to be applicable to all stakeholders. This has the potential to allow partners to do more than endorse educational efforts stemming from libraries.

Institutional
Owusu-Ansah (2001) acknowledged, "conflicts and tensions underlie the relationship between teaching faculty and academic librarians" (282). Badke (2005) confirmed that collaboration between faculty and librar-ians was not the norm, but argued for librarians to develop credibility by broadening goals through embedding information literacy credit-bearing courses within departments. In her article, "The Future of Information Literacy in Academic Libraries: a Delphi Study", Saunders (2009) estab-lished the most probable future of information literacy over the upcom-ing decade. Her study indicated, "The most heavily cited obstacle to the realization of any of the scenarios was faculty attitudes" (104–5). The study also revealed, "there is legitimate concern that neither current practitioners nor upcoming graduates are adequately prepared to adopt this role." And, "In particular if librarians hope to advise faculty on instruc-tional design and assignments or even take on a more full partnership role in instruction, they must be sure that they have learned the peda-gogical theory to support that role" (109–10). Information literacy is a product of transformative learning; and a complete paradigm shift has to be accepted institutionally by a majority of faculty members in order to slowly expand the number of departments that come on board with

curriculum reforms which would, in turn, foster sustainable consistency and alignment throughout the curriculum.

Professional

O'Connor (2009) conducted a critical analysis of information literacy documents (Presidential Committee on Information Literacy Final Report and Information Literacy Standards) in their historical context. She argues the documents emerged as a reaction for inclusion in educational reform conversations of the early 1980's. "Tying libraries and librarians directly to the educational mandates of the reform movement (and thus to funding) seemed and, perhaps, still seems critical to the survival of school and academic librarians" (80). Because these documents were created within the professional association's intensely layered structures of committees and subcommittees, the ideas they express have yet to trickle down to *all* academic librarians and all campuses across the nation. We don't intend to debate the political approach to this decision. Rather, we are interested in examining the impact this decision has had upon professional acceptance of information literacy and librarian responsibility as educators.

In his provocative article, "Information Literacy Makes All the Wrong Assumptions", Wilder (2005) disputes the benefits of embracing information literacy and instead suggests librarians should continue to focus on their disciplinary expertise as well as modeling reading and writing work at the reference desk. Wilder maintains teaching information literacy to all students would require "enormous and coordinated shifts in curricular emphases and resource allocation." (13) Six years later many academic librarians agree with Wilder. These oftentimes "silent resisters" oppose the notion of being an educator, strongly arguing they chose the field of librarianship to avoid the requirements of educating others. Library "instruction supporters" agree library instruction is a laudable endeavor. However, the idea of taking on new responsibilities such as applying learning theory and experimenting with pedagogy, especially when daily reality involves continuous change in the persistent information age, can preclude an instructional emphasis amongst library staff. Realistic librarian teaching loads and the provision of rewards for embarking upon instructional work oftentimes fall short of providing motivational incentives. This causes a situation in which librarians maintain that the faculty must teach the higher order thinking processes while simultaneously addressing plagiarism and copyright issues while librarians address other time-consuming responsibilities. The instruction librarians who have adopted education as a part of their dharma valiantly embrace the importance of evolving reference service and basic library instruction, but lack agreement as to how libraries should facilitate or incorporate information literacy. These instruction librarians believe integrated instruction will contribute to unprecedented shifts in curricular emphasis and that their teaching should be should be recognized, rewarded or compensated in some manner.

Instruction librarians Grassian and Kaplowitz acknowledge a professional debate amongst instructional librarians over where and how information literacy instruction should be taught.[3] Ultimately, they conclude "any of these formats may be useful and best suited to specific circumstances and environments" and "we need to focus on expanding our ILI menus so that we can offer more options to our learners" (Grassian and Kaplowitz 2009, 15). Rollins et al (2009) note their surveys indicate that "Most institutions agree on ALA's definition that information literacy is the set of abilities (or competencies) that enable an individual to recognize when information is needed, as well as the ability to locate, evaluate and use effectively that information; but a gap exists between the theoretical (intent) and the actual application (execution)." (453–4) Meanwhile, Budd (2009) notes an "apparent disagreement in the profession" about just how much librarians teach. Using the metaphor of a bridge, he notes "there is a considerable amount of tacit belief that libraries' instructional programs should stay on one side of the bridge, but some argue in favor of crossing it." He goes on to say "student learning is not in dispute, but the nature and degree of learning is the most profound" (12). The de-energizing and distracting nature of this constant debate needs attention and decisive action in order to move ahead. Regardless of whether librarians teach "one-shot" sessions, credit bearing courses or influence and encourage curricular changes across departments and at interdisciplinary levels, librarians need to know how to teach in order to have their instruction and curricular suggestions met with responsiveness.

Librarians can formally develop and hone their teaching skills in a two ways: via professional development trainings or academic coursework in an MLIS program. Edwards (2009) points out "interview data show that librarians receive minimal preparation for the teaching aspects of reference work either through pre-service education or on-the-job training."(35) To date, the best-known ACRL initiative for information literacy is its highly regarded Immersion programs that provide its participants opportunities to work exclusively with different facets of information literacy. The Immersion curriculum is known to keep pace with issues and trends facing academic librarians, and the program's graduates are often recognized as leaders in the information literacy movement. Despite the successes of the program, selection of participants is competitive and requires a financial commitment from participants or their home institutions. Other than Immersion, no other entity consistently offers workshops with intensive time and space for reflection that provides librarians professional development opportunities to examine information literacy in the academy.

The ACRL Board approved the Standards for Proficiencies for Instruction Librarians and Coordinators (2007) in order to both clarify the responsibilities of instruction coordinators as well as to create professional development opportunities for librarians with teaching responsibilities. These Standards can be used as a tool to foster conversations about cultural change and build a shared understanding of the future. Despite these efforts, a number of articles and studies suggest recent graduates moving into the academic library field were not prepared for instructional responsibilities. Julien (2005) located only one library and information science school that required students to complete a course on instruction. More recently, Spoles et al (2008) examined both the number of students exposed to the concept of information literacy in reference classes and the number of MLIS schools offering specific instruction classes. The authors conclude, "reference and IL instruction classes alone do not train students to become effective instruction librarians." Additionally, when a comparison was made between instruction course goals and outcomes and ACRL's 2007 Standards for Proficiencies for Instruction Librarians and Coordinators, "leadership, administration and assessment skills... are frequently understated." (207) Julien (2005) concludes her study, "It is inappropriate for senior library administrators to hire librarians for instructional roles who have no formal pedagogical training", and to do so, "raises serious questions about librarians' professionalism." (215)

The intersecting challenges, ranging from the lack of a national imperative through disagreements of how to facilitate or incorporate information literacy into LIS education or at a local level, affects all instruction librarians. Overall, this creates a compelling argument as to why information literacy has not achieved the cultural shift necessary for comprehensive program development.

Despite the fact guiding documents fail to mention educational duties, cited evidence indicates many librarians are participating more fully and accepting more responsibility in the educational process. Oakleaf (2011) notes, "not all academic libraries have embraced teaching and learning as a core value that infuses resource and service offerings, [but] many library departments and individual librarians have." (63) This has created cultural conflict within libraries between the traditional librarian dharma emphasizing service preeminence, and new librarian dharma emphasizing educator responsibilities. Ondrusek (2008) utilizes Kuhn's analysis of scientific revolutions as explanation of the phenomenon happening within the academic library profession. Kuhn laments that the "sources of authority" in a discipline typically "address themselves to an already articulated body of problems, data, and theory....to which the scientific community is already committed" (50). Academic librarians involved with information literacy programming and classroom or virtual

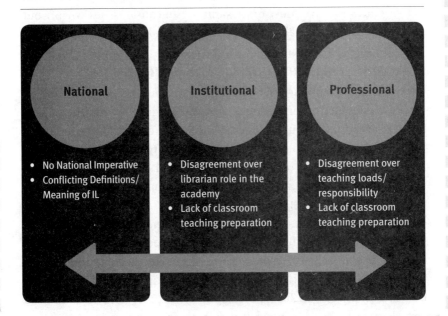

FIG 1.1
Intersections of Challenges Identified in Literature

National
- No National Imperative
- Conflicting Definitions/ Meaning of IL

Institutional
- Disagreement over librarian role in the academy
- Lack of classroom teaching preparation

Professional
- Disagreement over teaching loads/ responsibility
- Lack of classroom teaching preparation

instruction also have an articulated body of problems, data, and theory. Unfortunately, not all practitioners have acknowledged the invisible revolution, and library missions, policies and practices have yet to align with the vision of librarian involvement in educational reform.

In order to influence information literacy programming and culture on a campus or national level, instruction librarians must take the next step in the educational revolution by addressing the professional discord and tension surrounding information literacy. This is the elephant in the room in some library systems i.e. "a difficult issue that is commonly known to exist in an organization or community but is not discussed openly" (Heifetz et al 2009, 304). We believe the answer to the next step lies in what they call "courageous conversations" and "orchestrating the conflict" (304). A courageous conversation is "a dialogue designed to resolve competing priorities and beliefs while preserving relationships." Orchestrating the conflict is "designing and leading the process of getting parties with difference to work them through productively as distinguished from resolving the differences for them" (306). If instruction librarians remain complacent, settling for available resources and maintaining the status quo while ignoring the underlying issues, potential library contributions to educational reform in the form of comprehensive information literacy program development will not be fully realized. In order to begin to resolve the discord within our institutions and higher education, we must first examine the causal issues within our profession: interpersonal, structural, and cultural.

IV. IMMUNITY[4] AND RESISTANCE TO CHANGE ON THE INFORMATION LITERACY FRONTIER

Difficult issues such as conflicting dharma and language discrepancies exist beneath the surface of our information literacy programming efforts, and these issues are deeply embedded within the larger work culture of our libraries and institutions of higher education. ACRL (2007) began to address an evolving instructional culture with the adoption of the Standards and Proficiencies for Instruction Librarians and Coordinators, in part, to define skills needed to manage instructional programs. Despite this effort, "courageous conversations" regarding the interpersonal, structural, and cultural disconnects as they affect the practice of information literacy program development have been only lightly explored in the literature (Westbrock and Fabian 2010; Julien and Genuis (2011) and not addressed completely within the scholarship of instructional librarianship. Thus, this investigation of change resistance issues and related questions draws heavily on lived experience as well as leadership and transformational change literature.[5]

The concept of "immunity to change", gleaned from the work of Kegan and Lahey (2009), helps explain manifestations of resistance to change situated in information literacy programming efforts both individually and collectively. Essentially, "immunities" are blind spots that block further communication about challenges. Examples abound in information literacy settings. Results of an internal survey describing current instructional practice as a group of separate and unconnected efforts can be interpreted by colleagues as presumptuous. Or, a group process to write a comprehensive information literacy plan may unintentionally result in intense feelings of defensiveness and/or insecurity in some participants. Suggestions of change in current instructional practice can elicit avoidance behaviors and a discontinuation of communication. Our interpretations of Kegan and Lahey also reveal that resistance to change is basically human, and that even those of us who are trying to promote transformation within our work places can unconsciously and unintentionally hinder success because of unrecognized immunities that we, and our institutions, have. Because of these immunities, the everyday workplace frontier of information literacy practice presents issues that can be disheartening, isolating and de-energizing.

In information literacy programming development, the examination of current library structural and cultural issues, often blurred and further obscured by interpersonal issues, is critical. Both collective and individual immunities can benefit from individual and professional level conversations. Unfortunately, intersecting cultural, structural and interpersonal issues makes straightforward analysis challenging, and at times, elusive. Yet, we remain convinced that bringing these matters into the open will ultimately have a positive effect. With as much coherence as possible, we will describe the structural, cultural and interpersonal issues we understand from lived experience.

Cultural Issues

As we discussed previously, the educational roles academic librarians fulfill is evolving. The move from bibliographic instruction to information literacy, including the provision of credit-bearing courses in some institutions, has progressed. This educational change has created a cultural and dharma conflict within libraries, colliding service preeminence with educational responsibilities. Julien and Genuis (2011) outline a number of challenges that could be considered cultural in nature: "insufficient financial and technical support, insufficient time for preparation, and poor physical facilities" as well as "lack of commitment and professional support by library administrators, complex relationships with teaching faculty, and ambivalence about the teaching role." (103) Libraries also face rapid changes in service-oriented issues: a growing prevalence of digital content, consolidation of library space on campuses, and integration of subscription resources into common access portals (Schlosser 2011). The library environment is further complicated by intellectual property and copyright issues, open source, discovery tools, digitization, institutional repositories, and advances in scholarly communication. The ability to thoughtfully consider and carefully plan internal library initiatives is made more challenging when put into context of the relentless turmoil and upheaval in higher education. For example, administrative change at the top of the institution can alter strategic planning goals and suddenly influence library planning and priorities. Furthermore, technological change, economic issues, and the need to demonstrate value to the institution at large through accountability and assessment may suddenly hinder or advance library initiatives.

Information literacy programming competes for priority with these other pressing 21st century initiatives that require attention, and has successfully held a place in the matrix of change issues. Unfortunately, research indicates the sheer volume of continued change has the potential to lead to overload and fatigue (Kezar 2009). Continual change also has the ability to cultivate an immunity to change in individuals and organizations. (Kegan and Lahey 2009) One way libraries have attempted to cope with aforementioned competing priorities is to reassign responsibilities. In the case of information literacy, the trend is often to assign information literacy leadership and instruction to one position.

Structural Issues

Anecdotal evidence via professional contacts and postings on the ILI-L listserv indicate a trend of evolving instruction librarian positions into information literacy librarians or instructional coordinator positions. At the same time, new spots for information literacy leadership positions within a culture of existing instructional librarians have appeared. The effect these appointments have is organizationally progressive, but the cultural shift of staff acceptance and ownership of information literacy does not always happen simultaneously.

As a result, part of the difficulty for a newly formed position can be the absence of formal authority and power to make change. This is an example of a structural issue that crosses over to an interpersonal one. A library bureaucracy often contains structures that were formed many years ago. Libraries may have kept pace with many of the environmental and technological changes that have been necessary over the last twenty years, but the departmental structure and the autonomy of branch structures may remain relatively the same. If librarians who teach still report to their department heads, the incentive to change methods of pedagogy, collaboration, and/or the evaluation of teaching is low unless the department head or director encourages innovation and collaboration outside of departmental control. New instructional librarians tasked with program development in information literacy slowly learn that influence may be the only strategy open to them for creating change. Influence can be a powerful strategy of its own, but the learning curve for its techniques can be long. Situating information literacy efforts within an existing instructional tradition or experimenting with different pedagogical methods can lead unintentionally to deep resentment from co-workers.

In other cases, existing librarians expect the new Instruction or Information Literacy Librarian to do all of the teaching. A lack of communication about the role of a newly appointed instructional librarian or departmental directions may result in continuation of older teaching methods by some librarians and experimentation by others, thus dividing the workforce and preventing advancement at the programmatic level. In some systems, formal evaluation criteria do not assess teaching effectiveness by librarians. Again, the information literacy librarian may encounter a dead end when introducing new approaches and ideas. When only one librarian in an institution is charged with or expected to implement an information literacy program, and/or so many challenges and underlying issues exist within the profession, burnout can threaten to undermine positive advancement.

Interpersonal Issues

Acceptance and ownership of information literacy amongst library staff is often not embraced by all librarians in an institution. Julien and Pecoskie (2009) note, "Some librarians remain unconvinced of the value of information literacy instruction....and some express hostility toward the instructional expectations they feel towards the students they teach and toward the teaching faculty on campus." And, "This ambivalence undoubtedly affects students' learning experiences, compromising the potential success of instructional efforts." (149) Furthermore, Information Literacy Librarians or Instruction Coordinators are often charged with assessing both instruction programs and student learning, but lack the formal authority to established changes based on assessment. If the organizational structure does not allow librarian leaders the authority needed to mandate change, Information Literacy Librarians or Instruction Coordinators need to apply interpersonal skills in leadership, conflict resolution, negotiation, and advanced communication.

The ACRL 2007 Standards and Proficiencies for Instruction Librarians and Coordinators lists twelve important skill areas. They include administrative, assessment, teaching, presentation, communication, planning, and leadership skills, among others. But culture building, change agency, conflict negotiation, applications of emotional intelligence, and transformational learning are not on the list. A profession going through expansion and reform demands these skills in addition to the ones on the 2007 Proficiencies list. Our experience indicates that instructional librarians especially need emotional intelligence to navigate through carrying the role of change agent as they build programs for information literacy with their colleagues. Travis (2008) discusses change agency as a key part of integrating information literacy into the higher education curricula and points out that "librarians have rarely defined themselves as conscious change agents in library research." (21)

Palmer frames change agency in the larger context of educational reform and offers insight into the resistance that all agents of change face. He (1998, 164–6) explains reform and resistance as inseparable and we believe this may provide a template for recognizing underlying issues in information literacy program development. He acknowledges the paradoxical relationship between organizational resistance and social movements within organizations. He asks,

> Has significant social change ever been achieved in the face of massive institutional opposition? The answer seems clear: *only* in the face of such opposition has significant social change been achieved. If institutions had a capacity for constant evolution, there would have never been a crisis demanding transformation. (167)

He suggests, "If we want a movement for educational reform, we must learn to embrace this paradox" [which is the interdependency of reform and resistance] and, "We must also learn the logic of a movement, learn how a movement unfolds, partly so we know where we are located within it, partly so that we can help it along."(166)

Palmer names four essential stages that embody the dynamics of a movement: 1) "divided no more", 2) "communities of congruence", 3) "going public", and 4) "alternative rewards". Ultimately, he views resistance as "a source of energy". (165) Academic librarians have created professional communities of congruence and affinity around information literacy. While most of these communities rally around teaching techniques and effectiveness, there is scholarly evidence (Gibson 2007) of librarians' struggling to create comprehensive information literacy culture. Thus, the authors believe that, as a profession, we are ready to "go public" and address the cultural, structural and interpersonal underlying issues in information literacy scholarship and practice, framing resistance as a positive force.

Fortunately, Palmer's fourth stage offers further direction on how this reform movement can unfold through "alternative rewards", or "sustain(ing) the movement's vision and... put(ting) pressure for change on the standard institutional reward system" (166). He discusses resistance in positive terms because it fuels "imagining alternatives." Alternative rewards as well as cultural, structural and interpersonal change have been effectively explored in scholarship and applied successfully in organizational transformation. Thus, the following section reviews select organizational change literature. We hope this analysis maps the terrain of issues, suggests implications, and inspires ideas and action for information literacy program development.

V. UNDERSTANDING WHAT IS POSSIBLE

Heifetz et al (2009) provide insights into work cultures and change realities in his discussion of the "practice of adaptive leadership" that may offer highly applicable wisdom for information literacy program development.

"Adaptive leadership is the practice of mobilizing people to tackle tough challenges and thrive." (Heifetz et al 2009, 14) This form of leadership takes place in "an adaptive culture" which has "five distinguishing characteristics." These characteristics include "elephants [in the room] are named; responsibility for the organization is shared; independent judgment is expected; leadership capacity is developed; and reflection and continuous learning are institutionalized." (165) Part of the adaptive culture involves being able to tell the difference between a technical problem and an adaptive challenge. "Adaptive challenges can only be addressed through changes in people's priorities, beliefs, habits, and loyalties. Making progress requires going beyond any authoritative expertise to mobilize discovery, shedding certain entrenched ways, tolerating losses, and generating the new capacity to thrive anew." (19)

We think using the technique suggested by Heifetz et al called "getting on the balcony above the dance floor" (7) is appropriate to address cultural change in information literacy program development. It allows a big picture viewpoint to diagnose either systemic problems or something in yourself that is holding progress back (or both.) It allows really trying to understand the problems at hand in the context of adaptive challenge.

Another book (originally written for college students,) *Leadership for a Better World: Understanding the Social Change Model of Leadership Development* (Komives et al 2009), also offers relevant insight. It explains second order change as a goal of leadership. Its authors explain the difference between single order and second order change:

> *Single order change* involves structural or procedural changes that can be made within the organizations' current frameworks of rules, procedures, and leadership roles. Sometimes however, the current rules, procedures, or approaches to leadership are creating the problem. These situations call for *second-order change,* or changing the organization's fundamental values and assumptions. Second order change has been referred to as *transformative change*... which 1) alters the culture of the institution by changing select underlying assumptions and institutional behaviors, processes, and products; 2) is deep and pervasive, affecting the whole institution; 3) is intentional; and 4) occurs over time. (103)

Once we achieve an understanding of what the adaptive challenges and second order changes *are* on the frontier of leadership for the next decade of information literacy development, we can begin to plan with confidence. "Balcony thinking and diagnosis" requires identifying the underlying assumptions which produce immunities and routine behaviors and challenging those assumptions so that the culture of the organization begins to change.

Explanation for resistance to information literacy culture development range from competing priorities to threatening the time honored tradition and assumption that libraries are service institutions. Information literacy assumes a dharma change: instructional librarians are *educational* librarians and that the 21st century library is more than ever an environment for learning. Drawing on rich library history and strong relationship to education, the use of a learning model for organizational change seems like a logical next step in organizational planning. Service of the highest quality can exist side by side with progressive instructional programs in a blended community. It is not one or the other, either/or. Instead, both initiatives have the potential to exist under an umbrella of the learning organization.

Transformation and Learning within Organizations

Organizational change literature provides a glimpse of some possibilities for continual transformation and learning within organizations. Senge's *The Fifth Discipline: the Art & Practice of the Learning Organization* (1990[6]) defined a set of criteria for what constitutes a learning organization. The word "discipline" in the title refers to "a body of theory and technique that must be studied and mastered to be put into practice. A discipline is a developmental path for acquiring certain skills or competencies." (10) This discipline combines systems thinking, personal mastery, mental models, building a shared vision, and team learning, according to Senge, the learning organization is created and makes possible "a new wave of experimentation and advancement." (11)

Ten years ago, a new field of study and research began at the University of Michigan. Positive Organizational Scholarship, or POS, is dedicated to energizing and transforming organizations by linking positive emotion, resilience, virtues, leadership, thriving, and abundance in a scholarly context. "POS does not adopt one framework or theory but it draws upon the full spectrum of organizational theories to understand, explain and predict the occurrence, causes, and consequences of positivism. Research findings to date indicate the enabling positive qualities in individuals which lead to exceptional organizational performance." (Center for Positive Organizational Scholarship 2011)

Learning organizations, POS, and other organizational research may help library leaders identify and accelerate sustained transformative change. To illustrate academic library organizations that have utilized change strategies through learning, we offer the following examples:

Gilchrist (2007), in part, tells the story of instructional librarians' leadership for transformation and "their own professionalism as educators." (188) Overall, her dissertation is a phenomenological inquiry exploring the experiences of library leaders who worked together with disciplinary faculty to bring about instructional change using a process based learning pedagogy championed by an academic library. She looked at: "(a) library's role in instructional leadership; (b) experience of librarians leading instructional change; (c) experience of faculty members as they design assignments and modify courses to include process-based learning; and (d) prospect of process-based learning as a learning centered curricular tool" (abstract,1). Her work clarifies the critical leadership role academic libraries can have on their campuses by reframing curriculum reform and integrating student learning.

While not set in the context of information literacy, other librarians are transforming academic library cultures. Somerville (2009) brought leadership experience to her library from work as a non-profit executive director who "partnered with Fortune 50 corporations and higher education institutions." Her mentors "understood the strategic importance of creating workplace environments that constantly enhanced workers' capabilities to create" (v) and their approach was grounded in the work of Senge (1990). Somerville gives a glimpse into an academic library at Cal Poly San Luis Obispo, and reframes what is possible in a learning organization library, drawing, in part, on international information literacy research. She also discusses robust organizational change to address the centrality of learning at the University of Colorado at Denver. Based on a mix of theories and ideas relating to organizational change including those ideas of scholars in Sweden, the United Kingdom, the United States, Japan, and Australia, all of the changes at both libraries revolved around re-conceptualizing workplace environments as places where learning by everyone is essential for relevance in the present and future. Learning innovations resulted using multiple forms of collaboration between students, faculty, and librarians within the spaces of the library. Actual assessment of students' academic work affirmed advancements in students' research, publishing, communication, social structure, and technology competencies (Somerville 2009, 32).

Other academic library environments in the U.S. where initiatives to change to a learning culture include George Washington University Libraries and University of Nebraska Libraries. (Gieseke and Siggins 2010) Schlosser (2011) provides a literature review that includes a number of different approaches to strategic planning and other planning initiatives used in library systems. She then introduces Ohio State University (OSU) Libraries' grassroots, participatory planning process entitled OSUL2013 that emphasized culture as a "crucial element in organizational success." (156) The OSUL2013 process Schlosser reports on "operates according to a number of principles: grassroots participation and direction; an organic, "phased" process; a positive orientation[7]; and a focus on qualities, not processes." (157) She admits the focus on qualities instead of processes have made gauging success difficult, but participant evaluations were "largely positive." (167)

Each of the aforementioned libraries approached organizational transformation in a different fashion; yet they were all able to create, on some level, change within their respective organizations via learning and intimate staff involvement in change processes. We do not intend to prescribe a particular style of organizational change. Rather, we are interested in how organizational change through learning has the potential to remedy some of the cultural and structural issues that exist beneath the surface of information literacy program development. Further research and investigation into learning organizations and their potential for instructional librarianship is needed.

Considering Emotional Engagement in Organizational Transformation

On an individual, interpersonal level, Kegan and Lahey (2009) argue that adults can continue to learn throughout their lives and can change within the context of their work environments, once they overcome, (again in their words) "a kind of blind spot by getting some distance, or perspective, on a way of making meaning to which we had been captive." (167) The authors explore a "new way to understand change" and lay out what is necessary to accomplish the recognition of a personal immunity to change and the ways to address it effectively. Addressing the underlying emotional issues that accompany information literacy paradigm shifts has the potential to improve our day to day interpersonal relationships and foster the campus-wide culture we aim to develop. In order for such a climate to exist, emotion has to be framed first by leaders, and later by all by individuals as a source of strength and creativity, not a factor to avoid.

Leading thinkers (Cameron and Lavine 2006; Frost 2003; Kegan and Lahey 2009; Komives et al 2009; Lilius et al 2008; Spreitzer and Sonenshein 2003, 2004) on change note with certainty that engaging the emotions of employees in a workplace is an essential component of achieving significant goals. Kegan and Lahey (2009) point out contemporary leaders must find a more effective way to engage the emotional lives of their organizations and their leadership teams. They say:

> .....until we find a way to engage the emotional life of the workplace we will not succeed in meeting our most important goals. It means recognizing that hard-and-fast divisions between the public and the private, between the "work realm" and "the persona" are naïve and unproductive. (319)

Basically the Kegan and Lahey method of understanding change involves a deep understanding of oneself within the organizational context and uses emotional intelligence to unlock new insight. Would their method allow understanding that, in turn, opened a readiness to change in an information literacy leader, his or her cohort of instructional librarians and organizational administration? Each site must find the key to effectively begin to shake loose turf fears, workload perceptions, and comfort zones. Because it has worked for many other kinds of organizations over many years, we believe it will be effective for information literacy program development in all types of academic libraries.

Understanding the role of emotion in the workplace frontier of information literacy advancement is essential. Yet in the academic library instructional environment, not much is known about the affective realm. LIS literature certainly reflects research on the affective in student instruction (Schroeder and Cahoy 2010), emotional intelligence in academic librarian leaders (Herndon et al 2007), and information seeking for psychological or emotional reasons (Fourie 2009). Yet it is not easy to find research that directly addresses workplace emotions of librarians involved in information literacy program development.

Julien and Genuis (2009; 2011) provide two exceptions. They have published research results regarding emotion related to instruction librarianship and examined how library staff relate to instructional roles. Their findings indicate:

> Consistent with Nahl's (2007) assertion that the scholarly community must account for "the centrality of the affective domain in all human activity" (p. xix), data analysis revealed the central place of affect in the experiences of the librarians engaged in instructional work. Furthermore, a particularly salient theme that was manifest in the data was the expression of emotional labour, an occupational stressor identified by sociologist Arlie Hochschild (1983) in her classic book, *The Managed Heart: Commercialization of Human Feeling.* This book draws attention to work which "requires one to induce or suppress feeling in order to sustain the outward countenance that produces the proper state of mind in others... this kind of labor calls for a coordination of mind and feeling, and it sometimes draws on a source of self that we honor as deep and integral to our individuality (p. 7). (2009, 929)

Using phenomenological research methods including diary analysis and interviews, the authors found that instructional experiences of librarians ranged from "joy to misery." They concluded:

> Both individuals and organizations will benefit from considering the influence of emotional labour on library staff with instructional duties. Organizations, for example, might begin to address the invisibility of emotional labour performed as a part of the teaching role, perhaps providing opportunities for library staff to freely express their frustrations, their boredom, and their stresses. In addition, there may be implications for librarians' education. Those of us who educate librarians for their teaching roles, through courses in pedagogy and curriculum design for instance, ought to incorporate into our lessons understanding of affect and its impact on those in instructional roles. (2009, 934–5)

These findings move our focus beyond instrumental concerns that challenge successful information literacy instruction (e.g. a lack of instructors' training, and ubiquitous resource limits) to challenges which may seem even more insurmountable: changing workplace roles, and the sometimes invisible, but difficult emotional aspects of instructional work. At the very least, appreciation for the fact that these challenges exist, and emerging understanding of the ways in which such challenges are experienced by librarians with instructional responsibilities, may be a starting point for ameliorating them. (2009, 934–5)

Their follow-up 2011 article indicates that research on "highlighting the critical role of self-conception and the impact of intrapersonal factors on how library staff understand the fit of instructional work with their role within libraries" (109) is needed.

By approaching and working with emotion through mindful intention, we begin to not only witness our own thoughts, emotions and action patterns, but also mindfully intend to change the patterns that no longer serve our organizations or us. Redefining roles and building trust with integrity between library colleagues can allow for meaningful communication and genuine organizational progress. This holistic perspective implies great skill with application of emotional intelligence, modeling new behaviors, frequent respectful communication about emotions in the workplace, inner confidence, and boundless energy. Few among us can possess all of these traits. Yet, a workplace environment where effective and sustainable change can happen has to have these characteristics. Information literacy leaders can apply research findings, inaugurating a new area of investigation, that focus on bringing emotion positively into the workplace in order to enrich practice and provide energy for implementing positive learning results for students and librarians in the decade ahead.

There is a frontier of organizational change in information literacy program development. Additional research studies that provide an understanding of the emotional labor of leadership for instructional change or the emotional labor of facing and tolerating resistance do not yet exist.

We hope to see exploration of questions such as:

- Are there any information literacy programs where the findings of Positive Organizational Scholarship (POS) or other organizational change theories are being applied? If not, can studies begin?

- What are the components of emotional health in library work-places, and specifically, library workplaces where information literacy initiatives exist?
- Are information literacy librarians using emotional intelligence in their information literacy practice?
- Are there examples of successful information literacy programs where techniques such as appreciative inquiry have been applied?

In general, we sense that these are timely lines of inquiry and may unlock ideas for addressing the immunity to change raised earlier. It is clear the time has come to expand the range of strategies employed to achieve the goal of information literacy programmatic transformation.

A repertoire of research findings and applied techniques, some of which use emotion, are available to address ways in which organizational transformation and learning can be brought into the workplace.

Change Strategies for Experimentation

ACRL Information Literacy Immersion graduates and others will remember the impact of their reading of Palmer's book *The Courage to Teach: Exploring the Inner Landscape of a Teacher's Life*. Its central idea is that "good teaching cannot be reduced to technique; good teaching comes from the identity and integrity of the teacher" (10) reverberates for many and remains a central insight of importance. Palmer values the development of the self in teachers and asks: "How does the quality of selfhood form—or deform— the way I related to my students, my colleagues, my subject, my world?" (4) He also puts forward the idea that good teaching intertwines the intellectual, the emotional, and the spiritual and that they cannot be separated. (4–5) These ideas and values about the heart of the teacher and the integration of the intellectual, emotional and spiritual permeate the transformational and reform perspective that we are bringing to this analysis on behalf of information literacy program development in the coming decade.

From the writings examined regarding organizational change and the need to foster positive emotion as part of the change process, we have extracted a list of change techniques that may add vitality to information literacy program development. Though not all include emotional engagement, they all involve the individual in organizational life; many address

leading a group through change, sometimes with extraordinarily positive outcomes. The following lists are intended for two different types of
librarians: solo change agents and change agents who have the support
of a group of librarians or other campus stakeholders.

Individuals

- **Savoring:** "Savoring" adopts mindfulness practice from
  Buddhism. Savoring encourages participants to attend to and
  appreciate positive experiences. People who savor have far
  more positive experiences at work. (Bryant and Veroff 2006)
- **Reflected Best Self Exercise:** This exercise enables people
  to identify their unique strengths and talents, making it an
  excellent tool for personal development. Each participant
  requests positive feedback from significant people in his or
  her life and then synthesizes it into a cumulative portrait of
  his or her "best self." (Quinn et al 2004)
- **Energy Audit: A Tool for Restoration:** This focuses on personal sustainability over time and presents a rationale for
  NOT working at top speed daily. Spreitzer outlines four "key
  levers" for energy management and creates a pyramid dia-
  gram to illustrate them. With physical energy at the bottom
  of the pyramid, followed by mental, emotional and spiritual
  energy, she concludes, "the best long term performers tap into
  positive energy at all levels of the pyramid." (Spreitzer, 2011)
- **Using Influence as a Change Strategy:**
  - "Influencing Without Authority", a 2009 ACRL Active
    Guide, includes self help worksheets that the reader can
    fill out to guide insights and develop plans for influenc-
    ing others including peers, university faculty, adminis-
    trators and stakeholders in the higher education institu-
    tion. (This booklet does not introduce the complex cultural
    dynamics under the surface in a library workplace.)
  - Patterson and Grenny (2008) discuss the characteristics
    of leaders and scholars who have been successful influenc-
    ers by finding vital behaviors that work to change minds.
    They start by asking: "In order to improve our existing
    situation, what must people actually do?" And then they
    answer the question: "Give special attention to high

leverage behaviors....discover a few vital behaviors, change those, and problems-no matter what their size-topple like a house of cards."(28.) They outline six sources of influence which include: making the undesirable desirable; surpassing your own limits; harnessing peer pressure and finding strength in numbers through teamwork; designing rewards and demanding accountability; and actually changing things in the physical work environment and its structure to foster behavior change.

- Cohen and Bradford (2005) use an influence model in which "reciprocity and exchange are used to trade something the other values in return for what you want." (6) They clarify both internal and external barriers to change including the internal: "blinding attitudes, fear of reactions, and inability to focus on own needs and benefits to others" and the external: "different goals and priorities, incompatible measures and rewards, and rivalry, competitiveness, and jealousy." (8)

Groups

- **Positive Deviance:** Positive Deviance is a theory introduced in research by Spreitzer and Sonenshein (2004) which identifies extraordinary outcomes and works backwards to find out how they were accomplished.
- **Positive Organizational Scholarship (POS):** A variety of techniques, some listed individually above, can be explored in conjunction with POS. Many POS techniques suggest bringing emotion into the workplace in constructive ways to create organizations that build vitality into the workforce. Examples of these techniques discussed at the ALA/LLAMA 2010 Preconference (Christensen and Worline) include:
  - Challenging negative stereotypes in which we focus on negative emotions in the workplace. Negative emotions can be a signal to act. "Boredom and other deadened emotions in the workplace can be signals that something needs to change."
  - Cultivating an atmosphere where pride expressions are contagious. This encourages employees to think of their

workplaces as sources of pride, creativity and meaning, and effective collaborative work.

- **Appreciative Inquiry:** Appreciative inquiry rejects the diagnosis of problems as a route to change. (Cooperrider 1987) Instead, it suggests bringing an appreciative eye to what is working in an organization. According to Hammond, (1996) "The tangible result of the inquiry process is a series of statements that describe where the organization wants to be based on the high moments of where they have been. Because the statements are grounded in real experience and history people know how to repeat their success. Participants stir up memories of energizing moments of success creating a new energy that is positive and synergistic. (7) Sullivan (2004) explicates definitions, origins, and principles and assumptions of appreciative inquiry and discusses the practice of this technique within the larger context of library organizations. A key contribution of this article is Sullivan's application of appreciative inquiry and the learning organization to libraries.

- **Adaptive Personal Change:** Kegan and Lahey (2009) say "The hallmark of adaptive personal change is that one's grasp exceeds one's reach. "Good problems" we say, "solve us": They bring into being or strengthen our purchase on a whole new developmental plateau, a new self paradigm. Columbus was only looking to solve a navigational problem; instead his discoveries led to reimagining the world." (167)

- **Change Theory:** Travis (2008) defines change agency as "a framework that increases the likelihood of curriculum initiatives having an impact on student learning." (18) Travis recommends being aware of seven roles that are attributed to change: "developing the need for change, communicating the change, diagnosing the problems, creating the intent to change in the client, translating the action, stabilizing the change and developing self renewing behavior in the organization." (20)

- **Practice of Adaptive Leadership:** (see pages 19–21 this chapter)

- **Nemawashi:** Keyes and Namei (2010) explain nemawashi is "used figuratively and colloquially in Japan to describe a collective decision-making process that thoroughly considers all options prior to making a final decision in an effort to ensure that the solution can be implemented rapidly and smoothly." ["Literally, nemawashi refers to digging around the roots of a tree and carefully binding them before the process of transplantation."] (25)

These and other techniques may offer needed building blocks for the "deep, enterprise-level change" Gibson (2007, 24) discusses as necessary for the cultural shift to implement information literacy across our campuses. Overall, the high correlation between positive emotions and positive organizational change in many of these techniques indicates that it will be wise to pay deep attention to them for possible application to information literacy leadership.

CONCLUSION

Gibson (2008) closes his chapter on the history of information literacy by looking to the future. He notes:

> The transformation needed calls upon greater collaboration to advance sustained programmatic development to carry the classic aims of liberal education—a broad perspective on knowledge, a sympathy with a wide range of modes of inquiry, a capacity for critical thinking, flexible reasoning and adept problem-solving—into highly demanding work where the chief constants are innovation, technological change, and fluid and uncertain information resources. In these workplaces the chief expectations are collaborative ability, agility and adaptability, and constant learning while discarding settled ideas and assumptions— these abilities encompass "information fluent" behaviors and that are constantly needed in research, communication, and collaboration. (23)

In this summation, Gibson foreshadows the transformation needs we still see in 2011. Academic libraries need to consider the implications of becoming dynamic learning environments and shifting dharma in a way that enable librarians to better prepare students for academic and workplace success. To us "discarding settled ideas and assumptions" such as the library as exclusively a service organization, emotions as taboo in the workplace, and the fixed definition of information literacy are keys to achieving reform. Our suggested agenda for the individual academic library and the entire profession suggests embracing the past two decades of "mystery and marvel" (Cooperrider and Srivastava 1987). A foundation of impressive educational change and effective organizational growth allows for more experimentation with second order change techniques to advance information literacy with innovation, engagement, and vigorous positivism.

This chapter's research findings, insights from professional, lived experience, and ideas from transformational leadership writing, have resulted in a new vision of pathways to foster information literacy program culture and set new professional learning goals. The pathways point to: 1) a deeper engagement by practitioners with the findings of recent scholarship; 2) intentional building of robust institutional and professional information literacy cultures; 3) the need to acknowledge and engage with resistance issues in individual, structural, and cultural contexts; and finally; 4) the broad array of resistance and cultural change remedies available for experimentation and implementation in the future. Following these open pathways offers the promise of the true social change we envision for our field.

To close the chapter, we review core discoveries about information literacy culture development and make recommendations to individual instructional librarians, key campus stakeholders and ACRL leaders in the field.

ACRL Leaders

- Examine and revise guiding documents: Standards, Proficiencies, Bill of Rights and Code of Ethics to accurately reflect the 21st century educational responsibilities.

Key Campus Stakeholders

- Employ holistic change leadership to reinvent each library's instructional *community as a collaborative team or learning community* in order to build a culture of teaching and assessment; re-purposing an instructional workforce for student *and* librarian learning.
- Form and foster a team of information literacy stakeholders and keep it energized over time for a sustainable future.
- Resolve librarian instructional workload issues by working with key academic leaders and adopt realistic teaching expectations and rewards.

Individual Instruction Librarians

- Engage with the findings of recent LIS scholarship.
- Develop a common understanding of information literacy program techniques such as reflective practice, learning communities, and assessment.
- Advocate for language and definitional development, encourage enrichment of librarian instructional abilities, and start conversations about sustainable curricular reforms.

FIG 2.1
Core Values for "Deep, Enterprise-Wide Level Change" in IL Programming

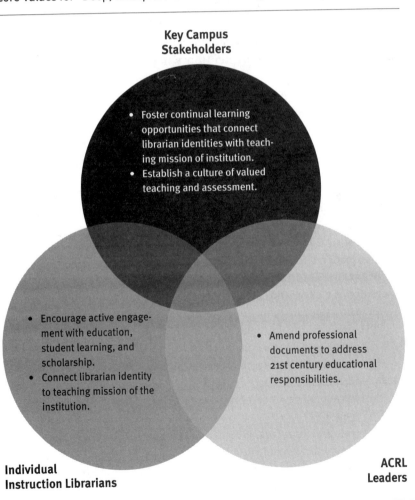

Key Campus Stakeholders

- Foster continual learning opportunities that connect librarian identities with teaching mission of institution.
- Establish a culture of valued teaching and assessment.

- Encourage active engagement with education, student learning, and scholarship.
- Connect librarian identity to teaching mission of the institution.

- Amend professional documents to address 21st century educational responsibilities.

Individual Instruction Librarians

ACRL Leaders

- Begin to relieve organizational discord and tension by identifying underlying issues and seeking resolution within the library instructional community.

Instruction Coordinators or Information Literacy Librarians, with the support of other librarians, other campus stakeholders and professional associations can create comprehensive information literacy culture. Kuhlthau, Budd, Elmborg, Bruce and Lloyd are situating information literacy within academic traditions and sociocultural perspectives. We argue it is time to bring that sort of academic understanding and thoughtful awareness to both affective and cognitive components of information literacy culture. Libraries and information literacy programming occupy complex spaces and intersecting identities. Awareness must be cultivated through many lenses: a candid acknowledgement of underlying issues that accompany paradigm shifts, recognition of emotion in change processes, mindful intention when applying research involving emotional engagement and/or transformational organization techniques, and holistic professional integrity.

References

American Library Association. 1996. "Library Bill of Rights." ALA. Accessed April 20, 2011. www.ala.org/ala/issuesadvocacy/intfreedom/librarybill/index.cfm.

———. 2008. "Code of Ethics." ALA. Accessed April 20, 2011. www.ala.org/ala/issuesadvocacy/proethics/codeofethics/codeethcis.cfm.

Andretta, Susie. 2007. "Phenomenography: a Conceptual Framework for Information Literacy Education." *Aslib Proceedings: New Information Perspectives* 59 (2):152–68.

Association of College and Research Libraries. 2007. "Standards for Proficiencies for Instruction Librarians and Coordinators." ACRL. Accessed March 21, 2011. www.ala.org/acrl/standards/profstandards.

———. 2010. *Value of Academic Libraries: A Comprehensive Research Review and Report*. Researched by Megan Oakleaf. Chicago: ACRL.

Badke, William B. 2005. "Can't Get No Respect: Helping Faculty to Understand the Educational Power of Information Literacy," *The Reference Librarian* 89/90: 63–80.

Barr, Robert B. and John Tagg. 1995. "From Teaching to Learning: A New Paradigm for Undergraduate Education." *Change Magazine* 27 (6): 12–25.

Branch, Katherine. 1998. "Librarians Value Service Most." *College and Research Libraries News* 59 (3): 176–7.

Bruce, Christine. 2008. *Informed Learning.* Chicago: ACRL.

Bryant, Fred and Joseph Veroff. 2007. *Savoring: A New Model of Positive Experience.* Mahwah, NJ: Lawrence Erlbaum Associates.

Budd, John M. 2008. "Cognitive Growth, Instruction and Student Success." *College and Research Libraries* 69 (4): 319–30.

———. 2009. *Framing Library Instruction: A View from Within and Without.* Chicago: ACRL.

Cameron, Kim S. and Marc Lavine. 2006. *Making the Impossible Possible: Leading Extraordinary Performance: the Rocky Flats Story.* San Francisco: Barrett-Koehler.

Center for Positive Organizational Scholarship. 2011. "Center & Its Mission." Accessed April 5. www.centerforpos.org/wp-content/uploads/2010/11/POS-Essence.pdf.

Christensen, Marlys and Monica C. Worline. 2010. "Is the Glass Half Full or Half Empty?" (morning presentations at American Library Association and Library Leadership & Management Association Preconference), American Library Association Conference, Washington D.C, June 25.

Cohen, Allen R. and David L. Bradford. 2005. *Influence Without Authority* Hoboken, NJ: John Wiley and Sons.

Cooperrider, David and S. Srivastava. 1987. "Appreciative Inquiry in Organizational Life." *Research on Organizational Change and Development.* Vol.1, edited by R.W. Woodman and W.A. Pasmore Greenwich, CT: JAI Press.

Desai, Christina M. and Stephanie J. Graves. 2006. "Instruction via Instant Messaging Reference: What's Happening?" *The Electronic Library* 24 (2):174–89.

Dole, Wanda V., Jitka M. Hurych, and Wallace C. Koehler. 2000. "Values for Librarians in the Information Age: an Expanded Examination." *Library Management* 21 (6): 285–97.

Edwards, Elizabeth Marie. 2009. "Examining the Preparation for Reference-Based Instruction Among Academic Librarians." Thesis, University of IL at Urbana-Champaign. Accessed March 21, 2011. http://hdl.handle.net/2142/9762.

Ekman, Richard. 2011. Emailed description of Workshops on "literacy" and "fluency". Council of Independent Colleges, April 14.

Elmborg, James K. 2005. "Libraries and Writing Centers in Collaboration: A Basis in Theory." In *Centers for Learning: Writing Centers and Libraries in Collaboration,* edited by James K. Elmborg and Sheril Hook, 1–20. Chicago: ACRL.

Fourie, Ina. 2009. "Learning from Research on the Information Behaviour of Healthcare Professionals: a Review of the Literature 2004–2008 with a Focus on Emotion." *Health Information and Libraries Journal* 26 (3): 171–86.

Frost, Peter J. 2003. *Toxic Emotions at Work: How Compassionate Managers Handle*

Pain and Conflict at Work. Boston: Harvard Business School Press.

Gibson, Craig. 2007. "Information Literacy and IT Fluency: Convergences and Divergences," *Reference and Users Services Quarterly* 46 (3): 23–6, 59.

———. 2008. "History of Information Literacy." In *Information Literacy Instruction Handbook*, edited by Christopher N. Cox and Elizabeth Blakesley Lindsay,10–25. Chicago: ACRL.

Gieseke, Joan and Jack Siggins. 2010. "Is the Glass Half Full or Half Empty?" (an afternoon panel presentation at American Library Association and Library Leadership & Management Association Preconference), American Library Association Conference, Washington D.C, June 25.

Gilchrist, Debra. 2007. "Academic Libraries at the Center of Instructional Change: Faculty and Library Leadership in the Transformation of Teacher and Learning." Dissertation, University of Oregon.

———. 2009. "A Twenty-Year Path: Leaning about Assessment; Learning from Assessment." *Communications in Information Literacy* 3 (2): 70–9.

Gilchrist, Debra and Anne Zald. 2008. "Instruction & Program Design through Assessment." *Information Literacy Handbook*, edited by Christopher N. Cox and Elizabeth Blakesley Lindsay, 164–192. Chicago: ACRL.

Grassian,Esther S. and Joan R. Kaplowitz. 2009. *Information Literacy Instruction Theory and Practice*, 2nd ed. New York: Neal-Schuman Publishers.

Hammond, Sue Annis. 1996. *The Thin Book of Appreciative Inquiry.* Plano, TX: CSS Publishing Company.

Hawks, Melanie. 2009. *Influencing Without Authority.* Chicago: ACRL.

Heifetz, Ronald, Alexander Grashow and Marty Linsky. 2009. *The Practice of Adaptive Leadership: Tools and Tactics for Changing your Organization and the World.* Boston: Harvard Business Press.

Herndon, Peter, Joan Gieseke, and Camila Alire. 2007. *Academic Librarians as Emotionally Intelligent Leaders.* Westport, CT: Libraries Unlimited.

Jacobs, Heidi L.M. 2008. "Information Literacy and Reflective Pedagogical Praxis." *The Journal of Academic Librarianship* 34 (3): 256–62.

Julien, Heidi. 2005. "Education for Information Literacy Instruction: A Global Perspective" *Journal of Education for Library and Information Science* 46 (3): 210–16.

Julien, Heidi and Shelagh K. Genuis. 2009. "Emotional Labour in Librarians Instructional Work" *Journal of Documentation* 65 (6): 926–37.

———. 2011. Librarians' Experiences of the Teaching Role: A National Survey of Librarians." *Library & Information Science Research* 33: 103–11.

Julien, Heidi and Jen Pecoskie. 2009. "Librarians' Experiences of the Teaching Role: Grounded in Campus Relationships." *Library & Information Science Research* 31: 149–54.

Komives, Susan R., Wendy Wagner, et al. 2009. *Leadership for a Better World: Understanding the Social Change Model of Leadership Development.* San

Francisco: Jossey Bass.

Kuhlthau, Carol C. 2004. *Seeking Meaning: A Process Approach to Library and Information Services,* 2nd ed. West Port, CN: Libraries Unlimited.

Kuhlthau, Carol C, Jannica Heinstorm and Ross J. Todd. 2008. "The 'Information Search Process' Revisited: Is the Model Still Useful?" *Information Research* 13 (4) paper 355. [Available at http://InformationR.net/ir/13-4/paper355.html].

Kegan, Robert and Lisa Laskow Lahey. 2009. *Immunity to Change: How to Overcome It and Unlock the Potential in Yourself and Your Organization.* Boston: Harvard Business Press.

Keyes, Charles and Elizabeth S. Namei. 2010. "Nemawashi: Integrating the Credit Information Literacy into a Community College Curriculum." *Best Practices for Credit Bearing Information Literacy Courses,* edited by Christopher Hollister, 25–41. Chicago: ALA.

Kezar, Adrianna. 2009. "Change in Higher Education: Not Enough or Too Much?" *Change Magazine,* Nov/Dec: 18–23.

Lilius, Jacoba M., Monica C. Worline, Sally Maitlis, Jason Kanov, Jane E. Dutton and Peter Frost. 2008. "Contours and Consequences of Compassion at Work." *Journal of Organizational Behavior* 29 (2): 193–218.

Lloyd, Annemaree. 2010. "Framing Information Literacy as an Information Practice: Site Ontology and Practice Theory." *Journal of Documentation* 66 (2): 245–58.

Mackey, Thomas P. and Trudi E. Jacobson. 2011. "Reframing Information Literacy as Metaliteracy." *College & Research Libraries* 72 (1): 62–78.

Maybee, Clarence. 2007. "Understanding Our Student Learners: A Phenomenographic Study Revealing the Ways that Undergraduate Women at Mills College Understand Using Information." *Reference Services Review* 35 (3): 452–462.

———. 2009. Understanding Undergraduates: What Does Phenomenography Tell Us About Learners?" *Proceedings of the 35th Annual LOEX Conference* San Diego, CA.

National Education Association. 2011. "Code of Ethics." National Education Association. Accessed March 21. www.nea.org/home/30442.htm.

Oakleaf, Megan. 2009. "Writing Information Literacy Assessment Plans: a Guide to Best Practice." *Communications in Information Literacy* 3(2): 80–9.

———. 2011. "Are They Learning? Are We? Learning and the Academic Library." *Library Quarterly* 81 (1): 61–82.

Oakleaf, Megan and Neal Kaske. 2009. "Guiding Questions for Assessing Information Literacy in Higher Education." *portal: Libraries and the Academy* 9 (2): 273–86.

Obama, Barack. 2009. Proclamation. National Information Literacy Awareness Month, Washington: The White House Office of the Press Secretary. Accessed December 16. www.whitehouse.gov/the_press_office/presidential

-proclamation-national-information-literacy-awareness-month/.

O'Connor, Lisa. 2009. "Information Literacy as Professional Legitimation: A Critical Analysis," *Journal of Education for Library and Information Science* 50 (2): 78–89.

Ondrusek, Anita. 2008. "Information Literacy." In *Academic Library Research Perspectives and Current Trends*, edited by Marie L. Radford and Pamela Snelson, 48–81. Chicago: ACRL.

Oud, Joanne. 2009. "Guidelines for Effective Online Instruction Using Multimedia Screencasts," *Reference Services Review* 37 (2): 164–77.

Owusu-Ansah, Edward K. 2001. "The Academic Library in the Enterprise of Colleges and Universities: Toward a New Paradigm." *The Journal of Academic Librarianship* 27(4): 282–94.

Palmer, Parker J. 1998. *The Courage to Teach: Exploring the Inner Landscape of a Teacher's Life*. San Francisco: Jossey-Bass, Inc.

Patterson, Kerry and Joseph Grenny. 2008. *Influencer: the Power to Change Anything* New York: McGraw-Hill.

Purdue, Jeff. 2003. "Stories, Not Information: Transforming Information Literacy", *portal: Libraries and the Academy* 3 (4): 653–62.

Quinn, Robert E., Jane E. Dutton and Gretchen M. Spreitzer. 2004. "Reflected Best Self Exercise: Assignment and Instructions to Participants." *Center for POS TeachingTool Series*. Accessed April 11, 2011. www.bus.umich.edu/positive/po-teaching-and-learning/reflectedbestselfexercise.htm.

Rollins, Debra Cox, Jessica Hutchings, Melissa Ursula Dawn Goldsmith, and Anthony J. Fonseca. 2009. "Are We There Yet? The Difficult Road to Re-Create Information Literacy," *portal: Libraries in the Academy* 9 (4): 453–73.

Saunders, Laura. 2009. "The Future of Information Literacy in Academic Libraries: a Delphi Study," *portal: Libraries and the Academy* 9 (1): 99–114.

Schiller, Nicholas. 2008. "A Portal to Student Learning: What Instruction Librarians Can Learn from Video Game Design." *Reference Services Review* 36 (4): 351–65.

Schlosser, Melanie. 2011. "OSUL2013: Fostering Organizational Change through a Grassroots Planning Process." *College & Research Libraries* 72 (2): 152–65.

Schroeder, Robert and Ellysa Stern Cahoy. 2010. "Valuing Information Literacy Affective Learning and the ACRL Standards." *portal: Libraries and the Academy*. 10 (2): 127–46.

Senge, Peter M. (1990) 2006. *The Fifth Discipline: the Art & Practice of the Learning Organization*. New York: Currency Doubleday. Citations refer to the 1990 edition.

Somerville, Mary M. 2009. *Working Together: Collaborative Information Practices for Organizational Learning*. Chicago: ACRL.

Sproles, Claudene, Anna Marie Johnson and Leslie Farison. 2008. "The Teachers are Teaching: How MLIS Programs Are Preparing Academic Librarians for Instructional Roles." *Journal of Education for Library and Information Science* 49 (3): 195–210.

Spreitzer, Gretchen M. 2011. "The Energy Audit: A Tool for Restoration." *POS Newsletter ("Teaching with an Impact" section)*, February 24. www.centerfor-pos.org/2011/02/the-energy-audit-a-tool-for-restoration.

Spreitzer, Gretchen M. and Scott Sonnenshein. 2003. "Positive Deviance and Extraordinary Organizing." *Positive Organizational Scholarship: Foundations for a New Discipline*, edited by Kim Cameron, Jane E. Dutton and Robert Quinn, 207–24. San Francisco: Berret-Koehler.

———. 2004. "Toward the Construct Definition of Positive Deviance." *American Behavioral Scientist* 47 (6): 828–47.

Sullivan, Maureen. 2004. "The Promise of Appreciative Inquiry in Library Organizations." *Library Trends* 53 (1): 218–29.

Symons, Ann K. and Carla J. Stoffle. 1998. "When Values Conflict." *American Libraries* 29 (5): 56–8.

Travis, Tiffani. 2008. "Librarians as Agents of Change: Working with Curriculum Committee Using Change Agency Theory." *New Directions for Teaching and Learning* 114: 17–33.

Walters, Scott. 2006. "Instructional Improvement: Building Capacity for the Professional Development of Librarians as Teachers," *Reference and User Services Quarterly* 45 (3): 213–8.

Westbrock, Theresa and Sarah Fabian. 2010. "Proficiencies for Instruction Librarians: Is There Still a Disconnect Between Professional Education and Professional Responsibilities?" *College & Research Libraries* 71 (6): 569–90.

Wilder, Stanley. 2005. "Information Literacy Makes All the Wrong Assumptions," *Chronicle of Higher Education,* January 7: 13.

Zauha, Janelle M. 2008. "The Importance of a Philosophy of Teaching Statement to the Teacher/Librarian." *Communications in Information Literacy* 2 (2): 64–66.

Notes

1. According to Elmborg LIS typically employs a scientific research model as opposed to a practice-based model. Hence research in teaching and learning has been accomplished by practicing professional librarians, not LIS research faculty.

2. Praxis, or "the interplay of theory and practice", Jacobs argues, "is vital to information literacy since it strives to ground theoretical ideas into practicable activities and use experiential knowledge to rethink and revision theoretical concepts". (260)

3. Some instruction librarians contend information literacy should be embed-

ded within departments or taught independently of other disciplines while others believe information literacy can be taught in "one-shot" course integration or its own credit course.

4. This section title took inspiration from Kegan and Lahey (2009) later referenced in the section.

5. To our knowledge, the vast body of literature about organizational change in academic libraries (Schlosser 2011; Somerville 2009) is general and does not deal with advancement of information literacy programs.

6. Note, Senge also published a second edition of the same title in 2006 as well as a Fieldbook in 1994.

7. This concept was influence by Maureen Sullivan's use of Appreciative Inquiry, discussed later in the text.

2

Ethnographic Study of Information Literacy Librarians' Work Experience: A Report from Two States

Celene Seymour

INTRODUCTION

This chapter reports on an ethnographic study of the experiences, practices and feelings of academic librarians who teach information literacy. Based on in-depth interviews with nine librarians who have information literacy responsibilities—five in West Virginia and four in Colorado—it examines the real-life work of practitioners in a wide variety of instructional environments. The research considers participants' preparation for their instructional role, ambiguity about the concept of information literacy, instructional challenges and professional practices. The authentic voices of instructional librarians provide insights into the roadblocks they face, success they experience and their expectations for the future.

The goal of this study is to explore the environment of information literacy instruction, especially in view of the paradigm shift associated with new information literacy initiatives described by Mitchell et al. (2001) and Ondrusek (2008). According to Ondrusek, "the custodial conception of the library no longer serves the societal good" and instruction is becoming the central role of college and university librarians under this new paradigm (2008, 59).

This research provides a valuable opportunity to illuminate the culture and context of instructional librarians' work environment that is not often available through information literacy literature.

ETHNOGRAPHIC RESEARCH: AN OVERVIEW

Ethnographic research seeks to understand and describe a culture by gathering perceptions of the people in that culture. "Ethnographic methods are used for capturing the largely unconscious cultural beliefs and practices" of participants (Hunter and Ward 2011, 265). By documenting these beliefs and practices and making implicit assumptions explicit, conclusions about how these assumptions impact behavior can be developed.

While quantitative or statistical research attempts to test a preconceived hypothesis by sampling large numbers of individuals, qualitative research such as ethnography generally focuses on a limited number of participants selected for the rich information they can contribute on a culture and issues related to that culture.

Once data is collected from interviews, observations, and other interactions with participants, it is sorted, reduced and analyzed. Interpretation of data, which has been called both an art and a science, consists of a close reading of accumulated information. Interview responses, for example, "are broken down into manageable sections or 'basic descriptive units', so that they may be more easily sorted, with the researcher concentrating on commonality of theme and pattern" (Maggs-Rapport 2000, 220).

Ethnography has been used by anthropologists to study exotic cultures for the past century, including Margaret Mead's *Coming of Age in Samoa* (1928). The following year Robert and Helen Lynd published a study of what was considered an average American small town, *Middletown: A Study of Contemporary American Culture*. Their research applied ethnographic research to Western cultures and helped to popularize the methodology. Clifford Geertz further established the theoretical foundations with such works as *Interpretation of Culture* (1973). The framework for ethnography to be applied to broader social sciences was developed in the 1980's and 1990's by theorists and researchers such as Lincoln and Guba (1985), Clifford and Marcus (1986) and Norman Denzin (1997).

Ethnography has been used extensively to study education, including the cultures of educational institutions, interactions between students and among educators and students. Early research studied the social life of students (Cusick 1973) and made an attempt to describe the classroom experience from the teacher's perspective (Smith and Geoffrey 1968). More recent research has studied learning from the perspective of minorities (Chang 1992) and the impact of emotions on teachers (Zembylas 2005).

While ethnography was an appropriate methodology to address the research goal of this chapter, it will not answer all questions pertaining to information literacy instruction or any other field. "The environment in which libraries exist increasingly requires them to possess a diverse and robust toolbox of research methods for understanding the rapidly changing needs and behaviors of students and faculty," according to Hunter and Ward (2011, 267). Some of the suggestions for further research mentioned in the conclusions are better suited to quantitative research or other tools in the research toolbox.

REVIEW OF THE LITERATURE

My dissertation research (Seymour 2008) was an ethnography that mirrors much of the research methodology and data analysis used in the study described in this chapter. I studied eight college writing teachers to uncover what texts college writing teachers used, both published textbooks and student-created texts, and explored how these texts reflected a theory of writing instruction. I interviewed participants, observed their writing classes, and convened focus groups of their students to enrich my understanding of how texts were used. Textual analysis of research notes and interview transcripts allowed me to make comparisons among participants and develop conclusions about the beliefs and experiences that inform their instruction and how these drive their practices.

The research on information literacy instruction described in this chapter is similar to the strategies I used in my dissertation research in several ways. In both cases primary research data is comprised of the words participants used to describe their beliefs and experiences. Their rich descriptions are intentionally used to understand the culture they work in and what impact their environment has on their practices.

There have been a number of other studies that have informed both the methodology and subject of information literacy instruction which focus this chapter.

Julien and Genuis (2009) used interviews and diaries to explore how "library staff relate to their instructional roles and the implications of those self-understandings for instructional outcomes" (926). The emotions they uncovered range from "significant pleasure" and "personal satisfaction" to "frustration, disappointment, and other negative emotions" (930). As "librarians have shifted from being straightforward service provides to trainers and then to teachers, this latter role assumes some level of expertise in pedagogy and curriculum design," what they found is related to "role stress" (926–927).

Julien and Given (2002/03) investigated "the discourse of librarians discussing their relationship with teaching faculty in postings to the Bibliographic Instruction/Information Literacy Instruction Listserve ... over the past seven years" (65). Researchers found that librarians "generally do not consider faculty members to be their clients—only those faculty members' students." (82).

Julien and Pecoskie (2009) looked at how librarians experience the teaching role. Interviews conducted with Canadian librarians with teaching responsibilities discovered ambivalence and even hostility. "One of the most salient themes identified in data analysis was the experience of complex and asymmetrical relationships between instructional librarians and teaching faculty at academic instructions." (150)

Sanders (2009) surveyed 13 information literacy experts, "library professionals who demonstrated high levels of participation and leadership in the field" (102–103), to document their expectations of how information literacy will evolve over the next decade. The study reveals that new librarians and even experienced practitioners are unprepared to fully partner with teaching faculty in instructional design. Sanders concluded that, "if librarians hope to advise faculty on instructional design and assignments or even take on a more full partnership role in instruction, they must be sure that they have learned the pedagogical theory to support the role" (109).

Cull (2005) used in-depth interviews of university teaching librarians to study their perceptions of information literacy instruction. He developed a description of academic librarians involved in information literacy instruction as "largely self-reflective, student focused, and pedagogically competent teachers who are passionate believers in the core role of information literacy in academic libraries" (1). Cull felt this type of research, which privileges the experiences and beliefs of information literacy instructors, was important because "few of their voices have been recorded in the professional literature" (2).

Ethnography has also been used to study issues related to student research and library usage. The University of Rochester hired Nancy Fried Foster, an anthropologist, to shed light on how students perform research and write papers by observing and interviewing them. The ethnographic study of undergraduate research practices by Foster and Gibbons (2007) "helped guide a library renovation, influence a Web-site redesign, led to changes in the way the library markets itself to students, and, in some cases, completely changed the image of undergraduates in the eyes of Rochester librarians" (Carlson 2007, 34).

Researchers have studied the various aspects of information literacy instruction—instructional (Julien and Pecoskie 2009; Cull 2005; Manus 2009), emotional (Julien and Genius 2009), cultural (Julien and Given 2002/03; Lister 2003) and institutional (Saunders 2009). The research described in this chapter seeks to integrate these four aspects of IL librarians' work in order to provide a unique understanding of their intersections and significance. What emerges is a holistic evaluation of their various effects on the viability and effectiveness of academic information literacy programs.

METHODOLOGY

Nine IL librarians, largely or primarily responsible for information literacy instruction in their academic libraries, were selected as participants because they were either recommended by the editors of this book or were librarians at colleges or universities known to the researcher. All participants—five from West Virginia and four from Colorado—are associated with colleges or universities accredited by the Higher Learning Commission, part of the North Central Association of Colleges and Schools, which assures the quality of the educational environment. Participants were included with no expectation that they would precisely "represent" the entire population of IL librarians but would shed light on common experiences and concerns.

Participants represent a variety of academic credentials and professional experiences. Three had completed library school in the past decade while two had received degrees before 1980. Six had additional master degrees, beyond the professional requirement of MLS or MLIS, or will complete a second degree within the next year. One participant had a Ph.D. in English. Two librarians in this study had degrees in education or significant experience teaching outside of library instruction.

The initial research instrument for this study was a list of 18 open-ended questions regarding experience with, practices in, and beliefs about information literacy instruction. "Generally, semi- or unstructured, opened ended, informal interviewing is preferred to allow for more flexibility and responsiveness to emerging themes for both the interviewer and the respondent." (Jackson et al 2007, 25) These questions are included as an appendix to this chapter.

Follow-up questions were developed after responses to the initial survey were reviewed. Most follow-up questions were individualized for a particular participant, based on his or her earlier responses in order to better understand or expand on these responses.

This research used emails to communicate between the researcher and participants. James, who studied the validity of email interviews in educational research, concluded that "email interviews create an arena in which the academic self could be articulated and explored, and in which the researcher could study and understand their lives" (James 2007, 973).

During this study, I found emails provided a rich text which was analyzed and comparisons among participates made. The informality and safety of emails, in addition to providing time for reflection and correction to assure accuracy, allowed the passion, humor, hope and discouragement of participants to surface.

Any similarities or differences between the two states in regard to providing information literacy instruction would enrich the study. Results shows IL instructors in the two states have similar backgrounds and experiences. They reported a range of support provided to information literacy programs and mirror the emotional and instructional terrain traveled.

This research provides a voice for those providing information literacy instruction on a daily basis. In this chapter I will not attribute individual quotes to specific participants. I will use the term Information Literacy instructor (IL instructor) to refer to all participants. For a list of participants, see the Acknowledgements section at the end of this chapter.

PREPARATION AND RESPONSIBILITIES

Preparation for their instructional responsibilities was a concern among participants. Only three of the nine participants took a course in library school devoted to instruction, others had no coursework focused on instruction and most indicated they feel this lack of training is problematic. Even those who completed library school since 2000 did not feel they were adequately prepared for information literacy instruction.

One IL instructor reported a need for a stronger pedagogical background. "My MLS program emphasized that we were to find the information that the user needed, not teach them how to find it." Another IL instructor reported having "absolutely no preparation for the pedagogical requirements of information literacy instruction." All participants have taken part in professional development activities and two have participated in ACRL's Information Literacy Immersion program.

One participant commented that librarians need the same instructional tools and training as faculty rather than those developed by and for librarians. "I feel that I have gained some of my best teaching skills from taking education classes and participating in teaching workshops designed for faculty."

There is not one simple description of the responsibilities the participants in this study fill. The number of students these programs serve, as reflected in student enrollment, varies substantially. Two institutions have fewer than 2,500 students and three have more than 29,000. One participant reported responsibility for 50,000 students across three institutions.

In larger universities, IL instructors would both manage the information literacy program and develop and provide instruction. As managers of information literacy instruction programs, participants report a significant amount of administrative responsibility. "As the Instruction Coordinator I plan and schedule the first-year writing workshops and general workshops and also manage the statistics and assessment analysis. I am also responsible for training the reference librarians on new instructional techniques, pedagogies, and technologies as appropriate. Finally, I also provide instruction for the reference librarians on the creation of Research Guides (LibGuides) and online tutorials."

Librarians in smaller colleges with limited (and sometimes rapidly diminishing) staff had general library duties such as covering the reference desk and providing assistance with technology in addition to their instructional duties.

An IL instructor said a broader responsibility is

> bringing emotion into the workplace constructively to make change with a team of librarians who agree to be part of a learning organization. It's not the teaching itself and it's not convincing the faculty of the need for collaborative instruction. It's the challenge right here in

our library workplaces to do things differently than ever before and talk together about whether and how we are going to face the intellectual and emotional demands of the 21st century academic library's educational mission together.

"This work is just plain hard," she further reported.

INFORMATION LITERACY INSTRUCTION CULTURE

Ethnography is a research methodology designed to explore and describe a culture that binds together individuals with similar values and interests. Although the information literacy instructors in this study do not share a physical environment or a common organizational structure, they do share the same responsibility for promoting student learning. An important goal in this research is to find out, based on the views of participants, if and how instructional librarians form a cohesive culture that can be studied and described and which supports their practices.

A description of the information literacy mission was provided by one participant. "We collaborate to facilitate student learning before the student is involved, we expect students to be part of the information retrieval and evaluation process, and we want them to reflect on the learning experience." But is there a culture which specifically supports the expectations of this mission?

According to participant responses, IL librarians share their experiences with others in the field through informal exchanges and more formally at state library conferences. Some reported that listservs or blogs add opportunities for sharing. But one stated that, while she "benefited from the information in blogs and lists, they don't compare to face to face communication."

One IL librarian did not feel these cultural expectations are met in day-to-day experiences. "I'm not sure if the culture exists and I've just never managed to really plug into it, or if most other librarians feel sort of isolated as well." Another reported that she is "incredibly busy, somewhat geographically isolated, and lacks access to funding for professional development activities." Another participant remarked that she "would welcome a discussion on shared beliefs and experiences regarding instruction with other librarians....But I do not remember that such a conversation has ever happened, regrettably." These appear to be common roadblocks to the creation of a viable information literacy instruction culture.

Opportunities for exchanging practices, questions and successes can lead to improved instruction by causing instructors to reflect on what they do. "I think anything that makes us think about what we do and why we do it can improve our instructional practices if we're willing to be lifelong leaders who can admit that we in fact don't know everything about our chosen fields and...still have things to learn," remarked one participant.

The difficulty of determining a shared culture of information literacy instruction is obvious from participants' comments and it is evident that IL instructors do not exist in one culture, but in several. They generally provide reference services along with other librarians, in addition to teaching, and share activities such as instructional design and delivery with non-library faculty.

Several participants reported that approximately 50% of their time is spent providing reference assistance and it isn't possible to differentiate between reference and instructional services. "Reference librarians provide services one-on-one to users *and* they teach. They have very demanding responsibilities that require a balance between service and education. This sets up a cultural conflict within their positions because a service culture and an instructional culture have different beliefs and pressures."

However, another participant describes the relationship between reference and instruction more positively.

> I consider reference and instruction to be two sides of the same coin—each reference encounter should be a teaching moment in helping students to develop information literacy skills and each instruction session (good ones anyway) should have hints of the reference interview as students are engaged in exploring what kinds of information resources are appropriate for a specific context.

In contrast, another participant commented that the gap between instructional librarians and librarians serving other functions is of real concern.

> Open dialogue between sub groups within each culture is not easy when it comes to the issues of territory, changing practices, sharing core principles, and areas of disagreement. It is well past time to stop walking away from talking to each other about these underlying issues of changing roles and new challenges.

Some participants reported their participation in the wider instructional culture, sharing with non-library faculty, is valuable. One participant reported that "I'm finding that talking with my non-library colleagues at the institution where I work in is very informative." She is currently collaborating with the campus Writing Center to provide research instruction. "The folks in the Writing Center are fueling my ideas for this project, not my colleagues in the library."

It is clear from responses that IL librarians exist in a complex environment that straddles the cultures of reference librarians and non-library faculty. As part of library culture but also part of the institution's overall instructional culture, it may be more constructive to understand how IL instructors interact with these cultures to serve both the library's mission and the overall instructional mission of the institution.

DEFINITION AND CONCEPT OF INFORMATION LITERACY

Participants in this study reflect an ambiguity in regard to the concept of information literacy and describe how our understanding of information literacy has changed over the past 20 years and continues to evolve.

"The concept of information literacy has its roots in the emergence of the information society, characterized by rapid growth in available information and accompanying changes in technology used to generate, disseminate, access and mange that information" (Bruce 1997, 2). In 1989 ALA defined information literacy as the ability to "recognize when information is needed and have the ability to locate, evaluate, and use effectively the needed information." Since that time the term has been challenged and debated. Shapiro and Hughes (1996) calls the term "an often-used but dangerously ambiguous concept." According to Budd, "coiners of the term probably meant something by it, but that meaning has been replaced by a circulating mélange of possible meanings" (Budd 2009, 63).

According to these IL instructors, there has been a shift in priorities from finding information to evaluating information and its appropriateness for meeting a particular need. Technology has also had a large impact on research and information gathering.

One IL instructor remarked that the 'means' of locating the information should be added to the description.

The 'tools' of 1989 were far different from the technological advances used in today's information searching. In fact, these advancements are coming or changing at a rate that is challenging to the information professional, and they are overwhelming to the general information seeker.

Another IL instructor remarked on the need to address the "instant information" world these students live in. "Rather than seeing Google and/or Wikipedia as the enemy, we need to teach students how and when to use these tools and when it is more appropriate to use a more 'academic' source."

One IL instructor reported the definition lacks attention to critical thinking.

Both the term and the definition have always bothered me....My cat processes information at this defined level. He hears the pantry door open and comes running. Library research involves higher cognitive functions and incorporate experience, prior learning and problem solving. Somehow that doesn't come across in the definition.

The need for librarians to keep alive the traditional standards for information evaluation in a culture where all information is considered equally valuable was voiced by one participant using a powerful mythological figure. He sees "the front lines of the information literacy battle today as more like Janus, the infamous two-headed god of the door, who looked both backward and forward simultaneously," occupying the middle ground between "barbarity and civilization."

Several IL instructors expressed the view that the concept of information literacy should not exist only within the walls of the academic library. Educators need to develop a culture of learning that extends beyond the wall of the classroom or the institution to the larger culture. The article by Shapiro and Hughes (1996) that presents information literacy as a "new liberal art" was quoted by one participant. Information literacy is a "new liberal art that extends from knowing how to use computers and access information to critical reflection on the nature of information itself, its technical infrastructure and its social, cultural, and philosophical context and impact".

The ability to ponder, refine, debate and challenge the definition of information literacy and the direction in which it is evolving reflects the exciting times these leaders in the field of information literacy instruction work in. Although many felt the existing term and associated concepts of bibliographic instruction and library instruction are inadequate or inaccurate, no one offered an alternative term. "Information literacy includes some admission of the inadequacy of those terms, but it does not replace them with a name that is sufficiency meaningful" (Budd 2009, 40).

Two participants defined information in the following way: "An information literate person has learned how to learn."

Describing it in a way that reflects learning skills rather than library skills, IL instructors can promote their critical function in the overall university curriculum.

> Libraries' instructional programs are invaluable to facilitating learning, knowledge growth, and communication. Librarians can enable understanding of the nature and purposes of communication, help students engage in dialogue with what others say, write, and show, and foster, through phenomenological cognitive action, student learning (Budd 2009).

By more precisely defining information literacy, both within the library profession and as individual IL instructors, practitioners will be better able to grasp the goals they are striving for and to articulate these goals to the university community.

INSTITUTIONAL SUPPORT FOR INSTRUCTION

None of the colleges or universities in this study has an institutional or state mandate to provide information literacy instruction. Several participating IL instructors indicated this lack of a mandate is a roadblock to successful and uniform information literacy instruction. Six of the nine participants responded that information literacy instruction is integrated into the First Year Experience, general studies program or other core curriculum. In describing the ideal information literacy program, several participants stated that the program would need to be required. But a requirement for information literacy is doubtful according to many participants. "The integration of information literacies across the curriculum is still only a dream," reported one IL instructor. Another participant reported that "attempts have been made to integrate IL into general students or the core curriculum, but that has proven very difficult."

As an example of institutional support for information literacy, one university offers a summer grant for faculty members to work with librarians to integrate information literacy instruction into their courses.

When participating IL instructors were asked to describe the institutional support their program received on a score from 1 (no support) to 5 (significant support), the wide range of perceived support became obvious. Some IL librarians reported support as low or non-existent (1 or 1.5) and others reported a high level of support (5 of a possible 5). The average score reported by Colorado librarians was 3.38, only somewhat higher than those reported by West Virginia participants (3.3).

Many participants reported that, while support from the library administration was high, support from the college or university administration was limited. Even within the library the support may vary from person to person. As one participant said, "the library administration does place a very high priority on information literacy. The rank and file may disagree with some of the administration's ideas and methods, but they do support it."

IL librarians may feel a lack of institutional support on a personal level. One participant reported a clear separation between librarians and non-library faculty and a distinction made by the university administration. "We do not generate FTE, there is no credit earning library courses. That places us low or nonexistent in the campus power structure. We are a service unit in the eyes of the university administration."

"The reality in this challenging economy is that we will not get all the resources we need to make the program ideal, but we are doing the best we can with what we have by being creative," is the philosophical and pragmatic way one participant described the need to "make do" with the financial support that is available. Without pressure from states and accreditation bodies, consistent and uniform support for information literacy instruction continues to be a problem in most institutions.

INSTRUCTIONAL TERRAIN

Although much of the discussion of information literacy focuses on broader conceptual and cultural issues, it is also important to understand what goes on in the information literacy classroom and how student learning is impacted, either positively or negatively, by these other issues. The study reported in this chapter allowed participants to explain the teaching and learning process as they understand it and what instructional practices they use in information literacy instruction. The issue of communication with faculty and students regarding instruction was also discussed.

Instructional Standards:

Any description of instruction should start with an understanding of the specific standards or learning objectives which focus that instruction. Most participating IL instructors reported they rely on ACRL *Information Literacy Competency Standards for Higher Education* (2000) to provide the focus for instruction. One IL instructor states, "They are the foundation for all that we do." According to another IL instructor, "We keep them in the back of our minds as we prepare for information literacy modules or present to classes." Several of the participants specifically post ACRL standards on their library instruction web sites to justify their programs and to educate teaching colleagues.

Other participants don't directly articulate these standards but they do use them to create appropriate learning objectives. "We build our own learning objectives off of ACRL standards, in consultation with the course professor and course goals," states one IL instructor. Another participant reported creating student learning objectives related to ACRL standards with faculty input.

Although standards and competencies are the starting point for instructional design, Budd argues these narrow competencies do not define learning. "The concentration on skills and competencies omit integrated informing, cognitive growth and learning." (Budd 2009, 40) Budd states they "signaled a noble effort informed by the best intentions" (2009, 40) but discusses the inadequacy of these standards. For example, "they *are definitely necessary for students' learning, but they are far from sufficient*" (italicizes origin), (41).

Instructional Practices:

Instructional programs described by participants show a variety of practices and strategies. Instruction strategies range from typical one-shot sessions (limited in scope and scalable to reach many students) to strategies that allow the librarian to fully participate in course design, delivery and assessment. Strategies, described below, are categorized as Low Integration to Full Integration to reflect the degree that instruction is designed for a specific class with the continued involvement of the librarian.

Low-Integration into Instruction: Strategies mentioned by participants are one-shot orientation sessions (generally focused on use of the online catalog and databases and maybe a tour of the library); drop-in workshops (which could be focused on information search strategies, term-paper writing, citation of sources, etc.); online tutorials and videos. Wimba is also used by some programs and is particularly useful for distant of non-traditional students.

Medium Integration into Instruction: Options mentioned by participants include on-demand instructional session customized to fit needs of an individual class; Libguides (online research guides) developed specifically for a discipline, a course or an assignment; and information literacy components integrated into discipline-specific courses.

High Integration into Instruction: Embedded Librarian programs were reported by two participants. This is the practice of assigning a librarian to take "an active role as a secondary instructor" and attends several or most class meetings in a particular for-credit course. "By teaching information-literacy sessions evaluating student assignments, and answering questions about research and writing, I have direct influence within the course", reports Manus (2009, 250). As reported by one IL instructor, this commitment is difficult to sustain and it was not known if the staff will be able to continue this workload in the future.

An IL instructor described the development of a new required writing course in which a librarian was involved in goal setting and course design. As a result "the mutuality of the goals and objectives of information literacy and writing instruction have come to the forefront for the writing faculty as well as for librarians."

Those strategies in which the librarian is fully integrated into instruction are problematic because of the time and effort involved given the tremendous demand on the IL librarian's time. Several participants reported having to cut back on some areas of instruction in order to sustain more intensive instructional efforts for other categories of students.

The degree to which library instruction can evolve from a cursory, one-shot orientation model, which Badke calls "remedial" (2010, 130), to one that allows a full range of involvement by a teacher librarian depends on the commitment of resources by the library and university administration and the willingness of faculty to share their instructional role.

Assessment of Learning:

Assessment of student learning is increasingly important as the demand for accountability in education grows. Assessment processes described by these IL instructors were uneven. Many programs rely on pre- and post-tests, minutes papers and surveys from students completing the instruction. There isn't much formal measurement of how much students gained from the instruction but librarians rely on informal feedback and anecdotal evidence to judge the success of instruction. In some cases instructors reported they had developed an assessment process but they were still collecting data and analyzing results.

One participant reported participating in the national assessment efforts *iSkills* (now *iCritical Thinking*) offered by the Educational Testing Service which provides national benchmarks for both information and computer literacy. But results were not useful in terms of an overall impact on the information literacy program.

An IL instructor recommends "grass roots" assessment, which she describes as assessment in which librarians and faculty work together to "identify what we thought every student should know (or have experience with) upon leaving our institution." This information then provides a foundation for the information literacy program and benchmarks for success.

Referring to assessment of the information literacy program, one participant described a program analysis she performed. "My findings were that we had a collection of instructional activities that were not directly or strategically linked to the mission of [the university] or each other from campus to campus." Although participants report greater emphasis on measurement of student learning, they are struggling to create a system where evidence of student success (or failure) can be used to improve instruction.

Communication Related to Instruction:

The most effective way to educate the university community about the library instruction program is individually through face-to-face communication, according to participants in this study. "I talk to a lot of people when they come for coffee," said one IL instructor. But, given the large number of faculty members some of these participants potentially collaborate with, more efficient ways are needed. Emails for a specific reason, such as reminding faculty of instructional services at the beginning of the fall semester, sometimes work but faculty are often overwhelmed by the volume of emails they receive.

Communication is further complicated when many faculty work part-time. One participating IL instructor reported the difficulty communicating with part-time faculty. "Many instructors are adjunct and re-education about the library's instruction program has to happen every year or every semester."

Some instruction librarians participate in or initiate more formal in-person presentations. They partner with specific departments or programs, attending their faculty meetings, or provide workshops. The program described by one IL instructor offers "general workshop each quarter on a variety of topics. These workshops are open to any member of the [university] community, but...more faculty have been attending the workshops themselves and have then been requesting similar workshops for their classes...My guess is that by coming to a workshop themselves, faculty have a better sense of the kind of instruction that the librarians can provide."

Virtually all participants maintain web sites for instructional services which allow faculty to schedule instruction and communicate with the librarian about instruction. Some of these web sites are extensive, articulating information literacy standards and other resources. However, no participants indicated it was a significant means of communicating with others about their program. The function of the library instruction web site and how well it serves that function should be a concern of library instruction programs.

Educators are challenged to communicate with and educate students who exist in a culture very different from the one they lived in as undergraduate students. This gap is sometimes manifested in a clash of values. According to one IL instructor, "I see so many undergraduates that don't seem to value education for the purpose of being educated. Every project and assignment is a series of checks to get the degree...to get the job." Another IL instructor has no problem bridging the gap between students and faculty and feels the key is continuous learning rather than refusal to evolve. "There is so much learning to keep up with that I feel we all need each other to act as mentors no matter what age we are."

The technology gap between students and librarians of a different generation may not be as big as reported, according to one participant. "I multi-task just as badly as the 20 something's. As old as I am, I love IM and flipping around media sources in order to find information. The human commonalities are far more important than differences." Another IL instructor acknowledges the challenges of engaging students who exist in a digital culture so different from the one she was raised in. "I try to bring them some pure energy about the excitement of learning every micro-change that I get. It's rewarding. Their eyes light up. The conversation happens."

According to Ondrusek, the instructional foundation of information literacy must be built on a teaching force who "strive to understand learning itself", who "form partnerships with an institution's teaching faculty" and understand that "assessment of learning must be integrated into the program..." (50). Participants in this study display an awareness of these requirements but are encountering roadblocks to addressing them given the failure of their institutions and a culture to fully support their endeavors.

THE EMOTIONAL TERRAIN

Throughout the interviews the emotions expressed by participants, both positive and negative, are of particular importance to a deep understanding of the cultural, instructional and institutional terrains they travel. It is "reasonable to surmise that negative instructional experiences influence librarians' efforts to educate learners" (Julien and Genuis 2009, 934). Therefore, exploring the emotional terrain associated with information literacy instruction and improving this environment should maximize the impact of instruction by minimizing negative instructional experiences.

In their study of how library staff members feel about their instructional responsibilities, Julien and Genuis found that "participants' effective response was strongly shaped by their relationship with students and faculty" (2009, 930). In that regard, a feeling of isolation was expressed by a number of participants in the current study. One aspect of this isolation is a disconnect they feel from librarians serving other functions.

In some regard this is because instruction programs are generally one-person operations with librarians from other departments filling in for a certain number or courses, but it is also because information literacy librarians see themselves as change agents. Their function is to upset the status quo which is no longer seen as effective.

One IL instructor reported being demoralized because "few of the librarians I work with seem to understand what I'm doing in the classroom. I feel they are only interested in providing reactive services from the reference desk; oftentimes when it is too late to impact assignment design. Because of these differing philosophies I've been accused of 'not doing my job.' Frankly it is very demoralizing." However, she realizes that "librarians not as heavily involved in instruction may not have had the time, space or circumstances to reflect on" information literacy.

Several participants report it is difficult to convince library faculty to upset the status quo. Another participant said "convincing teaching faulty that the move away from one-shot sessions to more of an embedded librarian approach is necessary." "I am isolated and solo change agents do not make much headway in certain respects," reported another IL instructor.

Because of the power structure of the library and the institution, IL librarians are frustrated by a lack of leverage to force change. "No one reports to me so there are no repercussions for refusing to pick up classes or failing to impart useful information to students in the classroom or at the reference desk", according to a participant. Another participant reported that she has no formal authority to promote change or authority to influence the integration of information literacy instruction except the power of influence.

Another emotional issue raised by participants is lack of acceptance as equals by non-library faculty members. The majority of participants reported that they have faculty status but not tenure. Some indicated they feel fully accepted by non-library faculty members, especially those they collaborate with, and serve on committees such as the Faculty Senate and participant in other important university functions. According to an IL instructor, "I think the faculty members who request presentations for their classes every semester respect my abilities and what I teach their students." She is not bothered by any perceived lack of respect.

But not all IL librarians are negatively impacted by this isolation and a number of participants addressed it in a positive way. "The more I accept myself as equal but unique in my own right, the better I feel." As another

IL instructor reported, "the more they see us and work with us in class-rooms throughout campus, the more they will understand and appreci-ate the unique instructional abilities of information literacy librarians."

All librarians who deal with the public directly, such as reference and circulation staff, face this "emotional labour" of providing service with a smile even at the most trying times and with the most trying patrons. But instructional librarians may face a different kind of emotional toll which requires proactive responses such as better preparation for and sup-port for their instructional responsibilities and a greater understanding of the emotional issues they face that stand in the way of their success.

"I am convinced that we can best move toward our professional goals buoyed by the supportive tide of collegiality," (Lister 2003, 34). The nur-turing of an information literacy culture could foster this collegiality and help IL librarians move toward their professional goals.

CHALLENGES

The primary roadblocks to information literacy programs, as reported by participants in this study, are institutional and cultural.

The lack of support from the institution, both the library and uni-versity administrations, is reflected in inadequate staffing and funding. This shortage of manpower was reflected in larger institutions that had to provide instruction for 50,000 students and smaller institutions, one of which is eliminating the instruction librarian position. A participat-ing IL instructor said, "Our strongest information literacy partner has been asking for more instruction and we simply can't provide it."

Getting information literacy taken seriously at the institutional level is a critical requirement to improving instructional success. These chal-lenges also involve the library culture. Although some participants report a "sea change" in support of information literacy from librarians and library staff, others says librarians are reluctant to change their traditional responsibilities to provide instruction or are unwilling to update their teach-ing skills to have greater impact on student learning.

One participant reported that the library's historical commitment to service is having a negative impact on instruction. "Information literacy program development is about learning outcomes and there is a very strong culture of service in our library system that unintentionally undermines advances in educational practices," according to one IL instructor.

SUCCESSES

Instructional success is primarily reflected in greater demand and an increase in number of students in sessions. One IL instructor reported providing information literacy instruction for 5,000 students each year. Another said 2,100 students participated in instruction each semester as part of the required writing course. One librarian who provides IL instruction (along with other public service duties) in a small institution with a very limited staff reported teaching 124 classes in the previous year.

Anecdotal evidence can also point to instructional successes. One instructor feels our assessment sometimes comes in informal encounters with students. The librarian told the following story to illustrate his point.

> I observed a young man explaining to a young lady how to construct a proper search in a complicated database. He [the young man] explained that her search was too broad and that she needed to add more search terms to her strategy in order to narrow the search....Then he told her to check the boxes for full-text and per-reviewed articles. Peer-reviewed were especially important, he instructed, because those articles were judged by a committee before they were published.

The librarian reported, "I was stunned. I asked him how he knew all of that, and he replied, 'You taught us that in my English 201 class four years ago.'" He was surprised and pleased. "Not only do they learn, but they teach their classmates."

Another instructor related student led instruction as an example of success. She described it as "students guiding the instruction, how it happens, and what they learn." She has found that

> students are more ready to learn, and more prepared to internalize what's happening in their class, if they are actively making choices about what and how they learn; if they are leading the conversations about what works in research and what doesn't, if they are guiding their own learning experience. It takes some effort from the instructor to prepare an environment where that can happen productively, but with that right environment, students can and will lead themselves into learning all the same things I want to teach them, without me having to tell them.

The excitement and satisfaction these instructors find in these examples of success is evident as they tell stories of interactions with learners.

It is clear these interactions enhance their professional work lives. On the other hand, the challenge of acceptance in the wider university environment and expectation that they will provide support for all learners without adequate support is also evident.

EXPECTATIONS FOR THE FUTURE

According to participants, information literacy programs in the future should be well-funded, mandated, assessed and focused on critical thinking. It would be both top down (fully supported by the administration) and bottom up (a grassroots movement by faculty, academic departments and students). The program should build on what had been taught at the K–12 level and would be developed and taught in collaboration with academic departments. Although many participants had clear views of what the ideal is, none felt the profession is close to meeting that ideal on any consistent level.

The challenges participants report are a result of a transformation in the profession and, hopefully, will be minimized by faculty, administrations and library staff who understand information literacy standards as learning standards relevant to all disciplines and lifelong learning. Preparing all librarians to carry out the instructional role and providing the institutional support to partner with non-library faculty should improve instruction and lessen the emotional labor.

One comment is particularly insightful in setting the context for this study and probably expresses the feeling of many of the exceptional librarians who are struggling to develop and maintain information literacy programs. "We are a teaching library." In her view, a library is not a building, a service desk or a passive collection of resources. It is part of an educational culture with the mission to provide instruction and support for learning throughout the institution.

CONCLUSIONS

Information literacy instruction has been "misunderstood and underestimated," according to Badke (2010, 132), and those who provide this instruction have been largely invisible. The goal of this study is to shed light on the complex environment in which information literacy instructors work by allowing practitioners an opportunity to describe the issues they face. It is necessary to understand these instructional, institutional, cultural and emotional aspects as inter-related and to address them in a holistic manner in order to fully support the library's instructional mission.

A paradigm shift in information literacy instruction which is both arduous and rewarding is described by participants. Historically, library instruction has been a service—an extension of reference desk activities to assist students in using library resources. The evolving expectation is that the information literacy program is part of the higher education curriculum, designed to provide instruction to all students as a valuable part of their course work and professional preparation. Support for instruction requires librarians committed to teaching, better prepared to design instruction and respected as equal partners with non-library faculty. It also requires institutions that support these information literacy competencies.

The primary roadblocks to meaningful and uniform instruction are a lack of institutional support, according to participants. "Until we convince the president, and the curriculum council that information literacy must be a required element of our students' education, we will never be able to reach each student with our program," according to another IL instructor.

Some participants see the lack of institutional support for their efforts as isolating and demoralizing. They view themselves as pioneers struggling to make headway in a challenging environment. As a result of their persistence and hard work, most participants report IL programs that are growing and increasingly integrated into the curriculum. Many report satisfaction and enthusiasm for the work they have undertaken but also alienation and frustration.

One possible solution to the frustration and isolation IL instructors feel is a better understanding of the culture in which they work. There is some evidence that a unique information literacy culture, allowing the systematic sharing of practices and concerns which could improve instruction, does not exist. Describing a unique culture which supports their instructional mission is problematic. But this complexity also makes it more important to understand and come to terms with this culture to fully support instructional practices and to address the emotional demands of IL instruction.

The IL instructors in this research come from the mountains of West Virginia and Colorado, but they provide a valuable map of the hills and valleys experienced by instructional librarians across the country. They are part of a profession that is struggling to come to terms with what information literacy is, how it can be given adequate respect in the academic culture, and the need for resources to build an effective and sustainable program.

Further research on the variety of issues uncovered in this study is needed. Institutional support for information literacy should be investigated, especially in terms of the budget reductions most institutions are dealing with. Is information literacy seen as a cost-effective way to prepare a workforce for the future, resulting in increased support, or is it viewed as an unnecessary addition to the curriculum which institutions are not able to fund?

Additional research on the existence of a unique information literacy culture and how this culture relates to the library culture and overall teaching culture of the institution is needed. The gap between instructional and other categories of librarians described by some participants may result in librarians working at cross-purposes or not fully understanding or supporting the different but related roles each serve.

Instructional practices, especially related to evidence of student learning, should also be investigated to uncover methods that provide effective and sustainable information literacy instruction to all students.

"Information literacy is conceivably the foundation for learning in our contemporary environment of continuous technological change" (Bruce 2004, 8). As the instructional, cultural, institutional and emotional pillars that support information literacy are strengthened, the overall academic learning environment will be enriched.

ACKNOWLEDGEMENTS

The author gratefully acknowledges the assistance of the following librarians for participating in this study and for their valuable insights:

Courtney Bruch, Front Range Community College (Colorado)
Lorrie Evans, University of Colorado—Denver
Carrie Forbes, University of Denver
Howard Hively, Fairmont State University (West Virginia)
Jennifer Knievel, University of Colorado—Boulder
Theodore Nesbitt, formerly of West Liberty University (West Virginia)
Beth Rogers, West Virginia Wesleyan College
Jennifer Sias, Marshall University (West Virginia)
Carroll Wilkinson, West Virginia University

APPENDIX 1
Initial Questionnaire: Questions for Information Literacy Ethnographic Study

Briefly describe your academic background—degrees, certification & years received.

Briefly describe your experience as a librarian and educator.

In 1989 ALA defined information literacy as follows: "To be information literate a person must be able to recognize when information is needed and have the ability to locate, evaluate, and use effectively the needed information." Do you think our understanding of information literacy has changed over the past 20 years? Does the traditional definition apply or can you suggest a better term for or description of this process?

How were you prepared for information literacy instruction in your formal library science degree program? Did you take any courses in instruction or teaching? Do you attend workshops or other development opportunities focused on information literacy?

Describe the history of information literacy at your university.

How does the information literacy program currently operate?

Within your library, how would you rate the priority placed on information literacy (5 being highest and 0 being the lowest)?

What library instruction do you provide for distant or online students?

What kind of support has information literacy received from the university administration in terms of funding, staffing or other encouragement?

Are you currently collaborating with other university departments or programs to provide information literacy instruction?

How do you access the impact of your information literacy efforts based on student learning?

How do you assess the overall effectiveness of your information literacy program? Have you found your program to be successful overall?

What roadblocks have you faced in developing a successful program?

What successes can you report?

Some people feel it is too late to teach information literacy when students are in college. Do you agree with this view?

Describe your ideal for information literacy instruction in the best possible situation.

How close do you think we are to reaching that ideal both locally and nationally?

Do you have other comments about information literacy pedagogy or how this pedagogy is applied?

References

American Library Association. (2000). *Information Literacy Competency Standards for Higher Education*. Chicago: ALA/ACRL.

Badke, William. 2010. "Why Information Literacy is Invisible." *Communications in Information Literacy* 4: 129–141.

Bruce, Christine. 1997. *The Seven Faces of Information Literacy*. Adelaide, AU: Auslib.

———. 2004. "Information Literacy as a Catalyst for Educational Change, A Background Paper." In Danaher, Patrick Alan, eds., Proceedings *Lifelong Learning: Whose responsibility and what is your contribution?*, the 3rd International Lifelong Learning Conference, Yeppoon, Queensland, AU.

Budd, John. 2009. *Framing Library Instruction*. Chicago: ACRL.

Carlson, Scott. 2007. "An Anthropologist in the Library." *Chronicle of Higher Education*, August 17: 34.

Chang, Heewon. 1992. *Adolescent Life and Ethics: An Ethnography of a U.S. High School*. Bristol, PA: Palmer Press.

Clifford, James, and George E. Marcus (Eds.). 1986. *Writing Culture: The Poetics of Ethnography*. Berkeley, CA: University of California.

Cull, Barry. 2005. "Voices in the Wilderness: A Report on Academic Information Literacy Instruction in Atlantic Canada." *Canadian Journal of Information and Library Science* 29: 1–26.

Cusick, Philip. 1973. *Inside High School: The Student's World*. New York: Holt McDougal.

Denzin, Norman K. 1997. *Interpretive Ethnography: Ethnographic Practices for the 21st Century*. Thousand Oaks, CA: Sage.

Foster, Nancy Fried, and Susan Gibbons (Eds.). 2007. *Studying Students: The Undergraduate Research Project at the University of Rochester*. Chicago: ACRL.

Geertz, Clifford. 1973. *Interpretation of Cultures*. New York: Basic Books.

Hunter, Gina and Dana Ward. 2011. "Students research the library: Using student-led ethnographic research to examine the changing role of campus libraries." *College & Research Libraries News* 72: 264–268.

Jackson, Ronald L., Darlene K. Drummond, and Sakile Camara. 2007. "What is Qualitative Research?" *Qualitative Research Reports in Communication* 8: 21–28.

James, Nalita. 2007. "The use of email interviewing as a qualitative method of inquiry in educational research." *British Educational Research Journal* 33: 963–976.

Julien, Heidi and Lisa Given. 2002/03. "Faculty-Librarian Relationships in the Information Literacy Context," *Canadian Journal of Information and Library Science* 27: 65–87.

Julien, Heidi and Shelagh K. Genuis. 2009. "Emotional Labour in Librarians' Instruction Work." *Journal of Documentation* 65: 926–937.

Julien, Heidi and Jen Pecoskie. 2009. "Librarians' Experiences of the Teaching Role: Grounded in Campus Relationships." *Library and Information Science Research* 31: 149–154.

Lincoln, Yvonna, and Egon Guba. 1985. *Naturalistic Inquiry.* Newbury Park, CA: Sage.

Lister, Lisa F. 2003. "Reference Services in the Context of Library Culture and Collegiality." *Reference Librarian* 83/84: 33–39.

Lynd, Robert S., and Helen Merrell Lynd. 1929. Middletown: *A Study of Contemporary American Culture.* New York: Harcourt Brace.

Maggs-Rapport, Frances. 2000. "Combining methodological approaches in research." *Journal of Advanced Nursing* 31: 219–225.

Manus, Sara J. Beutter. 2009. "Librarians in the Classroom." *Notes* 66: 249–261.

Mead, Margaret. 1928. *Coming of Age in Samoa.* New York: William Morrow.

Mitchell, Megan S., Cynthia H. Comer, Jennifer M. Starkey, and Eboni A. Francis. 2001. "Paradigm Shift in Reference Services at the Oberlin College Library". *Journal of Library Administration* 51:359–374.

Ondrusek, Anita. 2009. "Information Literacy," in *Academic Library Research: Perspectives and Current Trends,* eds. Maria Radford and Pamela Snelson, 48–81. Chicago, ACRL.

Sanders, Laura. 2009. "The Future of Information Literacy in Academic Libraries: A Delphi Study," *Libraries and the Academy* 9: 99–114.

Seymour, Celene. 1998. "Use of Instructional Texts in College Writing Courses as a Reflection of Teachers' Pedagogical Beliefs." PhD. diss., Indiana University of Pennsylvania.

Shapiro, Jeremy, and Shelley Hughes. 1996. "Information Literacy as a Liberal Art." *Educom Review* 31: 31–36.

Smith, Louise and William Geoffrey. 1968. *The Complexities of an Urban Classroom: An Analysis Toward a General Theory of Teaching.* New York: Holt, Rinehard & Winston.

Zembylas, Michalinos. 2005. "Beyond Teacher Cognition and Teacher Beliefs: The Value of the Ethnography of Emotions in Teaching." *International Journal of Qualitative Studies in Education* 18: 465–487.

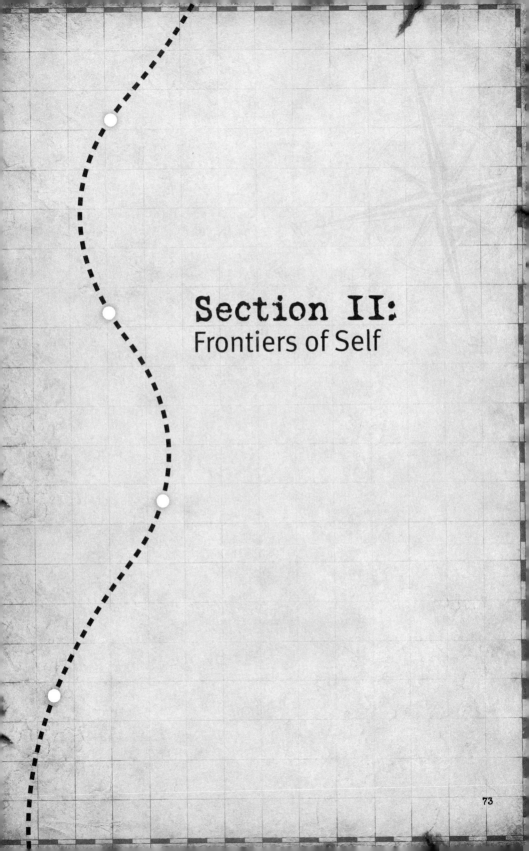

Section II:
Frontiers of Self

3

Critical Information Literacy: Definitions and Challenges

James Elmborg

After twenty years teaching English and composition, I became a librarian. I naturally brought many of the perspectives and issues of the English classroom to my work as a librarian, and I found my first position as a librarian working in "user education" as a liaison to composition and English. In this role, I faced immediate communication issues. Librarians I worked with rejected overly theoretical perspectives to their work. They saw tasks and jobs and looked for the most direct and efficient ways to do them. The professional literature modeled a problem-solving approach reflecting that mindset. Such research involved isolating variables around a problem and testing outcomes for the best solution, a solution we could replicate and apply broadly to library practice. In my own academic background and in my liaison work with English and composition, I found a dramatically different approach. There, instructors problematize incessantly and seek theoretical complexity as a way to continually re-frame their concerns. Each approach had its frustrations. Constant problematizing and theorizing can be paralyzing, since the problems never become stable enough to completely solve. On the other hand, the push to stabilize problems in order to solve them and to move immediately to practical solutions can mean over-simplifying underlying problems or seeking solutions to poorly understood problems. The tension between "problem setting" and "problem solving" made communication between the library and the academic unit difficult. In some ways, this tension seemed to reflect differences between working in a service role (distinctly defined problems and goal-driven solutions) and working in an instructional role (constantly shifting problems in murky contexts with competing agendas). As one charged with developing a teaching faculty in the library, I began to advocate that librarians become more engaged in theoretical questions of teaching and learning, and to bring those issues to the library and the classroom.

Upon becoming a faculty member in Library and Information Science, I became responsible for a research agenda, and my challenge has been to try to bridge this epistemological gap between two very different versions of knowledge-making. I have tried to be aggressive about problematizing academic library work, but I have tried to do so without veering entirely into the theoretical (and seemingly irrelevant). I was heavily influenced by the critical pedagogy movement in education and with how problematic teaching and learning can be if we take into account the social and cultural conflicts that shape our sense of what school should do. As a writing instructor, I found myself working with many students whose language was not Standard American English, and I found teaching writing to be a sometimes coercive activity that involved almost literally forcing students into linguistic constructions (and by extension, ways of thinking) that would make them sound "normal," which is to say "white" and "middle-class." While English and composition were acutely and painfully aware of the problems in this pedagogical position, the library literature rarely reflected any anxiety over the issue. My work as a scholar has largely been devoted to finding ways to initiate this discussion or to find others in the field to share the discussion with. In work like "Teaching at the Desk" (Elmborg, 2002), "Information Literacy and 'Real' Literacy" (Elmborg, 2004), and "Critical Information Literacy" (Elmborg, 2006) I aimed to bring critical perspectives to the field as both a practical and theoretical concern. As I continue to push forward with this work, my thinking has become increasingly challenging to (and critical of) the ways libraries and librarians tend to work. Some of us working in this field have come to call this approach "critical information literacy." This essay will explore "critical information literacy" as a concept that can inform the day-to-day practices of librarians. It will also extend this critical tradition established elsewhere in my work.

The tension between critical theory and social science methodologies outlined above manifests itself in a consistent question I get from librarians in practice. I am most often asked if I can provide clearer definitions or to provide examples of how we might practice critical information literacy. Because of the problems I have described already, I am wary of this effort to standardize and generalize theory. We are noun-driven in our discussions about research, easily turning ideas into concrete things so we can define, explore, and describe them. Michel Foucault described this process as the very essence of academia, the identification or creation of intellectual "objects" of study, whether those "objects" are literally physical objects or not (Foucault, 1982). Rather than seeing information literacy as a "thing" we can locate and define, I see it as a complicated set of interwoven practices. These practices are mobile, flexible, and malleable, residing in various places and in constant flux. In addition, these practices are not located in one place or person, but rather are shared across various sites and institutions, including information users (like students, and faculty) and those whose professional practices claim information literacy as their domain (librarians and IT staff) and among information producers (like authors, database vendors and publishers). Each of these roles involves people, values, and institutional cultures that shape practices. In order to understand information literacy, we must therefore ask a number of initial questions, including: Who is becoming information literate? What does becoming information literate mean? What can librarians do to help people become information literate? Who has a stake in what information literacy means? Information literacy thus bundles numerous dimensions into its central one.

This description of information literacy differs from the way we often see it depicted in official documents or practitioner literature. In these discussions of information literacy, we have aimed to stabilize the concepts as much as possible, that is, to make information literacy an abstract noun. When we begin to talk about critical information literacy, then, we find that all the various locations of literacy—the who, the what, and the how—become even more mobile and difficult to locate. Critical information literacy exists in relationships between people and information rather than as an identifiable thing in its own right. As we begin to engage the question of critical information literacy, it helps if we are careful with our language, to make sure we avoid reducing complex processes into overly simple concepts. The dynamism of critical information literacy needs to be reflected in our language. Christine Pawley has examined the ways that information literacy as a concept couples two "feel good" terms (information and literacy) in an attempt to gain traction for professional practice (Pawley, 2003). I agree with Pawley that our use of both "information" and "literacy" has tended to reify these concepts (to make them into unrealistically rigid and stable categories). I also think that by taking a critical approach to the language we use, we can open up these categories to move toward less mechanical and more rich and more human-centered understandings.

In adding the word "critical" to information literacy, I have two major intentions. The first is to recognize how "critical" it is for us to embrace and develop these new practices. In this sense, I intend the word to mean important and significant. It is "critical" that we do this and that we get it right. Secondly, I intend to be "critical," that is, to "criticize" our current practices. I intend to be critical as a way to improve our understanding, not out of meanness of spirit. I am critical of our tendency to treat information literacy as a "noun," for example, because focusing our attention on information literacy as an "thing" blinds us to the ways it must exist in people, practices, and process. I am critical of the Information Literacy Competency Standards, for example. I think they played a major role in turning information literacy into a "thing" we own, but which we aren't sure what to do with. This problem has defined our thinking and kept us from seeing other possibilities. In what follows, I intend to explore the central concepts involved in critical information literacy in order to open up the discussion of what it means to "do" critical information literacy. I will take each major term in turn—" "critical," and "information," and "literacy"—hoping to build as I go toward a useful conception of this admittedly difficult phrase.

WHAT IS LITERACY?

Historically, literacy has meant the ability to read and write. Etymologically related to "letters," literacy originally meant literally to "know one's letters." A general history of literacy reveals its relationship to power. In medieval times, the ability to read a text proved one's educational level, and consequently allowed one special treatment as a "gentleman" (the gendering of literacy is intentional since—except in only the rarest of circumstances—only males were allowed to be literate). Literacy levels have long been attached to Bible reading, and so literacy levels have been connected to piousness and right living. More recently functional literacy has been defined as the ability to use reading and writing to participate in the activities of the general society, especially the ability to sign financial instruments. In all these senses, reading and writing perform various social functions connected to power and class. Once they recognized the connection between power and literacy, societies found they could manipulate literacy levels to distribute power. Laws passed during the 19th century forbade the teaching of literacy skills to slaves, and women were long educated to read but not to write. Through such regulation, levels of power were distributed intentionally. Literacy has always been connected to power and to social class, and it has been intentionally deployed by societies to manage these categories and functions.

In the late 1990s, the concept of literacy began to expand and evolve as it became a catch-all metaphor for the skills that lead to success. Various words were coupled with literacy, including computer literacy, technological literacy, quantitative literacy, media literacy, financial literacy, and of course, information literacy. How can we account for this proliferation of literacies? Why literacy? In "Blinded by the Letter: Why are We Using Literacy as a Metaphor for Everything Else?" the questions of contemporary literacy are unpacked with an eye toward exploring the unspoken cultural work that the word "literacy" does today. Through analysis of old cowboy films and contemporary political rhetoric, Wysocki and Johnson-Eilola trace the ways reading and writing have been connected to the settling of the American West and to the vision of America's place in the unfolding future century. They cite President Clinton's creation of the National Institute for Literacy, which "was created to assistant in upgrading the workforce, reducing welfare dependency, raising the standard of literacy, and creating safer communities" (Wysocki and Johnson-Eilola 1999, 350–351). We often talk about literacy as a discrete set of skills that can be taught in relatively neutral ways. In Wysocki and Johnson-Eilola's analysis, the distribution of this set of skills pushes forward a national agenda of self-reliance and workforce ready citizens.

In many of these discussions, literacy is treated as a universal and relatively unproblematic good, one we can impart to people to give them a better life, and in the process, make them productive citizens rather than drags on society and the economy. In this vein, literacy levels are often cited as key for developing Third World countries into productive modern societies. Information literacy originated in this context as a form of literacy intended to connect to other literacies that make for productive citizens living productive lives. The origin of the phrase "information literacy" is generally credited to Paul Zurkowski, who was president of the Information Industry Association. According to Zurkowski, "People trained in the application of information resources to their work can be called information literates. They have learned techniques and skills for using the wide range of information tools as well as primary sources in molding information solutions to their problems" (Zurkowski 1974). The situating of information literacy in the workplace and the emphasis on skills and techniques to define information literacy connect it to other literacies designed to further the national economic and social good.

As we have come to see literacy as a "metaphor for everything else," the proliferation of literacies poses problems on two distinct levels. As Brian Street has persuasively argued, our past conceptions of literacy have been based on an "autonomous model" of literacy. In this model, the literate person is presumed to be an autonomous agent responsible for the accumulation of a certain set of skills that make him or her productive and useful. The failure to acquire such skills marks a person as inadequate, and we see illiteracy described in a number of ways that essentially blame illiterate people for their illiteracy. Street argues that contemporary social sciences have made a recent shift in how they see literacy, moving to what he calls the "ideological model" of literacy (Street 2001). The ideological model involves understanding all the social goods that have become attached to literacy. We also then must acknowledge that many of us have inherited these social goods as birthright, while others of us have not.

As we create new literacies by attaching various modifiers to the terms "literacy," we need to recognize the tensions set up by Street's dichotomy. If we see literacy as autonomous, then we assume that the skills that lead to literacy can be taught unproblematically. Like reading and writing, which we can teach phonetically as the relationship between sounds and written letters, other kinds of literacies can also be described as particular kinds of codes that lead to the ability to "read" other kinds of texts. Financial literacy becomes the ability to read and write checkbooks, mortgages, and tax documents. Quantitative literacy becomes the ability to read statistical data and to understand and explain what it demonstrates. Media literacy becomes the ability to read the television or computer screen to understand the message of the media. Fundamentally, the underlying metaphor of literacy involves "reading" and "writing." To read something skillfully is to be literate. To be able to write something is to master the literacy.

As we have already noted, the ability to read and write opens opportunities and constitutes a form of power. Marshall McLuhan argued that the phonetic alphabet allowed English speaking people to expand their global reach in that English "colonizes" all other languages by representing sounds rather than images (as do pictographic languages, for example). McLuhan connected the linear and logical structure of the written word with the militaristic logic of the Western mind (McLuhan 1999). McLuhan's Understanding Media was initially met with confusion and even scorn, but as English spreads to dominate online discourse (and by extension, all 21st century discourse), we can easily correlate the adoption of the English language with the communication channels of commerce that form the leading edge that spreads Western culture. In doing so, we must recognize that by adopting Western conceptions of literacy, a culture also tends to adopt Western values of capitalism with its patterns of production, consumption and worklife regimentation.

WHAT "CRITICAL" MEANS

In discussing literacy with my students, I am often challenged at this point to explain why this way of defining literacy is a problem. After all, capitalism (along with the rising middle class it has made possible) has made life infinitely better for those cultures that have adopted it. In introducing the concept of the critical, we risk positioning ourselves as outsiders who resist all the good things about the dominant culture rather than acknowledging all the great gains produced by literacy and its by-product, the Western middle class. In one recent discussion, students and I were exploring literacy's role in creating middle class values and the role of schools in linking these two concepts together. One student asked me sincerely, "Isn't that what we're supposed to be doing?" Indeed, we have come to accept the naturalness of literacy and its centrality for schools in creating Western prosperity and the Western worldview, so that anything critical of this process seems almost treasonous.

However, I want to take that risk because I think we have to acknowledge some basic problems with how we link literacy to cultural values. The first and most obvious problem is our assumption that the playing field in literacy education is equal. If we acknowledge that literacy significantly reproduces middle class identity, we must also acknowledge that lack of literacy excludes one from the middle class. In the autonomous model of literacy, the challenge for the autonomous individual (the non-literate student) is to gain the literacy skills required to enter the middle class. If we adopt the autonomous model, we frame this as a question of desire or will power. If students want to become literate, our schools stand ready to empower them. If not, they will be rejected from the system in favor of other students who want to succeed. James Gee has written about the ways that family literacy provides a framework for building future literacy skills. In essence, Gee argues that certain home literacies (notably middle-class literacies formed in English speaking homes with plenty of reading and writing) blend effortlessly into school, while the absence of such home literacies creates huge challenges for other students, challenges many of them never overcome (Gee 2001).

From a skills point of view, the challenges are formidable, but the challenges extend beyond just skills. If we consider the ideological model of literacy, we recognize that entangled with the Western middle-class performance of literacy are the cultural values McLuhan attaches to print literacy. These include the high value placed on autonomy (after all, reading mastery is achieved when one can completely internalize the reading process), competitiveness, and an acceptance of the justice of American capitalism's rise to global dominance. In essence, the story of literacy is the story of the Western rise to global domination. In I Won't Learn from You: The Role of Assent in Learning, Herbert Kohl describes a phenomenon he calls "learning refusal." He traces this "refusal" through various scenarios that represent students' intentional refusal to internalize the dominant culture around them because that culture devalues their lived experience by insisting that they accept the values embodied in the traditional literacy narrative (the story of the West, the story of the striving individual, the story of print literacy). He describes groups of Latino students in Texas who refuse to read history because their textbook starts the story of Texas with the coming of the white man. He describes students in New York who refuse to read and write without challenging the ways that language frames and reproduces gender, class, and ethnic techniques of domination (Kohl 1994). Kohl insists that we see these students as highly intelligent and extremely perceptive about how we use language. They intentionally refuse to adopt middle class literacy practices because those literacy practices come with a social and political "reality" that these students perceive and reject.

I have begun to assign a short story to my class in the course I teach on literacy: "The Ones Who Walk Away from Omelas" by Ursula Le Guin.

This brief science fiction tale describes a utopian society where everyone has everything they could want. They are happy and beautiful, intelligent and wise. At a certain point in their lives, in the middle teenage years, the young people go through a rite of passage. They are taken to a dungeon where a child lives in despair and squalor. This child is wretched and has no hopes for escaping the dungeon, and indeed, the child would not know what to do if liberated. The young people of Omelas then go on with their lives understanding that with all their happiness, wisdom, and beauty, a child exists in squalor in a dungeon. The child's condition is nobody's fault. However, the knowledge that the child exists creates such discomfort in some that they "walk away" from Omelas, unable to participate in a system with such a situation at its center (Le Guin 1975). The story is a parable, and as such it is simplistic and stark in its theme and message. Among many other things, it represents to me the origins of a critical consciousness, an awareness that material comforts and happiness depend on those in different circumstances who have yet to "make it" and who perhaps never will. The existence of such discrepancies poses a fundamental problem for us as educators. Once we are awake to the question, we can not "un-ask" it.

WHAT IS INFORMATION?

Of all the abstractions that we represent with nouns, perhaps the most problematic is the word "information." In The Problem of Information, Douglas Raber goes so far as to suggest that we should just give up on establishing a stable meaning for the term information "and embrace instead the idea that at least there will be times when it can be unambiguously identified (Raber 2007, 8). " "Information" does not exist in any tangible sense, of course, a fact we all know on some level. Derived from the verb "inform," information is literally any material thing that informs us. For something to be information, there must be a person who is informed. Information is therefore, literally, that substance which the informing material transmits to the person informed. At this point, we are veering close to pure metaphysical abstraction, interesting in its own right, but not terribly useful in moving our discussion forward. For our purposes, then, we can call the idea of "information" a useful fiction. While information is entirely abstract as a concept, we can very fruitfully treat it as a material reality in some cases. Indeed, information science as an intellectual field does precisely that. By applying scientific methodology to study information as if it were real and material, information science has been able to generate very useful observations about how information behaves and how it responds to those seeking to be informed.

Having conceded the usefulness of the fiction of information, I want to raise a concern about what happens if we treat information as if it were real, I do not aim to call all of information science (or its related fields of information retrieval and/or classification, etc.) into question. Rather, I want to draw reasonable parameters around what we can actually achieve by this move. Information science itself gestured toward this problem early in its formation as a field of study. Information scientists began to substitute the word "aboutness" for the more common library word "subject" (Raber 2003, 131–140). Information scientists were uncomfortable with the philosophical baggage that came along with the word "subject," in that by naming "subjects," we reinforced the illusion that information exists "out there" and apart from any person who is seeking to be informed. While we might debate whether a shift in terminology from "subject" to "aboutness" gains us philosophical ground, it does draw attention to a primary point worth emphasizing. Only a person seeking information can tell us whether a document or a statement provides information that he or she desires. In other word, the only judge of "aboutness" is the person who seeks to be informed "about" something.

Hope Olson has articulated the problems with our various versions of "subject" or "aboutness" by recognizing that our library tools, in identifying subjects, depend entirely on Western categories of meaning (Olson 2001). Rather than sliding easily over this observation, I want to pause to examine its significance. The power of classification to define legitimate subjects of inquiry is immense. Historically, libraries and librarians have constructed collections and tools treating the idea of "subject" as completely unproblematic. Indeed, in library rhetoric, "subjects" are real. They are also extremely powerful in that they reflect the authorized "subjects" in academic curricula. Like academic disciplines, library subjects are a natural part of how schools teach us to think. As useful fictions, "subjects" as ways of organizing "information" have served us well. Useful fictions present tricky challenges in that their usefulness can easily justify increased belief in their reality. To handle useful fictions we need to consciously suspend our disbelief. Ultimately, however, we can easily end up believing in useful fictions as if they are true. In such cases, we fail to recognize when the fictions take on a life of their own, and we allow these fictions to separate from their own stories.

In his impressive history of education as a colonial enterprise, John Willinsky argues that in "learning to divide the world" Western colonizers undertook a project that involved understanding cultural others as inferior objects of study. Following this ultimate classification (us=civilized, them=uncivilized), education began a program that involved dividing the world in ways that explained this "otherness" to the colonizers and the colonized. Willinsky claims that modern education grew out of the "ways in which imperialism was bent on taking a knowing possession of the world, on setting that world on public display for the edification of the West, and on developing the principal forms of schooling that might serve both colonial state and colonized native" (Willinsky 1998, 19) He argues that academic "subjects" were created to provide a seemingly neutral system for the imperialist mind to take "knowing possession" of the colonized. According to this analysis, "the five academic disciplines that have become staples of the school curriculum: history, geography, science, language and literature" reflect "traces of the colonial imagination that form part of how we have learned to divide the world." (Willinsky 1998, 19) Each subject in turn serves as a method for dividing the civilized "us" from the uncivilized "them."

When we allow the idea of "subjects," derived from school curriculum, to assume the status of reality in our minds, we separate the history of their evolution—indeed, the very reasons they exist—from their existence in our conception of professional practice. Controlled language, Library of Congress Subject Headings, and collections arranged by call numbers—all these represent significant ways that "subjects" have assumed the status of material reality in libraries, but they also carry the very obvious markings of their colonialist history. In relying on these subject categories to structure knowledge—and by extension to structure the ways that students learn—we in effect make judgments about legitimate and illegitimate questions based on whether the questions are represented as acceptable subjects. Subject categories impose a form of reality, but they do so in such passive and neutral ways that we can present them as "helpful" to students and researchers.

For this reason (at least in part) many people working in libraries continue to find the transformation of abstract classification into subjects unproblematic. In conversations with librarians-in-training about the classifying of information, I often reach the same point of impasse as in discussions of literacy: They ask "Isn't this what we are supposed to be doing?" While acknowledging useful fictions and their value, we also need to recognize the limits of these fictions and what gets hidden when we pretend that subject categories that we have invented for particular historic reasons are real. As one remedy for such simplifying of "information" into material category, Siva Vaidhyanathan proposes "critical information studies," which he says "interrogates the structures, functions, habits, norms, and practices that guide global flows of information" (Vaidhyanathan 2006, 303). This vision of Critical Information Studies "asks questions about access, costs, and chilling effects on, within, and among audiences" (Vaidhyanathan 2006, 303). Vaidhyanathan suggests that critical information studies should promote "the idea of 'semiotic democracy', or the ability of citizens to employ the signs and symbols ubiquitous in their environments in manners that they determine" Vaidhyanathan 2006, 305).

While different in many ways from critical information literacy, Vadhyanathan's critical information studies derives from the same need to get beyond surface descriptions of information to ask more fundamental question about "global flows of information." Doing so moves us away from defining information as a "thing" and toward understanding information as a repertoire of historically based social practices involving production, dissemination and reception. Such a discussion naturally leads us to ask more problematic questions about access, about who has access to information and who does not. Finally, and significantly, critical information studies connects access to information to "semiotic democracy," a wonderful phrase that concisely points to our inherent interests in a democratic society in making and expressing our own symbols and signs, rather than depending on externally generated concepts of "subject" or "aboutness."

In theory, all the impulses of critical information studies seem congruent with library philosophy, and indeed, in an era of where libraries advocate for open access publications to challenge publishers to open up their economic systems to bring down the walls between people and information, critical information studies would seem to provide a philosophical rationale and a way of conceptualizing information that might lead toward a liberating conception of libraries. However, we have much work to do in thinking about how this philosophy actually plays out in the roles librarians assume in educating students. One way of framing this question is to ask what would librarianship look like if it were viewed as a form of living and practicing critical information studies.

In some form, the question can be answered with critical information literacy.

WHAT IS CRITICAL INFORMATION LITERACY?

First of all, as one of the expanded concepts of literacy, information literacy has inherited assumptions about how literacy might be function in service of the national mission to maximize productivity and create a competitive workforce in the twenty-first century. Much of the rhetoric surrounding information literacy resonates with the language of productivity, and the Information Literacy Competency Standards have been rightly called to task for turning the research process into a formulaic and production-oriented concept. The Standards emphasize efficiency and their existence has made information literacy into a goal-driven, product-driven activity. Perhaps most damaging is the way the Standards have framed the student researcher. Though many readers will have intimate familiarity with the Standards, I reproduce them here for discussion:

An information literate individual is able to:

- Determine the extent of information needed
- Access the needed information effectively and efficiently
- Evaluate information and its sources critically
- Incorporate selected information into one's knowledge base
- Use information effectively to accomplish a specific purpose
- Understand the economic, legal, and social issues surrounding the use of information, and access and use information ethically and legally

As I have noted elsewhere, these Standards roughly emulate a process model (Elmborg 2006). The process is linear, moving from the determination of a need through access, evaluation and use. "Information" must be seen here as a fully reified concept, which means we must fully accept the "reality" of information as unproblematic. The Standards focus on efficiency and utility. Information literacy here emerges as a tool of the skilled knowledge worker, who becomes more information literate as she or he becomes a more efficient handler of information. At this point, we may well ask, "Isn't that what we're supposed to be doing?"

As suggested above, Information (and by extension information literacy) is a concept spread across multiple sites of meaning (including sites like the classroom, the reference desk, the lecture hall, and the dorm room) and with multiple participants (including the faculty member, the librarian, the IT staff, and the student) and various stakeholders (including the faculty, the library, the publishers, and future employers). However, the Standards ignore all aspects of information literacy except the student. In effect, by choosing to focus on defining the "information literate student," the Standards have adopted the autonomous model of literacy and put the entire responsibility for information literacy on the student. They do not call into question the ways all the other important players in the system might have competing or incompatible agendas in relation to that student. The student has become the "object" of information literacy, and by extension, the place where information literacy happens. The academic librarian (like all other stakeholders) can maintain a safe objective distance from this student and assess his or her progress toward information literacy using the measuring stick of the Standards.

Our first challenge in conceiving a critical information literacy is in rethinking this positioning of the student. Paulo Freire's work has been rightly invoked as a powerful alternative model for thinking about how this relationship might be conceived (Jacobs 2008). Freire argues that we need to break down the dichotomous relationship of students and teachers to conceive of a new way of thinking about students with teachers. Freire argues that "education must begin with the solution of the teacher-student contradiction, by reconciling the poles of the contradiction so that both are simultaneously teachers and students." (Freire 2002, 72). Freire describes the educational model represented by the Information Literacy Competency Standards as the "banking concept." In focusing on information as a tangible "thing," and information literacy as the set of skills for acquiring that "thing," we (perhaps unconsciously) have focused on teaching students to more efficiently "bank" knowledge. The logic of capitalism thus underlies the literacy narrative once again.

Freire argues that to combat this "banking" education, we need to develop "critical consciousness" in students and teachers. Freire argues that we "must reject the banking concept in its entirety, adopting instead a concept of women and men as conscious beings, and consciousness as consciousness intent on the world." (Freire 2002, 79) We must focus on "acts of cognition, not transferals of information." (Freire 2002, 79) Ultimately, according to Freire, a critical education "entails at the outset that the teacher-student contradiction be resolved." (Freire 2002, 79) Heidi Jacobs has perceptively argued that information literacy instruction needs to develop a critical praxis precisely to reposition the student in relation to what Freire calls "critical consciousness." Jacobs argues that "in terms of information literacy pedagogy, one of the best ways for us to encourage students to be engaged learners is for us to become engaged learners, delve deeply into our own problem posing, and embody the kind of engagement we want to see in our students." (Jacobs 2008, 261) Such "problem posing" is offered by Freire as an alternative to the banking concept. He describes a process of transforming banking education into problem posing education which means we stop seeing students as "objects" and repositories for information and begin seeing them as "historical beings necessarily engaged with other people in a movement of inquiry." He concludes that "any situation in which some individuals prevent others from engaging in the process of inquiry is one of violence. The means used are not important; to alienate human beings from their own decision-making is to change them into objects." (Freire 2002, 85)

Jacobs has provided a full analysis of the implications of bringing Freireian praxis into service as information literacy pedagogy (Jacobs 2008). Kopp and Olson-Kopp have written persuasively about the implications of conceiving information literacy work as developing Freireian critical consciousness (Kopp and Olson-Kopp 2010). I have argued the we have traditionally seen the library as an "information bank" in banking education (Elmborg 2004). In linking critical information literacy to Freireian pedagogy, a major question has remained somewhat unanswered. I think addressing this question directly might further push our understanding and perhaps open new lines of thinking. This question relates to the inherent problem of importing a pedagogy (and indeed an entire world view) from another time and place into twenty-first century education in Western developed nations. Paulo Freire was a Brazilian educator. He grew up among the poor in Brazil, and though he became highly educated, earning a law degree and spending his life as an educator, he maintained his identification with Brazilian peasants. His "pedagogy of the oppressed," which the banking concept and problem posing education exemplify, grew from his understanding of the way political power and education were deployed to oppress the peasant class in Brazil. Freire's pedagogy also derives from his Christian perspective, which drove his concern for the poor and which he coupled with a Marxist philosophy of class and power.

Any understanding of Freire's philosophy and praxis must on some level account for the translation of his work—deeply connected as it is to local historical and philosophical contexts—into modern (and postmodern) practices.

The first way to address this problem is to acknowledge it exists, to avoid reifying the banking concept as a concept and to treat it instead as a statement from a different time and place that can help us understand our own. Freire's commitment to a Christian concern for the poor and oppressed seems relatively unproblematic to me. Secular humanism (for lack of a better phrase) draws most of its moral framework from Judeo-Christian ethics, relying on questions of social justice and the responsibility of humans to take care of each other to guide its ethical positions. Concern with these issues is consistently raised in all major religions, making the ethic virtually universal in spite of specific dogmatic or ritual differences these religions might hold. I can certainly understand and respect resistance to any professional philosophy rooted in religious faith. However, it seems unwise to insist that education not have an ethical dimension of caring and responsibility at its core.

The concept of "oppression," however, presents more complicated problems. Freire developed his pedagogy in his work with oppressed working peasants in Brazil. For Freire, imparting reading and writing skills to these learners did not solve the central problems of literacy. In order to learn to read and write, these learners needed to develop a consciousness, a literate awareness of the power of having a mind, of having thoughts of one's own. They needed to move beyond thinking of the world as existing in a reified reality that they could experience but not change. They needed to develop agency, a sense of having a self that shapes and takes meaningful action in the world. For Freire, consciousness is central to literacy. In articulating a concept like the "banking concept," Freire wants to challenge the idea that we can deposit knowledge in people's minds while leaving them relatively unchanged in terms of how they see themselves in the world. For Freire, this "depositing" represents the ultimate fraud, a sort of parlor trick that separates real human growth from the accumulation of knowledge as thing. This trick is necessary to keep learners from asking fundamental questions about where they stand in this world and how it might be different. Viewed this way, "banking education" (rather than religion) is the opiate of the people.

In order to bring Freireian pedagogy into twenty-first century learning, we must ask questions about today's learners. Is "oppressed" the right word to describe students in contemporary Western societies? I can make no claim for privileged understanding of these learners. Having spent almost forty years in American schools working with various levels of learners, I reflect on the problems I have experienced trying to encourage students to own their consciousness and to see themselves as active agents in the world. I certainly recognize the "banking concept" with its technique of distilling powerful, highly political and ideological ideas into nicely teachable subjects, and I have seen the power of pretending that banking knowledge is neutral and unproblematic acquisition of information. I have felt the tension between educating students toward financial success rather than growth and actualization in the world. In retrospect, I have primarily experienced students as in some kind of suspended state, waiting for their moment to become "active" in the world (Lyotard 1984). I suspect that for many, this moment never comes, and they move from passive learners to passive employees almost seamlessly. Advertisements from financial management firms now promise that we will finally own our lives in retirement, when (as one current commercial ironically notes) we will travel the world, start a vineyard, or in some other way pursue the life we have been deferring since kindergarten.

But is this kind of education in contemporary society a form of "oppression" in the Freireian sense? One way to answer this question is to note the similar condition of the Brazilian peasant and the modern American student. Both are encouraged to see the world as static and unchangeable. Economic "realities" for both involve finding a place within a powerful system, a place where agency is limited and "critical consciousness" will only get you in trouble. We might easily see the American school system as a highly sophisticated technology that promises economic success (even extreme wealth) to students, if only they learn to play the game well enough. In response, some students see school as providing a secure and positive future, a path toward adulthood with some measure of guaranteed success. Other students see school as oppressive and detrimental to their identity, whether that identity is rooted in family, neighborhood, or some other group they identify with. And some students seem to see school as a game, easy enough to play but not meaningful in any important way.

At this point, we seem to have departed from Freire's "peasant narrative" toward a complex new "American student" narrative. The American student sees school through many different eyes. Most students understand school as primarily about power, power they can submit to, resist, or exploit. The game of school involves learning abstract and sometimes useless-seeming information, and learning to put that information into a framework with other information. The point of this game is not to make sense of the world, but rather to prove to teachers and future teachers and future employers that one can play this game. For many of the most sophisticated students, the game-within-the-game of school involves not being duped by the first game, not thinking the mental exercises of school really matter. The point of the game-within-the-game is to become an entrepreneur, to learn to make moves that upend the system and to become "above the rules" of the game. This response allows the student to stay in the game while not taking it too seriously. All around us today, we see these entrepreneurs glorified as the winners of this game. Many such entrepreneurs dismiss traditional education while deploying new and disruptive technologies, thereby accruing new levels of wealth and making a new game.

So to some extent, Freire provides us a way to see these students and their relationship to power, but at some point, this narrative ceases to really explain the position of today's learners in twentieth century Western schools. I have never been able to see twenty-first century students as "oppressed" in the Freireian sense. They generally do not accept their powerlessness in the world. They might walk away from school in protest, or they might submit to school because they see it as necessary to launch into the world of the active. As influential as Freire's "banking concept" has been, it has perhaps been overly reified as another "deposit" that schools of education put in the heads of future educators. If we read Pedagogy of the Oppressed with fresh eyes, we see that Freire anticipated this question. Indeed, Freire suggests that to avoid the stagnation of the banking concept, we need to turn to "problem-posing education" (Freire 2002).

Only by posing real problems in the world can we encourage students to see themselves as actors in the world. Freire creates a pedagogy of the "oppressed" because he sees oppression as the primary problem of the working peasant in Brazil. Whether we want to see the Western student as oppressed or not, I would contend that most of us see today's students as caught in a problematic educational system. Education is compulsory, but nearly all students struggle to reconcile the practices of school with their own evolving selves The problem of being a student involves finding a meaningful self, finding one's right relationship with the institutions that shape our lives, and finding the right relationship with our fellow humans. These goals are not explicitly part of what we traditionally define as "school." However, to practice a problem-posing pedagogy, we need to find ways to name this new kind of student's dilemma and to pose the problem of their condition to the students themselves.

CONCLUSION

Three problematic terms—critical, information, and literacy. Each term resists easy definition, and each term plays off the other two to create dynamism and avoid stasis. Having explored where these terms take us, perhaps we can return to the question most often posed about critical information literacy: what does it look like in practice? Perhaps at some unique institutions, critical information literacy might become a programmatic "thing," but I think in most cases, critical information literacy becomes an individual choice on the part of a librarian, a personal philosophy of librarianship. This person, the practicing critical information literacy librarian, seeks a way of engaging students as more than repositories of information. This critical information literacy librarian sees students as fragile human beings negotiating an unforgiving and highly competitive landscape. This librarian recognizes the need for young people to be more than consumers in a holding pattern waiting for an adulthood that will look very much like school. This librarian will have become "critical" of the ways that Western capitalism has restricted the meaning of our lives to getting and spending. This librarian will think it is "critical" that we find ways of being in the world and in our profession that are more rewarding and more humanizing.

This librarian will see "information" as one of the problems of our time, and will be troubled that information seems too easily treated "as if" it exists in some concrete form. This librarian will find important things missing from the Standards. The way that research is portrayed in the Standards will seem not so much wrong as one-dimensional and inadequate. The idea that we "recognize the need for information" will seem mechanical. The idea that we should aim to "access the needed information effectively and efficiently" will seem contrary to the slow and patient way that knowledge builds in the person. This librarian will be uncomfortable with the role of teaching students how to "evaluate information and its sources critically," especially if that evaluation involves formulaic value judgments about "good" and "bad" information. This librarian will be intrigued by the Standard that encourages us to "understand the economic, legal, and social issues surrounding the use of information," but will also be discouraged by how little of our professional discourse engages this question.

Finally, this librarian will recognize that being a literacy worker involves something other than imparting skills. It involves connecting daily work with students, colleagues, and institutions to larger ideological questions about who belongs in higher education and how to make higher education as accessible as possible to everyone. It involves putting ourselves on the level of students as co-questioners, co-doubters, even co-dreamers. In short, it involves an entire rethinking of the relationship between librarian and student. As radical as it might seem, the critical information literacy librarian may come be believe that we have no "thing" to teach to students. The critical information librarian will instead participate in Freire's ongoing questioning and struggling for meaning. To be a critical information librarian is to recognize that even with all our material success, there are those who have yet to "make it" in a world that is subtly but powerfully stacked against them. The critical information literacy librarian chooses not to walk away from the challenge posed by that problem, which seems to me the central educational and social problem of our time.

References

Elmborg, James. 2003. "Teaching at the Desk: Toward a Reference Pedagogy." *portal: Libraries and the Academy* 2 (3): 455–464.

———. 2004. "Literacies Large and Small: The Case of Information Literacy." *International Journal of Learning* 11: 1235–1239.

———. 2006. "Critical Information Literacy: Implications for Instructional Practice." *Journal of Academic Librarianship*. 32 (2) 192–199.

Foucault, Michel. 1982. *The Archaeology of Knowledge & The Discourse on Language*. New York: Pantheon Books.

Freire, Paulo. 2002. *Pedagogy of the Oppressed*. New York: Continuum.

Gee, James Paul. (1989) "Literacy, Discourse, and Linguistics and What is Literacy?" In *Literacy: A Critical Sourcebook*. Edited by Ellen Cushman, Eugene R. Kintgen, Barry M. Kroll, and Mike Rose. 525–544.

Jacobs, Heidi. 2008. "Information Literacy and Reflective Pedagogical Praxis." *Journal of Academic Librarianship*, 34(3): 256–262.

Kohl, Herbert. 1994. *I Won't Learn from You: The Role of Assent in Learning*. New York: The New Press.

Kopp, Bryan M. and Olson-Kopp, Kim. 2010. "Depositories of Knowledge: Library Instruction and the Development of Critical Consciousness."In *Critical Library Instruction: Theories and Methods*. Edited by Emily Drabinski, Alana Kumbier, and Maria Accardi. 55–67.

Le Guin, Ursula K. 1975. *The Wind's Twelve Quarters: Short Stories*. New York: Harper and Row.

Lyotard, Jean Francois. 1984. *The Postmodern Condition: A Report on Knowledge*. Minneapolis: University of Minnesota Press.

McLuhan, Marshall. 1999. *Understanding Media: The Extensions of Man*. Cambridge: MIT Press.

Olson, Hope. 2001. "Sameness and Difference: A Cultural Foundation of Classification." *Library Resources and Technical Services* 45 (3): 115–122.

Pawley, Christine. 2003. "Information Literacy: A Contradictory Coupling." *Library Quarterly*. 73 (4): 422–452.

Raber, Douglas. 2003. *The Problem of Information: An Introduction to Information Science*. Lanham: Scarecrow Press.

Street, Brian. 2001. "The New Literacy Studies." In *Literacy: A Critical Sourcebook*. Edited by Ellen Cushman, Eugene R. Kintgen, Barry M. Kroll, and Mike Rose. 430–432. New York: Bedford/St. Martin's.

Vaidhyanathan, Siva. Afterword: Critical Information Studies—A Manifesto." *Cultural Studies* 20(2–3): 292–315.

Willinsky, John. 1998. *Learning to Divide the World: Education at Empire's End*. Minneapolis: University of Minnesota Press.

Wysocki, Ann and Johnson-Eilola, Johndan. 1999. "Blinded by the Letter: Why Are We Using Literacy as a Metaphor for Everything Else?" In *Passions, Pedagogies, and 21st Century Technologies*. Edited by Gail E. Hawisher and Cynthia L. Selfe. 349–368. Logan: Utah State University Press.

Zurkowski, Paul G. 1974. "The Information Service Environment: Relationships and Priorities," *National Commission on Libraries and Information Science*, ED100391.

4

A Well-Worn Path... and Beyond: Charting Feminization in Academic Instruction Librarianship

Noël Kopriva

In this chapter, I survey the literature of feminization as it relates to women's library history in order to argue that information literacy instruction, connected as it is both to two feminized professions—teaching and librarianship—can be viewed as feminized a priori. As a result, some issues of authority and status that challenge instruction librarians can be connected not just to librarianship's feminized status but also to the feminized status of instruction librarianship. For librarianship as a whole, one successful strategy for achieving legitimacy has been to adopt a reformer's role. Within that framework, I contextualize arguments made for information literacy as both pedagogical and professional reform and trace them to their roots in nineteenth-century women librarians' success at framing librarianship in the language of social reform.

Librarianship, which achieved its first successes as a profession of reform, continues to reform and reinvent itself, and library instruction is no exception. Julien and Genuis (2009) discuss librarians' challenges with role ambiguity generally and with respect to teaching (104–105); Polger and Okamoto (2010) trace the evolution of teaching in librarianship from teaching primarily at the reference desk, to visiting classrooms in one-shot library workshops, to embedding ourselves into courses and teaching credit-bearing courses ourselves (3). Yet generally speaking, academic librarians who teach, like their colleagues in the teaching faculty, receive comparatively little instructional training while in graduate school and most, with the exception of school librarians, are not formally certified to teach (Julien and Genuis, 103; Polger and Okamoto, 1). In addition, the progress that instruction librarians have made in establishing recognized standards and standardized teacher training for information literacy instruction has been slow, especially when compared to the progress that has been made in integrating information literacy competencies for students into curricula and institutional strategic plans and mission statements. Thus, instruction librarians' teacher training and status are often ambiguous and defined by institutional context rather than by the profession as a whole or by any recognition of professional credentials by an academic library's parent institution. Complicating these issues is the tension which undoubtedly exists between librarians who practice instruction in libraries and library professors who write and teach about library instruction in library schools. As I attempt to show, at the center of this tension are issues of authority that can be linked to academic librarians' ambiguous status within the larger community of higher education.

Understanding that we work in a feminized specialty (teaching—or instruction, as we librarians call it) in a feminized profession (librarianship) has been, I argue, important to our success in raising the profile of information literacy and our profession as well. Though "librarians have traditionally played a key role ...in information literacy instruction" (Julien and Genuis 2009, 103), they also grapple with varying levels of support from administrators, from immediate colleagues, and from within themselves. Implicit in the challenges that librarians face is the need to assert authority, especially with respect to our colleagues in the teaching faculty. Discomfort with our status vis á vis teaching faculty has often meant that we dismiss, sometimes legitimately and sometimes prematurely, their requests or approaches to teaching and students. Similarly, I contend, discomfort with our status vis á vis library school faculty also causes instruction librarians to dismiss ideas about instruction coming from library school faculty as untested or even condescending. The latter scenario has played out vividly in a recent article in *Communications in Information Literacy*, which I discuss in some depth in order to tease out practicing librarians' attempts to assert their authority as teachers. Instruction librarians' attempts to dismiss library school faculty's theories about information literacy are reflective of our overall perception of teaching faculty as both allies and obstacles in our shared mission to help students become confident about finding and using information. It is time for the profession not only to admit, institutionally, that we *are* feminized but to take on issues of status at every possible level: in libraries and in library schools, but also at trustee and faculty senate meetings, and in workshops and classes organized to recognize, discuss and even examine remediation, not of our numerically feminized status, but of the issues that continue to challenge instruction librarians' status and indeed, librarians' status as a whole.

DEFINING FEMINIZATION

Dee Garrison (2003) used the term *feminization* to denote the process by which women "came to dominate [librarianship], at least numerically (12)". She notes that "in 1852 the first woman clerk was hired in the Boston Public Library; by 1878 fully two-thirds of the women there were female...by 1929 librarianship, composed of almost 90 per cent females, employed a larger percentage of women than either social work or teaching" (173). In short, Garrison believed that these numbers helped create a profession that was largely low-paid, ambiguously educated, and not, ultimately, in control of its own institutional funding, because women could not be well paid, well educated, or financially responsible without risking the kind of societal censure that would automatically exclude them from the profession in the first place. She also believed that "female dominance of librarianship did much to shape the inferior and precarious status of the public library as a cultural resource; it evolved into a kind of marginal public amusement service" (Garrison 2003, 174). This contention, about the status of not only public but all libraries, continues to haunt librarians and scholars of library history.

Later scholars of libraries and library history have explored the continuing effects of feminization on the profession, among them the lower salaries (Biggs 1982, 412–416; Passet 1996; Perret and Young 2011) and ambiguous academic status (Broidy 2007, 296–297; Bryan 2007, 781–784) that instruction librarians face each day. And though these and other challenges are frequently discussed or at least alluded to in the literature on information literacy (Knapp 1956; Lubans 1974; Hopkins 1982; Salony 1995), they are not explicitly connected to the feminization of the profession. This is a gap in the literature that my argument seeks to interrogate.

It is also impossible to ignore the fact that, as Sarah Pritchard (2004) says, "some things have changed for the better...there has been a noticeable shift in the leadership of the profession and in attention to issues of equity. Women hold a majority of leadership positions in ALA, research libraries, and large public libraries" (484). In addition, as Marta Mestrovic Deyrup (2004) shows, in the upper levels of administration in selected academic libraries, women have achieved dominance in terms of representation, with 52.1% of administrative positions in the Association of Research Libraries occupied by women. These same administrators earn 92% of the salaries of their male counterparts, a statistically insignificant difference (242). In the cases Deyrup presents, a feminized administrative profession is not necessarily an underpaid or marginalized one.

More encouraging still, women earned about 80% of what men earned in 2009 across all occupations (1), but women librarians earned about 94% of their male counterparts' salaries (US Bureau of Labor Statistics 2010, 13). These heartening increases in pay equity would be even more so if they pointed to a corresponding increase in librarians' status within higher education. Yet as Pritchard (2004) cautions,

> [Deyrup] barely scratches the surface of demonstrable problems such as occupational segregation within academic libraries, uneven treatment of women directors within the higher-level academic hierarchies of universities, pay equity at levels below the director (between librarianship and other fields requiring similar education), or situations like harassment or the lack of child care that still hinder women in all types of libraries (485).

In these areas, much study remains to be done. As long as information literacy agendas are adapted piecemeal or not at all, as long as we have to fight to increase our visibility, we continue to be challenged by our inheritance from the nineteenth and early twentieth century. If we contend with that inheritance knowingly, we have a better chance of shaping our professional futures, and those of our students, more deliberately and more successfully.

THE POLITICS OF REFORM IN LIBRARIES & HIGHER EDUCATION

Dee Garrison (2003) argued that public libraries, focused as they were on reform (36), were especially welcome sites of endeavor for "crusading women of the late nineteenth and early centuries to assume a new public role in many reform causes of the day" (12). Reform became an integral part of librarianship, especially as a means of establishing professional legitimacy. Information literacy practitioners and their predecessors in bibliographic instruction and library instruction are thus returning to their lineage when they deploy a reformist approach to convince sometimes reluctant administrators, faculty, and students about the importance of twenty-first century learning, critical thinking, and process-oriented research strategies that focus on invention, drafting, and revision—of keywords, not essays. But in using this strategy they are not alone: a focus on reform, as Craig Gibson (2008) has noted, seems to be a fixed characteristic of American higher education:

> One of the most striking features of the higher education system in the United States is the paradox of successive waves of reform...Reform movements arise in almost every generation, driven by societal, economic, demographic, and technological changes... (10).

Gibson points out that higher education, and academic library instruction by association, participates in a culture of cyclical reform. He further points out that the information literacy movement in fact emerged as a reform, of sorts, of the bibliographic instruction movement, though he traces the "notion of information literacy" all the way to Cardinal Newman's 'process approach' to liberal learning" in the mid-nineteenth century and then forward to Patricia B. Knapp's Monteith College experiment in the early 1960s (14). Gibson's main interest is in framing higher education reform as both cyclical and progressive. Mary Niles Maack (2002) has documented a similar paradigm in feminism in librarianship, as well (241). Her review of the seminal *On Account of Sex* series of bibliographies (McCook and Phenix 1984; Phenix et al 1989; Goetsch and Watstein 1993; Kruger and Larson 2000) and *The Role of Women in Librarianship, 1876-1976* (Weibel et al 1979) states that the latter's chronology makes it "possible to follow the flow of debates and trace the concerns of librarians" over time, from focusing on women's mere presence in the profession to issues of "status"—what I have tried to reframe as authority and legitimacy—as they came to dominate its landscape (243). She notes in her discussion of the *Account of Sex* bibliography that scholarship on women in librarianship has expanded past the borders of North America and the theoretical limits of library and information science, which she "strongly endorse[s]." Maack's own language smacks of reform as she exhorts her readers to believe "that library feminism is alive and that feminist librarians are still engaged in the 'struggle for equalization in one profession" (246).

Gibson's (2008) history, too, takes on a reformist agenda as he situates his initial exploration of the history of information literacy within the library profession, charting the development of information literacy's theoretical foundation in cognitive and learning theories, and then tracing its gradual advancement into the American Library Association's official apparatus. He notes that those interested in promoting information literacy began to believe that "program development for the information literacy agenda within the academy at large would need a set of 'content standards' to guide practitioners," (13) which resulted in the development of the *ACRL Information Literacy Competency Standards for Higher Education.* He shows the advancement of the Standards outside of academic librarianship proper, including their "endorsement by the former AAHE (American Association of Higher Education) in 1999," as well as "their later endorsement by the Council of Independent Colleges (CIC) in 2004." It is difficult to gauge the impact of the Standards on the academy at large because, as Gibson points out, higher education is "one sector of American education in which national norms have been noticeably absent" (18), but he believes that the development of these standards and their promotion at the national level is quite significant.

LIBRARIANS AND LIBRARY PROFESSORS: A PRODUCTIVE TENSION

At the same time, the library profession continues to interrogate the Standards. One significant recent example is John Budd's *Framing Library Instruction* (2009), in which he critiques the standards for what he sees as a "concentration on skills and competencies [that] omits integrated informing, cognitive growth, and learning" (40), among other issues, all of which culminate in a "necessary but not sufficient" (41) set of standards by which to measure student learning. *Communications in Information Literacy* recently published an editorial forum (Ragains et al 2010) in which four eminent academic instruction librarians (John J. Doherty, Debra Gilchrist, Esther Grassian, and James T. Nichols) examined Budd's argument and Budd himself was allowed to respond to their comments. The article presents an exemplary discussion between library professor and librarians of information literacy's meaning, its place in the profession, and the role of librarianship in academia.

Budd's argument centers around a critique of the ACRL Standards and generally accepted modes of teaching and learning by instruction librarians; in their place, Budd offers a philosophically driven approach to learning that he calls "phenomenological cognitive action" (33). Contending that information literacy as it is often taught pushes students to learn skills, not ways of thinking and knowing, Budd examines the ACRL Standards and finds that information literacy is "taken to be a field independent of the matter about which others speak, write, and show" (47). This is a problem, Budd believes, because it makes assessment difficult: "[s]ince the Standards are largely instrumental (skills-based), the evaluation that follows directly from them can only be instrumental as well" (43). In short, for Budd, the Standards, and by extension, most library instruction, emphasize acquiring skills rather than learning how to ask and answer research questions. His aim is nothing less than persuading practicing librarians to reject many accepted modes of practice and to change their thinking about learning.

Here the tension between Budd's push for reform on the one hand and practicing librarians' defense of current thinking on the standards should be extremely productive in terms of helping all librarians think about what they want information literacy to do, and more importantly, what information literacy—as the golden child of instruction librarianship—cannot accomplish for students, librarians or teaching faculty. For the most part, however, the librarians on the panel reject Budd's ideas on the grounds that they are too philosophical or not grounded in real-life experience—after all, they point out, Budd teaches aspiring librarians, not undergraduates. Debra Gilchrist notes: "librarians are already doing much of what Budd suggests" (Ragains et al 2010 116). Esther Grassian writes: "Reading Budd's book makes one wonder whether he has actually observed ILI in its various forms" (Ragains et al 2010, 117). Of course, many books on library instruction contain advice and observations on instructional methods already in practice, but Budd seems to have hit a nerve because of his teaching faculty status and perceived lack of library instruction experience.

I suggest that issues of authority over the topic and practice of information literacy and library instruction are at the bottom of the tension between Budd's book and its critics—not just between Budd himself but between teaching faculty and academic librarians; not just between teaching faculty and academic librarians, but between academic librarians and the apparatus of higher education. Julien and Genuis (2011) point out that

> Academic librarians' concern for developing information literacy skills, especially in undergraduate students, is centred in a desire for students' academic success, but is also driven by librarians' concerns for maintaining relevancy in an age where their professional expertise and value is contested (103).

In fact, as I hope I have shown, there has almost never been a moment in library history when librarians' professional expertise and value has been *un*contested. Frances L. Hopkins (1982) puts it this way: "[Instruction librarians] … in the academic environment … seek recognition of the educational value of bibliographic instruction; in their own professional environment, they seek its recognition as a core function of librarianship" (192). In other words, instructional librarians are very familiar with the struggle to sell themselves and their product to students and teaching faculty, and part of this process is establishing authority. When a member of the teaching faculty begins to analyze what instruction librarians regard as their main area of expertise, such an action might be perceived as a challenge to their authority, and thus their relevance.

Most important about the exchange between Budd and his critics for the purposes of this discussion is how it highlights tensions about authority and professionalism that librarians deal with on a nearly daily basis. As I have argued previously, Garrison (2003) and other scholars have shown that these issues of authority and professionalism have been part of librarianship almost from the beginning of its emergence *as* a profession. Too, librarians have always been drawn to reform as a mechanism by which to exercise authority and achieve relevance, but we are not always open to challenges to reform when they come from outside of our community. This includes professors in schools of information and library science.

Julien and Given (2002) note that "faculty-librarian collaboration is one of the most prevalent solutions offered in the LIS literature to the problem of faculty members' disengagement from the IL imperative" (70). Budd, in "Cognitive Growth, Instruction, and Student Success" (2008), presents a class curriculum that he developed in consultation with practicing librarians and LIS students (of which I was one) at the University of Missouri. A version of this class has been taught at the University of Missouri since Fall 2006. Budd notes that the course as first taught yielded a mix of negative and positive evaluations, the latter of which emphasized students' satisfaction with learning strategies for reading course assignments "and to understand the content of information sources to these assignments"(328). These reactions align with those of the practicing librarians in the panel discussion; for example, Debra Gilchrist notes that Budd's approach "encourages" a "dialogue ... between the student and the literature. This is very important to students as well as consistent with librarians' attachment to lifelong learning" (Ragains et al 2010, 119). In short, students who were encouraged to think about assignments broadly, in order to see connections between types of assignments and types of information sources, and furthermore, to reflect on their own process of making connections, are doing exactly what the course was designed to help them do—and what practicing librarians try to encourage in their instruction. In spite of this critical area of agreement between Budd and the panelists, the librarians' perceptions of the book and the class are quite disparaging.

It is unclear whether the librarian panelists looking at *Framing Library Instruction* (2009) had read Budd's earlier article (2008), so it is impossible to say that they ignored the collaborative aspects of the course. (Neither does Budd himself refer to the collaboration in detail in *Framing Library Instruction*.) Yet the partially collaborative aspect of the course points back to the tension over authority and professional legitimacy between librarians and faculty that I referred to earlier. Such tensions are discussed in detail by Julien and Given, who explore the complexity of instruction librarians' and teaching faculty members' relationships via an analysis of seven years' of conversations on the popular ILI-L listserv "from September 1995 to December 2002" (2002, 73).

Perhaps most relevant to the panel discussion of *Framing Instruction*, Julien and Given, LIS professors themselves, discuss practicing librarians' self-presentation not merely as faculty members, but as professors. When a librarian notes that she "considers [herself] a full-fledged professor with the assigned field of library science and/or information studies," Julien and Given (2002) note that "this statement is ... interesting ...given the fact that library and information studies itself is governed by professors of LIS" (81). Julien and Given's statement that LIS studies is "governed" by professors reflects a fundamental confusion about the field itself—do LIS professors, who teach and credential future librarians, really "govern" the field? Certainly professional librarians who participate in governing bodies such as the American Library Association's Council might disagree, since they too are part of the credentialing process and set professional standards. This disconnect between library faculty and librarians about where professional authority is located is profound; outside of the field, it is not surprising that teaching faculty might not understand why librarians should have a place at the campus community table.

According to Julien and Given, too, teaching faculty "typically engage in research and service activities—in addition to their teaching responsibilities—and generally hold doctorate degrees in their areas of specialty" and "to be equated with librarians, who may or may not do any research, and who typically hold masters-level degrees" might cause faculty to "rebel and further strive to define themselves as very different from the librarians on campus" (81). In fact, as the *AAUP Contingent Faculty Index* (2006) shows, teaching faculty positions of the type described by Julien and Given have decreased in the U.S. such that "these changes in the nature of faculty employment and faculty work have created a predominantly contingent faculty across the academy" (5). Such appointments tend not to support the research (and, it must be inferred, service) duties and opportunities that tenure-track faculty enjoy. The employment that Julien and Given describe does not exist in U.S. universities, and most practicing librarians located therein are aware of that fact. Julien and Given's ultimate conclusion, that librarians who call themselves "professors" without having a PhD or fulfilling service activities are risking alienation from those they most wish to help, is discouraging indeed to those who are doing no more than using their assigned titles. On the other hand, their plight might ring true for contingent faculty, whose job descriptions are ambiguous and who often do not fulfill research or service duties.

LIBRARY INSTRUCTION: WRITING FEMINIZATION IN

Information literacy's slow but steady incursion into higher education is encouraging but, I would suggest, complicated by academic librarians' professional status. Specifically, instruction librarians' authority in advocating for reform remains unclear to those outside the boundaries of the profession. Scholars of the profession examine librarians' reform efforts with an eye towards advancing instruction, or the status of women in libraries, though not usually both together. In this section I attempt to knit these two narratives together, at least in significant areas. For this I rely on Suzanne Hildenbrand's (2000) discussion of the phases of library women's history, which proposes an early dearth of authentic narratives about women in library history, followed by an intense focus on what she terms the "equity orientation" of the nineteen-sixties through the nineteen-nineties' more specialized studies focused beyond early foundational issues such as pay equity, career advancement, and a basic presence in library history (51).

Library instruction began as an integral part of academic librarianship but its importance soon decreased in favor of other roles that librarians believed to be more appropriate to their role as they understood it at the time. Often the terms of appropriateness seem to match up with librarians' quests for professional legitimacy and better status within their college and university communities. For example, Mary Salony (1995) traces academic library instruction in this country back to the early nineteenth century, but notes that "toward the end of the nineteenth century, libraries often offered a credit course in bibliography" (33) aimed at both educating students to use the library and "bringing [the library] more fully into the teaching learning process"(31). Yet at that same time, "head librarians ... were being pushed from the teaching role by collection growth" (Hopkins 1982, 194) and the educational role that librarians aspired to was becoming largely administrative; thus began a trend of rejecting teaching, which was seen as less influential. Georgia Higley (1996) sees the ascendance of the administrative role more positively (indeed, a current metric for measuring women's parity in librarianship is the presence of women in administrative roles). In her revisionist history of women librarians in the U.S. West, Higley documents the activities of women librarians in land grant colleges, themselves instruments of reform conceived of as "instrument[s] for social betterment" (193), with an eye to showing that "despite the poor salary, ambiguous job descriptions, and hardship conditions, women librarians found western land-grant college places where personal ability, not gender, determined position and stature" (74). Higley's emphasis on librarians as administrators and Hopkins' on librarians as teachers, however, have the same aim: to increase the perceived status of women in libraries.

After a good start, then, library instruction programs in the United States actually declined in the first decade of the twentieth century (35); in the following decade, librarians struggled to prove that a need for instruction existed and to fit it into college schedules in a way that would not interfere with students' regular classes. Thus librarians' teaching took place, almost from the beginning, outside of regular classroom teaching—which implied a certain lack of importance, even as librarians would try to convince students otherwise. These continued as librarians revised their approaches to instruction and their attempts to integrate it more closely into the college curriculum, with varying degrees of success. For example, during this time, orientations to the library during Freshman Week became a popular strategy (Salony 1995, 36–37). Interestingly, Hopkins believed, however, that many librarians trained by Melvil Dewey and other library schools at this time, who were often female and middle-class, "were neither the intellectual nor social equals of academic faculty" and that "there is no doubt that Dewey's good intentions depressed the profession as a whole"(194). Her observation seems emblematic of the "expansion" of the "equity tradition" that Hildenbrand identifies, wherein the gains made by the women's movement allowed for some security in which to make admissions about the level of training and education women had and its possible negative effects on the profession—made of course, in such a way as to encourage better training and education for women, not to disparage their presence in the profession in the first place (57).

In 1952, Patricia K. Knapp noted that "planned instruction in the use of the library at the college level is still quite generally limited to one or two orientation lectures and perhaps a 'library paper' in Freshman English" (224). She argued that though "college instructors" might "assume that most college students acquire [library and research] skills as a natural by-product of their work in content courses … college librarians know better"

(225). In spite of the energy of her argument, what she called "planned instruction" and librarians later called bibliographic instruction (BI), did not gain real momentum until the 1960s and 1970s. This is likely because the 1960s and 1970s were a time that saw increased empowerment of women and librarians.

In fact, most scholars agree that the rise of bibliographic instruction, with its emphasis on empowering the user and advancing democracy, was part of a wide-ranging platform of social change that also included the women's movement, and it is true that the women who dominated the profession sought to raise their own status within it. Yet works such as the aforesaid Weibel, et al's (1979) *The Role of Women in Librarianship 1876–1976* and the *On Account of Sex* bibliographies (Heim and Phenix 1984; Phenix et al 1989; Goetsch and Watstein 1993; Kruger and Larson 2000) do a splendid job of documenting the women's liberation movement in libraries without any in-depth mention of library instruction. Women in libraries—their employment prospects, the effects of marriage on their careers, and salaries—such foundational issues dominate these scholars' focus rather than the current age of teasing out the intricate, devilish details of intra-academic status. For example, Patricia Layzell Ward's (1979) "Women and Librarianship" is one such study investigating the "social wastage of women, particularly those who are graduates and who hold a professional qualification" who have left librarianship to marry and raise families (159). Anita R. Schiller (1979) asks, poignantly, "did feminization bring low salaries, or vice versa?" and concludes that "women predominate in librarianship because salaries are low," not the reverse (240). These are merely samples of the important work happening as women began to study their own status in the profession, and it makes sense that in the beginning, the issue of library instruction was not linked to feminization.

MOVING INTO THE THIRD DECADE

As librarians move further into their teaching roles and become more engaged with instruction, we are also differently engaged with our campus communities. Teaching, bibliographic instruction, information literacy: librarians interested in classroom teaching of any kind continue to search out ways to assert themselves as authorities, even as their status as members of a feminized profession presents an ongoing challenge to doing so successfully. I would suggest that current conversations on evolving "from information to meaning" also provide an interesting site for observing issues of authority (Kuhlthau 2008, 66). Kuhlthau proposes that "innovative approaches to interaction between people and information are needed to bridge the divide between information behavior, information literacy and the impact of information in order to seek meaning" (72). Her address seeks to tie librarianship and information science together more closely—the immediate benefits of which would be better communication between the professions; but perhaps indirectly, information literacy, long the province of librarians, would gain currency with information technologists, thus raising the status of instruction librarians within the information community. James Elmborg (2006) suggests that there has been "an evolution in what librarians do, and moving from service provider to active educator challenges librarians and library educators" (192), a statement that not only reflects current reality but also hints at the struggles for legitimacy librarians experience as they shift roles.

Heidi Julien and Shelagh Genuis (2009; 2011) have done great work on the role of instruction librarians, using sociological theoretical interpretations of their data to show that teaching librarians are often self-conflicted. Julien and Genuis specifically note that instruction librarians faced "external contextual challenges" that were beyond the librarian's control, including administration, facilities, and technology; "challenges arising from interaction with instructional clients and teaching faculty," and "intrapersonal challenges" having to do with self-confidence and personality (Julien and Genuis 2011, 103–104). These issues are certainly related to instruction's taking place within the sprawling bureaucracies of higher education. They also reflect a lack of autonomy discussed in my introduction and can be traced back to a tradition of librarians being dependent on outside entities for funding, support, and the institutional cachet to initiate and carry through curricular reforms such as integrated information literacy programming.

Ellen Broidy (2007) documents the challenges that instruction librarians face and foregrounds them in a feminist context as she discusses her experience of proposing, designing, and teaching a class on "Gender and the Politics of Information," an undergraduate seminar taught at the University of California Irvine. For example, she notes because of prior relationships she had built within the department of women's studies, she did not have to "convince the department of the need for a library-focused course, nor...negotiate for time in the schedule of classes" (496). These two bugbears—selling the need for sustained library instruction and asking for time in another faculty member's course schedule—plague all instruction librarians from time to time and Broidy's freedom from them is, all too sadly, worthy of note. She also provides a reason for why the course was initially approved: "It was perceived as a course that 'belonged' to an academic department *and not to a library*" (499, emphasis added). As such, the gender studies aspect of the course contained the important "intellectual content" while "incorporation of skills became a covert activity" (Broidy 2007, 499). This conflict between instruction (which is the presentation of library skills) and real teaching (which has to do with intellectual content) continues throughout Broidy's account.

Such a conflict seems to me emblematic of the problems librarians face in convincing teaching faculty to let them into their classrooms—but in this case it is the librarian herself struggling to justify teaching information literacy skills and concepts. Indeed, later on in the article, Broidy seems to correct herself, contending that teaching library research skills was not the reason she "proposed the seminar;" the far meatier topic of "open[ing] up a dialog with our students about the very nature of information" was the real issue at stake in teaching the course (500). It is probably indisputable that a discussion of the gendered nature of information seems more appropriate for upper-division work than does a discussion of subject and keyword searching (which was also covered). Yet the need to discuss both is equally great for students who wish to access, understand, and use information in a sophisticated and ethical manner.

Broidy and her colleague were able to get around the need for "covert" instruction by having the student teach other via seminar presentations (499, 500, 506). This strategy, which decentralizes power and builds community, also provided the instructors with an "easy way to introduce the concept of subject headings, keywords, and other possible points of entry" (499) into information literacy concepts. Perhaps needless to say, Broidy's course was a success, so much so that when she left UC Irvine for UCLA, she turned it into a graduate seminar (506). She concludes by going outside of her own course experiences to argue for more classes in gender and information studies and more broadly and significantly, for a "reconceptualization of what we do in the classroom" (507). She believes that "we need to begin this reconsideration in library school" and contends that the challenges of "convincing library school faculty and administrators to add yet another course to an already crowded curriculum" might be "outweighed by the benefits" (507). These benefits would all serve to increase librarians' legitimacy and authority by adding to our ability to shape students' understanding of information in more sophisticated ways "while underscoring the significance of our contributions to the academic enterprise" (507). Broidy's skillful recounting of her equally skillful incursion into mainstream classroom instruction embodies the shift from standalone instruction to integrated information literacy that she first envisioned. It also provides a roadmap for those of us who wish to transform our classrooms into sites where "instruction" becomes teaching.

Though some librarians have enthusiastically embraced assessment and some have resisted it, there is no question that the conversations we are having about assessment have provoked a new wave of self-reflection about what it means to design, teach, and measure student learning experiences. As documented their website, Megan Oakleaf and her colleagues in the RAILS project have reinvigorated the academic discussion about the uses of rubrics, for example, and Project Information Literacy, also through its website, consistently provides useful data to the librarian community. Although some might find the emphasis on assessment superfluous to what librarians are really supposed to be doing—James G. Neal (2011) provides an impassioned appeal against Return On Investment (ROI) studies, for example—there is no lack of agreement about the need for libraries to prevent professional obsolescence in new and convincing ways. Proving the importance and effectiveness of our instructional role is one important goal in our current strategy.

As noted in my earlier discussion of librarian-faculty relationships, there continues to be tension between how librarians perceive themselves and their roles and how faculty members perceive librarians as well. This tension, while obviously challenging in short-term classroom situations, has yielded much helpful research. It turns out instruction librarians experience "ambivalence about the teaching role" (103). When librarians themselves doubt the importance of what they are doing, it is difficult to unequivocally insist on the importance of their jobs in instruction. Other issues are at play as well: often librarians and library workers who do instruction are told, not asked, to do this work, and resentment or resistance can be the result (Julien and Genuis 2011, 104). Those of us who want to teach face other barriers: Ellen Broidy's experiences show that sustained course time is the exception, not the norm, for example. The analysis of practicing librarians' resounding rejection of the bulk of John Budd's *Framing Library Instruction* mirrors the strain between practicing librarians' ongoing struggle for legitimacy and their fear that library school professors who "govern"(Julien and Given 2002, 81) their profession ultimately set the rules and hold authority, regardless of their own affiliations with organizations such as ACRL that set competency standards for information literacy instruction.

At the bottom of this tension, I contend, is not only role ambiguity but a credentialing issue: who decides that a person is competent to practice as a librarian? Who decides that a person is achieving competence in her profession in such a way that others outside the profession (teaching faculty) recognize and respect that competence? These questions have never been satisfactorily answered, and they lead, as so many issues under discussion in this article do, to the ongoing challenge of librarians' status. Are we faculty or academic professionals? Do we have tenured status or are we regularly reappointed? Are we allowed participation in faculty governance, and when we gain it, are we represented on a par with our teaching colleagues? In short, in this discussion of the feminization of the profession and its continuing effects on our attempts to promote information literacy in higher education, what should stand out most clearly to the reader are the research gaps. Histories of information literacy abound, and so do histories of women in librarianship, as well as studies of the feminized profession. Studies that link these important issues together are less common and would serve a catalytic function in helping to define information literacy—not only in terms of what it is and what it does, but in terms of the librarians who promote it, what they do, and what systemic challenges face them as they move into the third decade of information literacy teaching and programming.

References

Association of College and Research Libraries. National Conference. 2011. "Peer Revered: Proceedings of the Fifteenth National Conference of the Association of College and Research Libraries, March 30–April 2, Philadelphia, Pennsylvania." Association of College and Research Libraries, 2011. Accessed January 3, 2012. www.ala.org/acrl/sites/ala.org.acrl/files/content/conferences/confsandpreconfs/national/2011/papers/stop_the_madness.pdf.

Biggs, Mary. 1982. "Librarians and the 'Woman Question': An Inquiry into Conservatism." *The Journal of Library History (1974–1987)* 17: 409–428. Accessed June 28, 2011. www.jstor.org/stable/25541321.

Broidy, Ellen. 2007. "Gender and the Politics of Information: Reflections on Bringing the Library into the Classroom." *Library Trends* 56: 494–508. Accessed March 1, 2011. http://search.ebscohost.com/login.aspx?direct=true&db=a9h&AN=28817877&site=ehost-live.

Bryan, Jacalyn E. 2007. "The Question of Faculty Status for Academic Librarians." *Library Review* 56 (781–787). Accessed June 29, 2011. doi: 10.1108/00242530710831220.

Budd, John M. 2008. "Cognitive Growth, Instruction, and Student Success." *College & Research Libraries* 69: 319–330. Accessed April 02, 2011. http://search.ebscohost.com/login.aspx?direct=true&db=llh&AN=BLIB08109041&site=ehost-live.

———. 2008. *Framing Library Instruction.* Chicago: Association of College and Research Libraries.

Cox, Christopher N. and Elizabeth Blakesley Lindsay. 2008. *Information Literacy Instruction Handbook.* Chicago: Association of College and Research Libraries.

Curtis, John W., and Monica F. Jacobe. 2006. "Consequences: an Increasingly Contingent Faculty." In *AAUP Contingency Faculty Index 2006,* 5–16. Association of American University Professors: Washington, DC. 2006. Accessed April 13, 2011. www.aaup.org/NR/rdonlyres/F05FF88E-B2A8-4052-8373-AF0FDAE060AC/0/ConsequencesAnIncreasinglyContingentFaculty.pdf.

Deyrup, Marta Mestrovic. 2004."Is the Revolution Over? Gender, Economic, and Professional Parity in Academic Library Leadership Positions." *College & Research Libraries* 65: 242–250. Accessed March 23, 2011. http://search.ebscohost.com/login.aspx?direct=true&db=a9h&AN=13330819&site=ehost-live.

Elmborg, James. 2006."Critical Information Literacy: Implications for Instructional Practice." *Journal of Academic Librarianship* 32: 192–199. Accessed November 12, 2010. http://search.ebscohost.com/login.aspx?direct=true&db=a9h&AN=20712045&site=ehost-live.

Garrison, Dee. (2003). *Apostles of Culture,* second edition. Madison, WI: University of Wisconsin Press.

Gibson, Craig. 2008. "History of Information Literacy Instruction." In *Information Literacy Instruction Handbook,* edited by Christopher N. Cox and Elizabeth Blakesley Lindsay, 10–25. Chicago: Association of College and Research Libraries.

Heim, Kathleen M., Dianne J. Ellsworth, and Kathleen Weibel. 1979. *The Role of Women in Librarianship 1876–1976: The Entry, Advancement, and Struggle for Equalization in One Profession.* London: Mansell.

Higley, Georgia Metos. 1996. "College, Community, and Librarianship: Women Librarians at the Western Land-Grant Colleges." In *Reclaiming the American Library Past*. Ablex. http://search.ebscohost.com/login.aspx?direct=true| &db=llh&AN=BLIB97011223&site=ehost-live.

Hildenbrand, Suzanne. 2000. "Library Feminism and Library Women's History: Activism and Scholarship, Equity and Culture." *Libraries & Culture* 35: 51–65. Accessed June 22, 2011. http://search.ebscohost.com/login.aspx ?direct=true&db=llh&AN=BLIB00005153&site=ehost-live.

Hopkins, Frances L. 1982. "A Century of Bibliographic Instruction: The Historical Claim to Professional and Academic Legitimacy." *College and Research Libraries* 43: 192–98. Accessed November 12, 2010.

Julien, Heidi and Lisa M. Given. 2002."Faculty-Librarian Relationships in the Information Literacy Context: A Content Analysis of Librarians' Expressed Attitudes and Experiences." *Canadian Journal of Information & Library Sciences* 27: 65–87. http://search.ebscohost.com/login.aspx?direct=true &db=lxh&AN=11075533&site=ehost-live.

Julien, Heidi and Shelagh K. Genuis. 2009. "Emotional Labour in Librarians' Instructional Work." *Journal of Documentation* 65: 926–937. Accessed April 15, 2011. http://search.ebscohost.com/login.aspx?direct=true&db=llh &AN=BLIB10110243&site=ehost-live.

———. 2011."Librarians' Experiences of the Teaching Role: A National Survey of Librarians." *Library & Information Science Research* 33: 103–111. Accessed April 13, 2011. doi:10.1016/j.lisr.2010.09.005.

Knapp, Patricia B. 1956. "A Suggested Program of College Instruction in the use of the Library." *The Library Quarterly* 26: 224–231. Accessed November 12, 2010. www.jstor.org/stable/4304554.

Kuhlthau, Carol Collier. 2008. "From Information to Meaning: Confronting Challenges of the Twenty-First Century." *Libri* 58: 66–73. Accessed November 11, 2010.

Maack, Mary Niles. 2002. "Documenting One Hundred Twenty Years of Writings on Women's Entry, Advancement, and Struggle for Equalization in Librarianship." *Library Quarterly* 72: 241–246. Accessed May 20, 2011. http://search.ebscohost.com/login.aspx?direct=true&db=a9h&AN =6626283&site=ehost-live.

McCook, Kathleen de la Peña and Katharine Phenix. 1984. *On Account of Sex: An Annotated Bibliography on the Status of Women in Librarianship, 1977–1981*. Chicago: American Library Association.

Neal, James G. 2011. "Stop the Madness: the Insanity of ROI and the Need for New Qualitative Measures of Academic Library Success." In *Association of College and Research Libraries. National Conference. Peer Revered: Proceedings of the Fifteenth National Conference of the Association of College and Research Libraries, March 30–April 2, Philadelphia, Pennsylvania*, 424–429. Accessed

on April 15, 2011. www.ala.org/acrl/sites/ala.org.acrl/files/content/confer-
ences/confsandpreconfs/national/2011/papers/stop_the_madness.pdf.

Oakleaf, Megan. "RAILS." http://meganoakleaf.info/rails.html. Accessed May
12, 2012.

———. "Rubric Assessment of Information Literacy Skills." Institute of Museum
and Library Services grant project. In http://railsontrack.info. Accessed May
12, 2011.

Passet, Joanne E. 1996. "You Do Not have to Pay Librarians:" Women, Salaries,
and Status in the Early 20th Century." In *Reclaiming the American Library
Past*, edited by Suzanne Hildenbrand, 207–219. Norwood, NJ: Ablex.

Robert Perret and Nancy J. Young. 2011. "Economic Status of Academic
Librarians." *portal*: *Libraries and the Academy* 11, no. 2 (2011): 703–715.
http://muse.jhu.edu/ (accessed June 6, 2011).

Polger, Mark Aaron and Karen Okamoto. 2010. "Can't Anyone be a Teacher
Anyway?: Student Perceptions of Academic Librarians as Teachers." *Library
Philosophy & Practice* 12: 1–16. Accessed June 22, 2011. http://search.ebscohost
.com/login.aspx?direct=true&db=lxh&AN=56660151&site=ehost-live.

Pritchard, Sarah M. 2004. "Apostles of Culture: The Public Librarian and
American Society, 1876—1920." *Library Quarterly* 74: 477–486. Accessed
March 23, 2011. http://search.ebscohost.com/login.aspx?direct=true&db=a
9h&AN=16628729&site=ehost-live.

Ragains, Patrick, John M. Budd, John J. Doherty, Debra Gilchrist, Esther
Grassian, and James T. Nichols. 2010. "Teaching Matters: A Panel Critique
of Budd's Framing Library Instruction and the Author's Rejoinder."
Communications in Information Literacy 4: 112–128. Accessed May 12, 2011.
www.comminfolit.org/index.php/cil/article/view/Vol4-2010ED2.

Salony, Mary F. 1995. "The History of Bibliographic Instruction: Changing
Trends from Books to the Electronic World." *Reference Librarian* 51–52:
31–51.

Schiller, Anita. "The Disadvantaged Majority." In *The Role of Women in
Librarianship, 1876–1976: The Entry, Advancement, and Struggle for
Equalization in One Profession*, 222–240. edited by Kathleen Weibel,
Kathleen de la Peña McCook, and Dianne J. Ellsworth. Phoenix: AZ: Oryx.

United States Bureau of Labor Statistics. 2010. *Highlights of Women's Earnings in
2009*. Report 1025. Washington, DC: US Census Bureau. Accessed April 15,
2011. www.bls.gov/cps/cpswom2009.pdf.

Ward, Patricia Layzell. 1979. "An Investigation into Certain Problems of Library
Staffing." In *The Role of Women in Librarianship, 1876–1976: The Entry,
Advancement, and Struggle for Equalization in One* Profession, 159–. edited by
Kathleen Weibel, Kathleen de la Peña McCook, and Dianne J. Ellsworth.
Phoenix: AZ: Oryx.

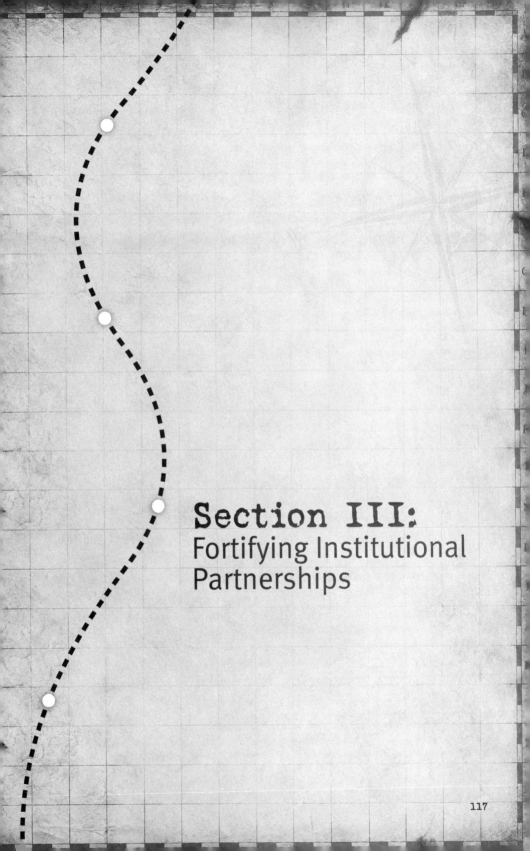

Section III:
Fortifying Institutional Partnerships

5

Hitching your Wagon to Institutional Goals

Anne E. Zald and Michelle Millet

THE THIRD DECADE AND ACCOUNTABILITY

As we enter the Third Decade of academic information literacy programming, institutional integration is a critical strategy we must employ to achieve sustained transformation. Connecting library programs to institutional accreditation processes is a lever which must be utilized with a broad understanding of its benefits and limitations. To quickly recap the decennial framework, during the first decade of information literacy programming the foundation was established, culminating in the 1989 ALA President's Commission definition of information literacy (American Library Association 1989) and articulating the role of various stakeholders in promoting the societal value of information literacy. During the second decade ACRL issued the Information Literacy Competency Standards for Higher Education (Association of College & Research Libraries, 2000) and sought partnerships with higher education associations and accrediting agencies to align information literacy with the broader discussions of teaching and learning in higher education (Thompson 2002) . This second decade brought widespread innovation within academic libraries to implement strategies and programs to move library instruction into a curricular context. The third decade is characterized by a growing clamor for change in higher education both from within and without the academy. Academic librarians must now ensure that programmatic educational initiatives are attentive to institutional context and priorities which, increasingly are being driven by external calls for accountability (McLendon, Hearn, and Deaton 2006).

The social consensus defining higher education as a "common good" worthy of extensive public financial support is coming under increasing scrutiny, critique (Hacker, Andrew, and Claudia Dreifus 2010; Kamenetz 2007) and, not to be underestimated, increasing competition (Kamenetz 2010; Wilson 2010). In 2006 the Spellings Commission (The Secretary of Education's Commission on the Future of Higher Education 2006) brought these debates into high relief, followed by the contentious 2008 reauthorization of the Higher Education Act (Lowry 2009). In response to the Spellings Commission report and state legislative mandates, accreditation processes are evolving toward increasing transparency and accountability (Brittingham 2008) and librarians must be cognizant of and active in all the assessment and accountability processes which the institution is engaging. These issues remain contentious for higher education years after the Spellings Commission debate as illustrated by the 2011 publication of *Academically Adrift: Limited Learning on College Campuses* and the *Degree Qualifications Profile* from the Lumina foundation (Anonymous. January 18, 2011; Lumina Foundations 2011).

Since the 1940's as federal funds became an increasingly important component of the higher education financial model (e.g. student financial aid, research funding, etc.) accreditation by the regional agencies shifted from a voluntary process to a de facto requirement with federal recognition of the regional agencies as the arbiter of quality. It is important to recognize that the Spellings Report and other critics of higher education are challenging the underlying rationale of the accreditation process.

> Accreditation serves two functions: institutional quality improvement among its members (the "private" function) and quality assurance (the "public" function) ... The role of accreditors as gatekeepers for federal funds has brought increasing expectations that accreditation serve the public interest by focusing more directly...on educational effectiveness as indicated by student learning and success. It is the quality-assurance function that is under question (Brittingham 2008, 32–33).

Critics of federally sanctioned accreditation assert that accreditation is part of the problem.

> The accreditation process suffers from structural problems: secrecy, low standards, and little interest in learning outcomes...The accredi-

tors have been able to carve up the country into regional cartels... accreditors have been able to apply intrusive, prescriptive standards (Neal 2008, 27).

Alternatively, critics claim that through transparency in the marketplace institutions should be held accountable to, "...the people who matter: the students, parents, and taxpayers who fund higher education" (Neal 2008, 28). Although the recommendations of the Spellings Commission, emphasizing consumer accountability and performance outcomes such as student learning and completion rates were not implemented at that time through federal law or regulation, they do have an ongoing influence. Several of the six regional accrediting agencies have revised their standards since the appearance of the Spellings Report in 2006. The ongoing national dialog around institutional and student learning assessment has intensified and voluntary associations of higher education institutions have been established to address issues of consumer value and transparency. Both the Voluntary System of Accountability (VSA) and the University and College Accountability Network (U-CAN) are building publicly accessible data repositories, institutional profiles and cost comparisons to assist prospective students and their families. In addition the VSA, with support from the Fund for Improvement of Post-Secondary Education (FIPSE) and the Lumina Foundation, is conducting research to determine the comparability of existing measures of student learning (Voluntary System of Accountability 2010).

In this shifting landscape of accreditation and accountability the key questions for library managers are also shifting away from those emphasized under the "quality assurance" function of accreditation which emphasized collection volume counts and adequacy of facilities. The question libraries increasingly need to answer is, "How does the library advance the missions of the institution?" (Association of College & Research Libraries 2010, 11). Institutions are increasingly being asked to define their mission and value in terms of student learning rather than by number of degrees conferred. Therefore, librarians must actively participate in local efforts to define learning outcomes and demonstrate added value to student learning in response to these increasing calls for accountability not only from university administrators but also from consumers, federal and state legislators and funding agencies. Information literacy in the third decade engages librarians in the paradigm shift from facility- and collection-centric services to an institutionally-integrated approach to the educational role of libraries and librarians. As accreditation, assessment and accountability in higher education increasingly focus upon student learning outcomes, information literacy is much more firmly grounded as an institutional outcome addressed in the learning outcomes of general education and the majors to which the library can make significant contributions in the areas of definition, implementation, and collaboration on faculty development to address course and program redesign.

A CASE STUDY: EXTERNAL PRESSURE, AN ACCREDITATION OPPORTUNITY AND FACULTY SUPPORT THROUGH CURRICULAR CHANGE

As is the case in many academic libraries the Coates Library at Trinity University, a selective liberal arts institution in San Antonio, Texas, implemented the liaison librarian model where librarians were partnered with academic departments, building individual librarian-faculty partnerships to enact a course-integrated approach to library instruction. This model is typical of the second decade of information literacy described earlier in this chapter. Statistics showed the "program" to be growing; the number of sessions was increasing and librarians were certainly teaching more classes than ever. There was, however, a critical component missing. In this situation there was no larger curriculum map that illustrated how or where information literacy was "happening" across the liberal arts disciplines. Neither the Library nor the institution could demonstrate student achievement of this learning outcome as a part of a Trinity University degree. Achieving that larger vision, effecting a transformation, would require the Library to be connected in a substantial way to a curricular need. The Library's challenge was to demonstrate the value of information literacy to student learning and shift the responsibility for information literacy as a student learning outcome back into the hands of the teaching faculty who are responsible for creating curriculum.

Librarians constantly seek opportunities to make the case that information literacy is an intellectual competency critical to success in all the disciplines and, indeed, a foundation for lifelong learning. Informally, through conversations with faculty, and formally through internal institutional processes such as curriculum and program reviews, librarians can create those opportunities. However, external processes such as accreditation can be more powerful for many reasons, not the least of which is their institution-wide scope.

Regional higher education organizations which include accreditation among their responsibilities are looking for ways to enhance student learning. This is in part a response to external critics but also a result of extended discussion within higher education circles over the past decades. The reaffirmation of accreditation process that libraries are most familiar with remains in place and involves documenting past and present practice in a format now called the "Compliance Certification" documentation. Compliance Certification addresses the bean counting of input/output documentation such as tracking down transcripts, figuring out student-to-faculty ratios and, for the library, providing volume counts for academic departments. Rather than depending exclusively on this input-output accounting, institutions in the Southern Association of Colleges & Schools (SACS) have the opportunity to select and develop a Quality Enhancement Plan (QEP) as part of the reaffirmation process. The QEP became part of reaffirmations in 2005 and served as a way for the academic institutions under the purview of SACS to be forward thinking.

According to SACS, the Quality Enhancement Plan "describes a carefully designed and focused course of action that addresses a well-defined topic or issue(s) related to enhancing student learning" (Southern Association of Colleges and Schools Commission on Colleges 2004, 24). Each institution within the SACS region develops its own plan for choosing and implementing a QEP. The directions on how to implement a plan are not mandated or sanctioned from SACS itself. The Southern Association merely requires that a QEP demonstrate the following criteria: it enhances student learning; shows broad-based institutional participation; reviews current best practices in the topic; be supported financially by the institution; state a clear timeline and responsibilities; and demonstrate that the QEP topic is feasible and assessable (Southern Association of Colleges and Schools Commission on Colleges 2004, 3).

At Trinity, the president appointed a 15-member committee to review proposals submitted by students, staff, and faculty from all over campus. Twelve proposals in total were submitted which the committee narrowed first to six and then to three after public discussion and presentation of each proposal. Anyone from the university could comment on the proposals and there was opportunity for both face-to-face questioning and write-in questions and comments. The three finalist proposals were forwarded to the president for final selection (Millet 2010).

THE CASE STUDY OF A QEP: BEING PREPARED TO PROVIDE YOUR DATA

The Coates Library at Trinity read eagerly about the Quality Enhancement Plan requirement for schools within the Southern Association of Colleges & Schools (SACS) and the precedent established by the "information fluency" QEP at the University of Central Florida (University of Central Florida 2006). The Library seized on the QEP process as an opportunity to impact student learning by creating a plan for systematically integrating information literacy across the curriculum. The idea was not to promote the library's instruction program, but rather to transform the library's teaching mission from one-shot instruction occurring in a scattered manner throughout the curriculum to an approach that emphasized working with faculty to create a year-by-year approach across the curriculum to create, implement, and measure specific learning goals for individual courses and even academic departments. The QEP process put the Library into competition with other proposals submitted across the campus. The Library QEP proposal provided both a plan and a structure for Trinity University to articulate and implement campus-wide learning outcomes for both undergraduate and graduate students. Major features of the proposal were course and assignment redesign structured in a multi-year plan that progressed through the curriculum and faculty development through summer and mid-semester workshops. In addition to focusing each year of the plan on a progressive level of the curriculum, departments were also able to work closely with their liaison librarian to define department-specific learning objectives if they wished.

A number of factors contributed to the president's selection of the Libraries Information Literacy Across the Curriculum program as the campus-wide Quality Enhancement Plan initiative. For the four years prior, librarians had gathered and used data in conversations with faculty to elicit what the faculty wanted students to learn and to share what librarians could see happening. Through this legwork, librarian by librarian, liaison to department, the topic of information literacy was familiar to a broad cross section of the faculty. By tracking data and understanding student learning the Library QEP proposal was able to demonstrate feasibility as well as a track record of demonstrable impact.

WHAT WE KNEW: ADDING VALUE

In addition to the groundwork laid through the liaison program, the Information Literacy Coordinator spearheaded a variety of assessment instruments for the teaching librarians to employ in their instruction individually in classes, while also taking part in larger assessments such as the First Year Information Literacy in the Liberal Arts Assessment (FYILLAA) project, which was based at Carleton College at the time. This tool, in particular, provided Trinity with data comparing itself to elite liberal arts colleges around the country. Results from this study showed that Trinity students had less research and information literacy experience coming into college than those at peer institutions, yet also had a higher self confidence in their abilities (Trinity University 2008). By working with the faculty in small groups over lunch conversations about what they wished their students could do, the library learned that evidence from more prestigious institutions often held sway with many teaching faculty. Comparative data from aspirant peer institutions can be a powerful tool.

Assessment of student learning became an integral part of the information literacy program at Trinity before the QEP even presented itself because the Library had a strong working relationship with the office responsible for campus assessment. For libraries and librarians this is another way to get a seat at the table and be prepared for the larger opportunities that come along, i.e. contributing a question or two to the survey administered to graduating seniors asking about their critical thinking skills, or having access to institutional data from large scale assessments like the National Survey of Student Engagement (NSSE) or the College Student Experience Questionnaire (CSEQ).

In addition to these efforts to gather quantitative data, the Information Literacy Coordinator and University Librarian held regular focus-group type luncheons for teaching faculty to talk about ways in which they felt their students' work could be bettered and strengthened with collaboration between librarians and faculty. Instruction within the Libraries saw an increase of over 50% from 2003 to 2007 (the year the QEP was chosen), an indicator of increased collaboration between librarians and faculty, and growing familiarity with the Library as an instructional partner.

The heart of the Trinity QEP was placing a financial value on working closely with faculty, with the right personnel, to develop assignments and redesign courses to integrate information literacy (Millet, Michelle S., Donald, Jeremy, Wilson, David W. 2009). The largest portion of the QEP budget was allocated to three activities; 1) to provide grants for creating new and redesigning existing courses, 2) to bring in experts and outside teaching faculty to provide faculty development workshops, and 3) to offer stipends to teaching faculty to attend annual and mid-semester gatherings where they learned more about information literacy and the course grant opportunities. Each summer faculty teaching courses that paralleled the goals of the QEP or who showed an interest in redesigning their course to integrate information literacy objectives were invited to workshops. The emphasis of the workshops was to ensure that student information literacy learning would be evaluated in the context of the assignments. Integration into the curriculum often, but not always, resulted in library instruction as a part of the course. The Library made clear to faculty participants that the goal of the QEP was not merely to increase the number of library instruction sessions. Through these collaborations the QEP could achieve the related goals of strengthening the place of information literacy on campus, building faculty acceptance of the responsibility to address information literacy in their teaching, building teaching partnerships between faculty and librarians, and expanding the perception of the educational role of libraries and librarians.

CONCLUSION: GENERAL LESSONS FROM THE CASE STUDY

This case study illustrates that for transformational impact, a library instruction program must be actively engaged outside of the library in partnership with the academic departments and administrative structures that govern the curriculum. In addition the case study points to both the strengths and the limitations of an instruction program built exclusively on individual teaching partnerships forged by liaison librarians. Those partnerships are critical for building knowledge on the part of both members of the partnership, e.g. the librarian gains knowledge both of faculty teaching practices and challenges as well as student information behavior and needs, while faculty gain knowledge of the contributions that librarians can make to student learning. Faculty-librarian partnerships also provide opportunities to gather data, both qualitative and quantitative, that can be used to demonstrate the library's impact on student learning. However, successful teaching partnerships can only take a library instruction program so far. Ultimately a library instruction program built entirely upon course-level partnerships is not sustainable and cannot support consistent student achievement of institutional learning outcomes. Curricular integration requires the full engagement of those responsible for creating curriculum, e.g. the faculty. Full responsibility for the partnerships required for curricular integration cannot lie solely at the course level with the liaison librarian, instruction coordinator or department head. Institutional impact requires a corresponding engagement of the library administration in advocating for the educational mission of the library and paving pathways for partnerships to address curriculum at the institutional level of departments, schools and colleges.

This case study also points to several principles for institutional engagement which librarians and library administrators can employ to achieve sustainable and transformative information literacy programming. First, regardless of which regional accrediting agency governs your institution connect the libraries to all the relevant standards, processes and priorities which that agency establishes for your institution, paying attention not only to collections and facilities but also to the institution's educational mission. By identifying information literacy as the library's contribution to the educational mission of the institution, librarians stake a role in furthering progress on institutional challenges. Second, connect the libraries to institutional participation in alternative assessment or value initiatives, e.g. VSA, U-CAN, thereby contributing to the measures your institution has identified as vital to communicating value to external stakeholders. Third, connect the libraries to institutional assessment initiatives that are underway including participation at the national, state, consortial or peer institution level [see www.learningoutcomeassessment.org/surveys.htm for information about additional national surveys in which your institution may participate]. Fourth, connect the libraries to formal or informal initiatives focused upon student learning assessment, curriculum or program reviews, the scholarship of teaching and learning (SoTL), etc. Many institutions have a center which focuses on faculty development related to teaching and learning. If such an obvious starting point does not exist, take the next step and consider how the library can initiate those conversations. The library, situated at the cross roads of many institutional priorities, may have knowledge about where conversation about teaching and learning is occurring, who is participating in that conversation, and the broader range of expertise that can be drawn into the conversation, e.g. computing and assessment professionals, instructional designers and technologists, etc. Librarians are very good at organizational processes, meeting facilitation, and working on cross-functional teams. Play a leadership role at your institution by identifying needs related to the institution's educational mission and organizing ways to meet those needs.

What a library organization will learn and how it will act based upon engaging these principles will vary. Institutional culture and practices are deeply engrained and will influence strategies and objectives. These principles require administrative engagement, political savvy, and persistence to influence cultural change. Articulating the library's contribution to issues of institutional, consortia, state or regional importance will raise difficult questions that libraries may be unaccustomed to answering, or do not yet have a methodology to answer. In this they will join their faculty and administrative colleagues in grappling with a changing higher education environment and forging new partnerships to improve institutional performance.

References

News: Academically adrift. January 18, 2011. *Inside Higher Ed.*, www.insidehighered.com/news/2011/01/18/study_finds_large_numbers_of_college_students_don_t_learn_much.

American Library Association. American library association presidential committee on information literacy: Final report. in American Library Association [database online]. Chicago, IL, 1989 [cited 12/5/2010 2010]. Available from www.ala.org/ala/mgrps/divs/acrl/publications/whitepapers/presidential.cfm (accessed 12/5/2010).

Association of College & Research Libraries. 2010. *Value of academic libraries: A comprehensive research review and report.* Chicago, IL: Association of College & Research Libraries, www.acrl.ala.org/value/ (accessed December 13, 2010).

———. Information literacy competency standards for higher education. [cited 12/5/2010 2010]. Available from www.ala.org/acrl/standards/information-literacycompetency (accessed 12/5/2010).

Brittingham, Barbara. 2008. An uneasy partnership: Accreditation and the federal government. *Change* 40 (5) (September/October 2008): 32–8.

Hacker, Andrew, and Claudia Dreifus. 2010. *Higher education? how colleges are wasting our money and failing our kids—and what we can do about it.* New York: Times Books, Henry Holt and Company.

Kamenetz, Anya. 2010. *DIY U: Edupunks, edupreneurs, and the coming transfor-*

mation of higher education. White River Junction, Vermont: Chelsea Green Publishing.

———. 2007. Generation debt: How our future was sold out for student loans, credit cards, bad jobs, no benefits, and tax cuts for rich geezers—and how to fight back.

Lowry, Robert C. 2009. Reauthorization of the federal higher education act and accountability for student learning: The dog that didn't bark. *Publius: The Journal of Federalism* 39 (3): 506–26 (accessed September 12, 2010).

Lumina Foundations. 2011. *Degree qualifications profile.* , www.luminafoundation .org/publications/The_Degree_Qualifications_Profile.pdf.

McLendon, Michael K., James C. Hearn, and Russ Deaton. 2006. Called to account: Analyzing the origins and spread of state performance-account ability policies for higher education. *Educational Evaluation and Policy Analysis* 28 (1): 1–24.

Millet, Michelle. 2010. Be prepared for the opportunity: Foundations, information literacy, and a QEP. *LOEX Quarterly* 37 (1): 8–9.

Millet, Michelle S., Donald, Jeremy, Wilson, David W. 2009. Information literacy across the curriculum: Expanding horizons. *College & Undergraduate Libraries* 16 (2/3) (April/September 2009): 180–93.

Neal, Anne D. 2008. Seeking higher-ed accountability: Ending federal accreditation. *Change* 40 (5) (September/October 2008): 24–9.

Southern Association of Colleges and Schools Commission on Colleges. 2004. *Handbook for reaffirmation of accreditation.*

The Secretary of Education's Commission on the Future of Higher Education. 2006. *A test of leadership: Charting the future of U.S. higher education.* Washington D.C.: U.S. Department of Education, , www.ed.gov/about/ bdscomm/list/hiedfuture/index.html.

Thompson, Gary B. 2002. Information literacy accreditation mandates: What they mean for faculty and librarians. *Library Trends* 51 (2) (Fall 2002): 218–41.

Trinity University. Expanding horizons: Using information in the 21st century. A quality enhancement plan for trinity university 2008–2013. San Antonio, TX, 2008 [cited January 31 Available from www.trinity.edu/departments/ academic_affairs/qep/ExpandingHorizonsQEPpublic.pdf.

University of Central Florida. What if? A foundation for information fluency. university of central florida enhancement plan 2006–2011. 2006 [cited January 31 2011].

Voluntary System of Accountability. 2010. VSA research & presentations. [cited December 7 2010]. Available from www.voluntarysystem.org/index. cfm?page=research.

Wilson, Robin. 2010. For profit colleges change higher education's landscape: Nimble companies gain a fast-growing share of enrollments. *The Chronicle of Higher Education*, February 7, 2010, 2010, sec News: Administration. http://chronicle.com/article/For-Profit-Colleges-Change/64012/?otd=Y2xp Y2t0aHJ1Ojo6c293aWRnZXQ6OjpjaGFubmVsOmNvbW1lbnRhcmnksYXJ0 aWNsZTpmb3ItcHJvZml0LWNvbGxlZ2VzLWRlc2VydmUtc29tZS1yZXN wZWN0Ojo6Y2hhbm5lbDphZG1pbmlzdHJhdGlvbixhcnRpY2xlOmZvc i1wcm9maXQtY29sbGVnZXMtY2hhbmdlLWhpZ2hlci1lZHVjYXRpb25z LWxhbmRzY2FwZQ== (accessed December 6, 2010).

6

Merging Critical Thinking and Information Literacy Outcomes— Making Meaning or Making Strategic Partnerships?

Robert Schroeder

INTRODUCTION

Information literacy and critical thinking—what is the relationship? Many librarians have sensed a connection. When discussing the myriad literacies popularized in the 21st century Patricia Senn Brevik (2005, 23) states, "...information literacy is a kind of critical thinking ability; often the terms are used interchangeably." It is true that in library literature critical thinking and information literacy are often combined, merged, entangled and subsumed within each other. What does this mean for academic instruction and information literacy librarians who are working to teach students the requisite information literacy skills? If critical thinking and information literacy outcomes become blended at academic institutions, how should librarians react? Is a close relationship between the two concepts in the form of a combined outcome to be applauded and supported, or should such unions be avoided at all costs? The following chapter will look at critical thinking, how librarians perceive its relationship to information literacy, and what useful strategies can result when these two concepts are combined.

To set the stage a few of the major psychological and philosophical theories of critical thinking will be briefly noted. In order to gauge our profession's understanding of critical thinking and its relationship to information literacy, a survey of library literature will be performed. The more rigorous articles from this survey will then be discussed in order to discern the range of positions librarians have taken on the relationship of these two concepts. Moving from theory to practice, the next section will showcase five different models of campus-wide learning outcomes that combine critical thinking and information literacy into one outcome. A special note will be made of unique features of each of the combined outcomes, in the hopes that readers will find that one or more of the models resonate with the learning outcomes at their own institution. Next a recent survey of almost 200 librarians will be analyzed to discover librarians' feelings around the idea of a merged critical thinking and information literacy outcome, as well as the perceived benefits and liabilities of such a merger. Finally, for those information literacy librarians considering adopting strategic partnerships (such as combining critical thinking and information literacy at their campus), some practical advice will be given.

CRITICAL THINKING

Initially one factor that makes this line of inquiry particularly tenuous is that currently in the field of education there is no agreed upon definition of critical thinking. As Jennifer Reed succinctly states in her 1998 dissertation;

> A review of literature in the field of critical thinking revealed a general lack of consensus on how critical thinking is best defined, on what critical thinking skills can and should be taught, and on determining the most appropriate framework for this teaching. As a whole, educational reformers have not even agreed on terminology. ..The relationship among "critical thinking," "higher order thinking," "thinking skills" and other terms such as "informal logic," "informal reasoning," "problem solving," "argumentation," "critical reflection," "reflective judgment," and "metacognition" have further complicated the issue. Other areas of disagreement and concern include (a) the extent to which critical thinking is subject specific, (b) differences between expert and novice thinking in a discipline and the extent to which novices can learn to think more like experts, (c) dif-

ficulties in separating higher order and lower order thinking skills for instructional purposes, and (d) whether critical thinking should be considered a process or a set of skills (Reed 1998, 28).

Another reason there is controversy in defining critical thinking is that in the later part of the 20th century definitions of critical thinking converged on educators from two separate disciplines—philosophy and psychology (Gibson 1995, 28). Many philosophical definitions of critical thinking tend to be based on or related to the concept of informal logic, while psychological definitions are most often based on theories of cognition or neuroscience.

The lack of consensus on a definition of critical thinking has not stopped philosophers, psychologists, and educators from attempting to pin it down. The short discussion below is not meant to thoroughly examine the breadth and nuances of the critical thinking landscape, but rather it is meant to touch upon a few of the major definitions in order to give the reader an idea of their scope and range.[1] For example, according to the philosopher Robert Ennis (1962, 83), "As a root notion *critical thinking* is taken to be *the correct assessing of statements.*" Ennis (Table 6.1) goes on to further refine this definition in logical terms with twelve aspects of critical thinking (84).

TABLE 6.1
Ennis' twelve aspects of critical thinking

1. Grasping the meaning of a statement
2. Judging whether there is ambiguity in a line of reasoning
3. Judging whether certain statements contradict each other
4. Judging whether a conclusion follows necessarily
5. Judging whether a statement is specific enough
6. Judging whether a statement is actually the application of a certain principle
7. Judging whether an observation statement is reliable
8. Judging whether an inductive conclusion is warranted
9. Judging whether the problem has been identified
10. Judging whether something is an assumption
11. Judging whether a definition is adequate
12. Judging whether a statement made by an alleged authority is acceptable

Another philosopher, Richard Raul, moved beyond informal logic into the realm of metacognition when he stated;

> The idea of critical thinking, stripped to its essentials, can be expressed in a number of ways. Here's one: critical thinking is the art of thinking about thinking in an intellectually disciplined manner. Critical thinkers explicitly focus on thinking in three interrelated phases. They *analyze* thinking, they *assess* thinking, and the *improve* thinking (as a result). (Paul 2005, 28)

Paul also defines the intellectual traits that a critical thinker possesses as, intellectual integrity, intellectual humility, fair-mindedness, intellectual perseverance, confidence in reason, intellectual courage, intellectual empathy, and intellectual autonomy (33).

In the late 1980s Peter Facione conducted a Delphi study to find out if there was a consensus on a definition of critical thinking in higher education and to see how critical thinking might best be taught and assessed. The Delphi panel consisted of forty-six experts—philosophers, educators and social scientists and their definition of critical thinking went even farther into the affective realm by positing the dispositions of a critical thinker. It reads in part;

> The ideal critical thinker is habitually inquisitive, well-informed, trustful of reason, open-minded, flexible, fair-minded in evaluation, honest in facing personal biases, prudent in making judgments, willing to reconsider, clear about issues, orderly in complex matters, diligent in seeking relevant information, reasonable in the selection of criteria, focused in inquiry, and persistent in seeking results which are as precise as the subject and the circumstances of inquiry permit (Facione 1990, 3).

CRITICAL THINKING IN LIBRARY LITERATURE

With these, and many other definitions of critical thinking swirling around academe for at least forty or fifty years, what does library literature have to say about the relationship of critical thinking (any definition) and information literacy? At first blush, a lot. Searching indexes to library literature (Library Literature and Information Science, LISTA, and ERIC) hundreds of hits are found with the query *"information literacy" and "critical thinking"*. Unfortunately if one is looking for a rigorous mapping of critical thinking to the ACRL Information Literacy Competency Standards for Higher Education (ACRL Standards) one will be disappointed in the search results. Craig Gibson (1995, 27) notes, "Interest in critical thinking is not new among librarians. Even though library literature abounds with references to critical thinking, such references often lead only to brief discussions with imprecise definitions of the term." Regarding the ACRL Standards, Dean Cody (2006, 404) insightfully notes that "ACRL dances around the issue of defining critical thinking; however it recognizes its importance." The author would add that ACRL also dances around the issue of how information literacy is related to critical thinking. The vast majority of the articles found by the author in library literature typically would also assert, without evidence, that information literacy was related in some natural and intimate fashion to critical thinking and then launch into an example how "critical thinking information literacy skills" were taught at a certain university. So many of the articles were of this ilk that the author at first doubted his searching skills and so set out to confirm if the above generalizations about the literature on the relationship between critical thinking and information literacy might be true.

Library Literature and Information Science Full Text, LISTA, ERIC, and Education Full Text were searched on the subject terms "critical thinking" and "information literacy."[2] Two-hundred and twenty one articles were found that matched these search criteria. After eliminating the duplicate articles 199 unique articles remained. In order to have a confidence level of 95% and a confidence interval of 10% a random sample of 65 articles was chosen from this set to be tested.

The first question asked of the articles was whether "information Literacy" was defined. Twenty-nine (45%) of the articles contained no definition of information literacy. Twenty-two (34%) of the articles contained a minimal one to two sentence definition, while the remaining 14 (22%) gave more that a minimal definition. Thirty-one (48%) of the articles mentioned a set of existing information literacy standards. Most of the articles with an academic focus mentioned either the ACRL or earlier ALA definitions of information literacy, while a few also referred to the British (CILIP), Australian or New Zealand (CAUL or ANZIIL), or the Alexandria definitions. The rest of the articles that mentioned a set of standards were either K–12 focused and so mentioned the AASL or Big 6 standards, or mentioned institutions that developed home grown standards on their own. As "information literacy" is a concept conceived of by librarians and ubiquitous now in library cultures, perhaps it is reasonable to assume extensive definitions of information literacy would not be needed.

The next question asked of the articles was if critical thinking was defined. All of the articles were indexed on the subject term "critical thinking" so a minimal definition of the term might be expected. Nearly three-quarters of the articles in the sample (48 or 74%) contained *no definition* of critical thinking. While the term "critical thinking" was mentioned in passing in this portion of the sample, it was left up to the reader to imagine what this concept might be. Eight articles (12%) had a bare minimum of a definition—usually consisting of one or two sentences. The remaining 9 (14%) had a definition that went beyond two sentences. The 14 articles that did mention an existing model referred either to the major models mentioned above (Ennis, Paul, or Facione) or to "homegrown" models developed by the authors or their institutions.

This survey confirms the author's suspicions as well as Gibson's observation above to lack of rigor in librarians' discussions and explorations of the concept of critical thinking in regards to information literacy. The articles in the survey were indexed both under the subject terms "critical thinking" and "information literacy". For this reason it could be expected the set of results would contain a fair amount of articles that would go beyond a shallow discussion of both of these issues and the relationship between the two. However only 22% of the articles went beyond a minimal definition of information literacy, and only 14% did the same for the concept of critical thinking.

CRITICAL THINKING AND INFORMATION LITERACY

Much of the library literature that does focus on the subject of critical thinking and its relationship to information literacy tends to be overly optimistic, imagining linkages in spite of the lack of much real evidence.[3] Rebecca Albitz (2007,100) notes that some of the criteria in classical critical thinking models, such as Ennis', imply a critical thinker would need to know research skills, but nowhere in the definition of critical thinking is this relationship made explicit. Many other writers make the point that evaluating information sources is an obvious example of critical thinking (see McCormick 1983, 340; Bodi 1988, 150; and Herro 2000, 556). There are, however, two articles that take a more rigorous and sustained look at critical thinking and its relationship to information literacy.

Craig Gibson's thoughtful 1995 article, *Critical Thinking: Implications for Instruction*, is a great primer on the subject of critical thinking and information literacy instruction. In it he describes the state of critical thinking, controversies within the movement, and assessment of critical thinking. He mentions the "back-to-basics" movement within library instruction that came about as a reaction to the development of the concept information literacy and its attempt to link itself to critical thinking. Members of this movement, such as Cheryl LaGuardia (1992,16) held that what should best be taught in library instruction sessions are practical skills rather than conceptual skills that fall under the rubric of critical thinking. Gibson remarks that "this is a very undesirable scenario for librarians who wish to be part of the educational mission of their institutions" (Gibson 1995, 31). He address many of the issues librarians face when teaching critical thinking in library sessions and asserts, "Learning to question well, reason out research problems, predict with confidence the location (or even the existence) of information, as well as evaluating the information found—these are the core skills" (33).

Dean Cody, in his article "Critical Thoughts on Critical Thinking" (2006, 404), notes that ..." a survey of library literature reveals a lack of agreement among librarians upon a definition of critical thinking," and he goes on to state that "Librarians *acknowledge* that there is little agreement concerning the definition of critical thinking" (405; italics added by author). He would appear to be an ally of the back-to-basics movement alluded to by Gibson above. Even though he is in a minority opinion among librarians, he makes a logical case for shunning a union between critical thinking and information literacy. Because there is no agreed upon definition of critical thinking, he argues that our claims to be teaching it via information literacy instruction are baseless. An individual's "thinking" is hard enough to measure, and many definitions of critical thinking relate it to attitudes and dispositions of the thinkers. How could we teach and assess if our students were thinking critically, especially within our normal parameters of the 50-minute library session? Taking a behaviorist approach he argues that in order to measure student learning outcomes we need to look only at the outputs of student's research work, such as successful database searches. He suggests that, "...the new criterion for evaluating students' work is control. Students need to exhibit control over database search interfaces in order to attain relevant retrieval, regardless of their attitude" (Cody 2006, 406).

CRITICAL THINKING, INFORMATION LITERACY AND LEARNING OUTCOMES

In library literature many librarians have given their often uncritical support to the union of critical thinking and information literacy. But have these two concepts been successfully linked in practice, and how has this merger fared? A few colleges and universities in the United States have created campus-wide outcomes that join critical thinking and information together. In the discussion below five models that combine critical thinking and information literacy will be discussed, and the unique features of each model will be highlighted.

These liaisons have taken a variety of forms. At Portland State University the "Critical and Creative Thinking Learning Outcome" (Table 6.2) looks suspiciously like a curt definition of information literacy (Portland State 2011).

While the title of the outcome does not explicitly state the term information literacy, many of the words in the body of the outcome (italicized in Table 6.2) reflect information literacy goals. The outcome is terse and rather broad, and comingles critical thinking outcomes with those of information literacy. The draft "Inquiry and Critical Thinking Outcome" at the University of Nevada (Table 6.3) is written in a similar vein (University of Nevada 2008).

While this outcome is more fully articulated than the one from Portland State University, the title still does not use the term information literacy and the information literacy portions of the outcome are interspersed with those of critical thinking.

The "Analysis, Problem Solving, and Information Literacy Outcome" from Spokane Falls Community College (Table 6.4) represents a slightly different take on a merged outcome (Spokane Falls 2011).

Information literacy is specifically mentioned in the title, while critical thinking is implied only by the mention of two components of criti-

TABLE 6.2

Portland State University Critical and Creative Thinking Outcome

Students will develop the *disposition and skills to strategize, gather, organize*, create, refine, *analyze, and evaluate the credibility of relevant information* and ideas

TABLE 6.3
University of Nevada

(Information literacy components italicized).

2. Inquiry and Critical Thinking Outcome—Use qualitative and quantitative reasoning and *appropriate research methods to guide the collection*, analysis, and use of *information*

Competence in the Inquiry and Critical Thinking outcome is defined by the following objectives:

1. Analyze problems, articulate questions or hypotheses, *and determine the need for information.*
2. *Access and collect the needed information from appropriate primary and secondary sources.*
3. Use quantitative and qualitative reasoning, including the ability recognize assumptions, draw inferences, make deductions, and interpret information to analyze problems in context and draw conclusions.
4. Recognize complexity of problems, tolerate ambiguity when appropriate and identify different perspectives from which problems and questions can be viewed.
5. Evaluate and report on conclusions, including discussing the basis for and strength of findings, and *identify areas where further inquiry is needed.*
6. Use results of inquiry and analysis to make judgments and guide actions.

cal thinking, analysis and problem solving. The information literacy and critical thinking components are interspersed, and like the University of Nevada's outcome the larger "ability" is parsed out into smaller, more easily assessed "learning outcomes".

Laney College in Oakland California (Table 6.5) has conceived of a slightly different form for their combined outcome (Laney College 201).

They have repacked their general education outcomes, often organized by courses, into more conceptual categories. Outcomes from the mathematics and computer literacy courses are combined with information literacy in the "Critical Thinking and Information Literacy" outcome. Each of them however remains a distinct unit within the more general outcome. The University of Maryland (Table 6.6) takes this segregation to the extreme in their bifurcation of critical thinking into undergraduate and graduate abilities (Office of Outcomes 2006). While both the undergraduate and graduate abilities are labeled "critical thinking" the undergraduate proficiency is clearly the classic ACRL Standards' definition of

TABLE 6.4

Spokane Falls Community College Analysis, Problem Solving and Information Literacy

(Information literacy components italicized).

Ability

- Students will *access, evaluate and apply information from a variety of sources* and in a variety of contexts.

Learning Outcomes

- A. Make accurate observations, isolate issues, and formulate questions
- B. *Recognize the need for both quantitative and qualitative information.*
- C. *Identify, locate, and access potential sources of information.*
- D. *Evaluate information on the basis of its origin, viewpoint, currency, relevance, and completeness.*
- E. Analyze information using available technologies and analytical methods.
- F. Make justifiable inferences and suggest viable solutions/interpretations.
- G. Evaluate solutions/interpretations for validity and appropriateness, and make necessary adjustments.
- H. *Use information ethically.*

TABLE 6.5

Laney College General Education Outcomes

(Information literacy components italicized).

Critical Thinking and Information Literacy

- A. Solve quantitative problems using numerical, graphical, and algebraic methods. *(Area 4b: Mathematics)*
- B. Demonstrate proficiency in using a computer and computer applications, including the Internet, to accomplish personal, academic, and/or professional tasks. *(Area 4c: Computer Literacy)*
- C. *Locate and cite appropriately information from a variety of sources (books, databases, internet, primary sources) in various formats (print, online, multimedia); evaluate information for relevance and reliability, and incorporate it effectively into written work. (Information Competency)*

information literacy, while the graduate ability more closely maps to classical definitions of critical thinking.

MERGING OUTCOMES—WHAT DO LIBRARIANS THINK?

Much of library literature assumes, in a hopeful manner, that information literacy and critical thinking are somehow easily and meaningfully merged. At some academic institutions, like those showcased above, campus-wide learning outcomes have been created that merge these two concepts in intriguing ways. Regardless of whether this is a meaningful merger of these two concepts, or a mere opportunistic or strategic conflation, it is a pragmatic way librarians and other faculty at a few institutions have seen fit to acknowledge information literacy at their institution. But what does the rest of our profession think about such mergers? What are the benefits and the challenges of such a pact?

In mid March 2010, academic librarians were surveyed in order to discover how they felt about the merger of critical thinking and information

TABLE 6.6
University of Maryland

(Information literacy components italicized).

Within the School of Undergraduate Studies, proficiency in critical thinking is demonstrated through the through the ability to:

- *Determine the nature and extent of information needed;*
- *Evaluate information and sources critically;*
- *Incorporate information into a personal knowledge base;*
- *Support positions with credible reasoning and evidence;*
- *Use information effectively to accomplish a specific purpose; and*
- *Use information ethically and legally.*

Within the Graduate School of Management and Technology proficiency in critical thinking is demonstrated through the ability to:

- Develop credible responses to complex questions;
- *Gather appropriate evidence;*
- Evaluate alternative solutions with respect to evidence; and
- Choose the solution that best fits the evidence.

literacy into one outcome. The survey asked them to envision working with a combined outcome and to reflect on what advantages and disadvantages might arise from such a merger. The survey was posted to the Information Literacy Listserv and almost 200 librarians responded. No effort was made to gather a statistically valid sample of academic librarians and the survey was open to anyone who wanted to reply, so no statistically meaningful inferences can be made from the data. But many of the author's initial reflections on the pros and cons of merging the two outcomes into one were confirmed, and many new ideas surfaced as well.

The first question in the survey asked for the librarians' opinions about the relationship of critical thinking to information literacy. Neither critical thinking nor information literacy were defined at this point of the survey, as it was hoped that each librarian would rely on his or her own internalized impressions of these concepts in order to answer the first question. Five responses were given from which to choose, ranging from

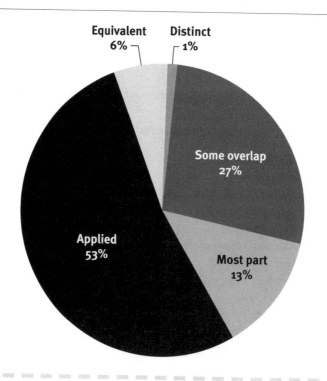

FIGURE 6.1

Information Literacy's Relationship to Critical Thinking

"Information literacy is distinct from critical thinking", to "Information literacy *is* critical thinking".[4] A small minority of those surveyed chose either one of these two extreme responses. Only 1% (3) said that the two outcomes were totally distinct, while 6% (12) agreed that they were exactly the same. 27% (54) said that there was some overlap between the two, and 13 % (25) agreed that information literacy was for the most part, critical thinking. The majority of respondents, 53% (104), thought that information literacy was critical thinking applied to information. In spite of the fact that library literature has not provided us with a wealth of rigorous articles clearly linking critical thinking and information literacy, it seems that academic librarians *feel* there is a strong and obvious relationship between information literacy and critical thinking.

A slightly modified version of the Portland State University "Critical and Creative Thinking" outcome above was used as an example outcome in the rest of the survey, as this definition merged part of each of the concepts

FIGURE 6.2
Affective Reaction to Example of Merged Outcome

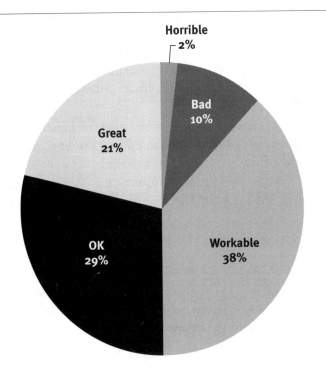

in a relatively concise manner (see Table 6.7 for the exact wording of the definition used in the survey).

Each respondent was to imagine that she or he worked as an instruction librarian at a four-year college that had the outcome above as the only campus-wide outcome for student learning. Hoping again to get a visceral and emotional response, the second question asked, "As an instruction librarian, concerned about teaching information literacy to students, your reaction to this outcome and its definition would be ..." Then a range of five possible responses were given that ranged from "horrible" to "great".

About one-eighth of the respondents felt extremely negative about the example outcome. 2% (4) said that it was horrible and as an instruction librarian they wouldn't be able to work with it at all, while 10% (19) said that it was bad—perhaps it wasn't the worst outcome they could imagine but it was pretty close. However the vast majority of the librarians surveyed had more positive feelings towards this entwined outcome. 38% (75) thought they could work with this definition, and 50% (98) of those surveyed were very positive about it—29% (57) thought it was "pretty much OK" and 21% (41) thought it was a great outcome. Again, even with an outcome that was short and obviously not overly descriptive of critical thinking or information literacy, librarians responded positively. The author was surprised with the amount of acceptance this outcome garnered from the academic librarians surveyed. It would seem to indicate that most librarians take a pragmatic and flexible stance when faced with such non-traditional definitions that conflate information literacy and critical thinking.

The third question of the survey asked what was missing from the survey's critical thinking outcome (see Table 6.7 for wording). As the survey's definition was rather terse it was not surprising that most of the respondents noted that pieces of the ACRL Information Literacy Standards were not addressed. Most notably the specifics of finding information; the

TABLE 6.7
Wording of Critical Thinking Outcome Used in Survey

"Students will develop skills to strategize, gather, organize, create, refine, analyze, and evaluate the credibility of relevant information and ideas."

ethical and legal uses of information; and that the information found needs to be applied or used in some manner. Many others noted that the definition wasn't clear or well written, it was too broad and didn't show examples of actual outcomes, and that it wasn't really a definition of critical thinking. When one appreciates that this definition was an artifact of years of meetings of diverse faculty from across the Portland State campus, many of these defects become more understandable. The politics of creating such campus-wide outcomes on any campus often lead to such imprecise definitions as seen from the point of view of instruction librarians. The real question for an instruction librarian concerned with the success of an information literacy programs is, "What level of trade off is acceptable in order to get the majority of my information literacy goals met?"

The forth survey question asked, "What do you see as the advantages of having the critical thinking outcome (in Table 6.7), but no articulated information literacy outcome at all." A great many librarians responded that just being called a "critical thinking" outcome was a great plus, even if most of the text of the outcome described information literacy as well. This renaming helps to move information literacy from mere skills to the more conceptual level of thinking and reasoning. Because the concept of critical thinking has been discussed and debated for many years on colleges campuses, many if not most academic institutions have accepted some flavor of critical thinking as a campus-wide learning outcome. As the definition of critical thinking has been articulated by a local community of faculty there is often a huge amount of buy-in for the concept. Anyone using the term critical thinking in an outcome would have no need start afresh to explain a new term (like information literacy) and there would be no need to start at ground level to build consensus around it across campus. The fact that this outcome to some extent encapsulates information literacy, without using the term information literacy or library jargon, could make it much easier to promote on many campuses. This would potentially free up a lot of time and energy librarians currently spend to educate and promote a concept new, foreign, and sometimes threatening to teaching faculty. One librarian responded, "Information literacy still draws a complete blank among non-librarian academics, whereas all professors promote critical thinking."

The survey respondents noted another advantage of such an outcome— that it is short yet broad, and allows for creativity and flexibility in its interpretation by librarians. Librarians would be able to rationalize and adapt many different models of information literacy instruction under the aegis of this somewhat ambiguous outcome. As one respondent noted, "This is broadly inclusive and may actually provide the assertive librarian free reign. I don't see anything here preventing the librarian from pursuing an information agenda with specific, measurable outcomes." With the outcome recognized as critical thinking, the whole campus would "own" the outcome, not just librarians. Faculty across disciplines already see critical thinking as germane to all of their students, and it would be much easier to build librarian-faculty partnerships around such an outcome.

The fifth survey question asked, "What do you see as the disadvantages of having the above Critical Thinking outcome and no Information Literacy outcome at all?" The respondents overwhelmingly lamented the lack of an explicit tie-in to the library. Instead of spending our time and energy educating faculty to the existence of, and the need for, information literacy, many thought that the battle now would be showing that the library and librarians can and do teach critical thinking. While many respondents thought there were no disadvantages with the outcome as stated, others reiterated their concerns about what was missing in this definition from question three above. They mentioned it was too broad, unclear, and seemed unmeasurable as written. A few respondents also implied that it was important that students know that what they are learning is information literacy (not critical thinking) and somehow with the outcome defined as critical thinking this would not be possible. A few also noted that many accrediting bodies now assess for information literacy at colleges, and the lack of an outcome explicitly called information literacy could make it harder to prove that information literacy is indeed valued and assessed at an institution.

STRATEGIC PARTNERSHIPS AND THE FUTURE OF INFORMATION LITERACY PROGRAMS

Library literature shows us that there is a strong current of sentiment that links critical thinking to information literacy, even though in most articles critical thinking is not well defined, if at all. Many of the articles written about the relationship of these two concepts vaguely and hopefully hint that the linkages between the two are strong and obvious. On a practical level, over the last forty years most academic institutions have acknowledged critical thinking as an outcome of student learning, and many have embraced some form of critical thinking as a campus wide goal for all of their students. What does this mean for future librarians charged with integrating information literacy into their campuses?

Critical thinking can be a "strategic partner" in achieving our goals as information literacy librarians. Information literacy has not been as broadly accepted as a campus-wide outcome for a variety of reasons, but there is evidence that, at some institutions at least, information literacy has been creatively combined with critical thinking. The author has been involved with the creation and revision of such hybrid outcomes at two institutions—Spokane Falls Community College and Portland State University. The process of creating campus-wide outcomes is often long, intense, and intensely political. For pragmatic reasons, at least at the two schools mentioned above, over the course of long discussions with dozens of faculty groups, information literacy became merged with critical thinking into one combined outcome.

For many of the librarians involved in these processes, the author included, the question then arises—to what extent can this resulting outcome be considered a success or a failure? Over the course of creating these campus-wide outcomes this "new" concept of information literacy and the library's role in teaching it became clear to many faculty, and teaching faculty and librarians had many fruitful discussions as to its merit and place amongst all the other literacies swirling around academe today. If our goal as instruction librarians is to teach our students (and faculty) the information skills and concepts they need to become better scholars and ultimately better citizens, then surely this can be done under the aegis of such a combined goal. Many survey respondents pointed out that currently librarians spend great amounts of energy on introducing and advocating for information literacy. By partnering with critical thinking advocates on campus, the energy being spent in getting the term "information literacy" recognized and accepted by an often over burdened and over assessed faculty can be channeled elsewhere. One respondent remarked, "Well, you have info literacy as an outcome—if political factors keep you from having one labeled as such, you've achieved it anyway."

When outcomes are forged by committees over long periods of time all of what we as academic librarians know to be information literacy will surely not ultimately end up reflected in the final draft. All instruction librarians involved with information literacy programs have numerous goals for their programs—the question then becomes will we only accept "perfection" (one-hundred percent of our goals being accepted), or "good enough"?

From the survey results above it is obvious that many librarians feel that a learning outcome that combines information literacy with critical thinking is at least "good enough". While it is not a perfect outcome many of the survey comments suggest the challenges created by merging the two are not insurmountable. Many librarians even consider strategically partnering around such an outcome a success. At institutions where classic educational and philosophical definitions of critical thinking have been adopted information literacy is often an implied requisite, and it would be easy for librarians to link these two concepts. For example, following Ennis' definition of critical thinking, without adequate research and evaluative skills how could a student judge"...whether a statement made by an alleged authority is acceptable" (Ennis 1962, 84)? If Facione's definition of critical thinking were adopted at an institution information literacy skills would definitely be required in order for a student to be "... diligent in seeking relevant information" (Facione, 1990, 3).

Ultimately however, it comes down to each individual librarian and the environment and culture at each institution. At any institution where critical thinking/information literacy is an accepted campus-wide outcome faculty in every discipline, not just the library, will need to customize and adapt the general outcome to make sense in disciplinary terms. As Joanne Kurfiss writes in *Helping Faculty Foster Students' Critical Thinking in the Disciplines* (1989, 42) , " In spite of clear difference among the disciplines, common elements of reasoning exist. Critical thinking in all disciplines involves both discovery and justification of ideas." Engineering professors will call their application "problem solving", Mathematicians "logic", and English faculty will be teaching varieties of literary criticism like "post-modernism", "reader response" or "post-colonialism". Just as other faculty project their own disciplines' definitions onto critical thinking, librarians too can operationalize critical thinking in the realm of research as "information literacy".

We know our students need information literacy skills to succeed in their inquiry and exploration in academe, and to prosper as informed professionals and citizens in the 21st century. And we know too that librarians will be central in delivering these important skills. At many institutions we may have a campus-wide outcome for information literacy; at others we may only be able to project information literacy onto other goals, such as critical thinking. In merging these concepts we have seen that some meaning has been made, but more importantly we also realize that finding strategic allies on campus, like those groups promoting critical thinking, can be a viable strategy for pragmatically reaching our long term goals as information literacy librarians.

APPENDIX A:
Critical Thinking /Information Literacy Survey

1. In your opinion which sentence below best describes Information Literacy's relationship to Critical Thinking?
   A. Information literacy is distinct from critical thinking.
   B. Information literacy has some overlap with critical thinking.
   C. Information literacy is, for the most part, critical thinking.
   D. Information literacy is critical thinking applied to information.
   E. Information literacy is critical thinking.

For the next few questions imagine you have just been hired at an instruction librarian at a 4-year college. They only have one college-wide outcome for their students—"Critical Thinking". They define "Critical Thinking" as:

"Critical Thinking Outcome: Students will develop skills to strategize, gather, organize, create, refine, analyze, and evaluate the credibility of relevant information and ideas."

2. As an instruction librarian, concerned about teaching information literacy to students, your reaction to this outcome and its definition would be most like:
   A. ARGH! I won't be able to work with this definition at all.
   B. It could be worse (but not much worse).
   C. I can see working with this definition.
   D. This is pretty much OK.
   E. WOW! This couldn't be better.
3. As an instruction librarian, concerned with information literacy, what is missing in your opinion from the above definition? *Text box...*
4. What do you see as the advantages of having the above definition of Critical Thinking outcome and no Information Literacy outcome at all? *Text box...*
5. What do you see as the disadvantages of having the above definition of Critical Thinking outcome and no Information Literacy outcome at all? *Text box...*
6. Anything else you would like to mention in regards to critical thinking and information literacy? *Text box...*

References

Albitz, Rebecca S. 2007. "The What and Who of Information Literacy and Critical Thinking in Higher Education." *portal: Libraries and the Academy* 7: 97–109.

Bodi, Sonia. 1988. "Critical Thinking and Bibliographic Instruction: The Relationship." *The Journal of Academic Librarianship* 14: 150–153.

Brevik , Patricia Senn. 2005. "21st Century Learning and Information Literacy." *Change* 37: 20–28.

Cody, Dean E. 2006. "Critical thoughts on Critical Thinking." *The Journal of Academic Librarianship* 32: 403—407.

Ennis, Robert H. 1962. "A Concept of Critical Thinking: A Proposed Basis for Research in the Teaching and Evaluation of Critical Thinking Ability." *Harvard Educational Review* 32: 81–111.

Facione, Peter A. 1990. *Critical Thinking: A Statement of Expert Consensus for Purpose of Educational Assessment and Instruction. Research Findings and Recommendations,* Newark Del.: American Philosophical Association.

Gibson, Craig. 1995. "Critical Thinking: Implications for Instruction." *RQ* 35: 27–35.

Herro, Steven J. 2000. "Bibliographic Instruction and Critical Thinking." *Journal of Adolescent and Adult Literacy* 43: 554–558.

Kurfiss, Joanne Gainen. 1989. "Helping Faculty Foster Students' Critical Thinking in the Disciplines." In *The Department Chairperson's Role in Enhancing College Teaching* (*New Directions for Teaching and Learning No 37,* edited by Ann F. Lucas, 41–50. San Francisco: Josey-Bass.

LaGuardia, Cheryl. 1992. "Renegade Library Instruction," *Library Journal* 117: 51–53.

Laney College, 2011. "General Education Outcomes." Accessed March 21. www.laney.peralta.edu/apps/comm.asp?$1=31347 .

McCormick, Mona. 1983. "Critical Thinking and Library Instruction." *RQ* 22: 339–342.

Office of Outcomes Assessment University of Maryland University College. 2006. "Critical Thinking as a Core Academic Skill: A Review of Literature." Accessed March 21, 2011. www.umuc.edu/outcomes/pdfs/CRITICAL%20 THINKING%20LITERATURE%20REVIEW.pdf .

Paul , "Richard . 2005. The State of Critical Thinking Today." In *Critical Thinking: Unfinished Business* edited by Christine M. McMahon, 27–38. San Francisco: Jossey-Bass.

Portland State University Institutional Assessment Council. 2011. "Critical and Creative Thinking." Accessed March 21. www.iac.pdx.edu/content/critical -and-creative-thinking .

Reed, Jennifer H. 1998. "Effect of a Model for Critical Thinking on Student Achievement in Primary Source Document Analysis and Interpretation, Argumentative Reasoning, Critical Thinking Dispositions, and History Content in a Community College History Course." PhD diss. University of South Florida.

Spokane Falls Community College, 2011. "Analysis, Problem Solving, and Information Literacy." Accessed March 21. www.spokanefalls.edu/College/Outcomes/Analysis.aspx .

University of Nevada. 2008. "Gen Ed Advisory Committee Report on Undergraduate Learning Outcomes." Accessed March 21 2011. http://generaled.unlv.edu/geac/Gen_Ed_Report_on_Outcomes_DRAFT_OUTLINE_12_Nov_2008.pdf .

Notes

1. For short overviews of critical thinking in education see:
   Bailin, S. 1994. "Critical Thinking: Philosophical Issues." In *The International Encyclopedia of Education 2nd ed.*, edited by Torsten Husen and T. Neville Postlethwaite, 1204–1208. Oxford: Pergamon.
   Schrag, Francis. 1992. "Critical Thinking." In the *Encyclopedia of Educational Research 6th ed.,* edited by Marvin C. Alkin, 254–256. New York: Macmillan. See also Cassel, Jeris F. and Robert J. Congleton. 1993. *Critical Thinking an Annotated Bibliography*. Metuchen, N.J.: Scarecrow Press.

2. The database Library Literature and Information Science Full Text did not have a subject term for "information literacy" so it was searched in this database as a keyword phrase.

3. For a bibliography see Ellis, Erin L. 2008. "The Evolution of Critical thinking Skills in Library Instruction, 1986 – 2006: A Selected and Annotated Bibliography and review of Selected Programs." *College & Undergraduate Libraries* 15: 5–20.

4. For the whole survey see Appendix A.

7

Crossing the Instructional Divide: Supporting K–20 Information Literacy Initiatives

Jo Ann Carr

INTRODUCTION

Although the American Library Association has a common definition of information literacy as a "set of abilities requiring individuals to 'recognize when information is needed and have the ability to locate, evaluate, and use effectively the needed information" (ALA, 1989), the development of a seamless information literacy curriculum across the education spectrum is as great a challenge as the development of a true K–20 curriculum for any other subject area. This is despite the efforts of ALA, its divisions, and individual librarians, libraries, and library teams to develop and support K–20 information literacy initiatives.

Information about collaborative information literacy activities and projects between K–12 and academic libraries has long been detailed in library literature and was comprehensively explored by the 1998 AASL/ ACRL Taskforce on the Educational Role of Libraries. Their "Blueprint for Collaboration" also included an ambitious list of recommendations for fostering collaboration across the K–20 information literacy spectrum. These recommendations focused on collaboration, on joint association activities, on continuing education for librarians and on outreach. (AASL/ACRL 1998)

To continue the work of the 1998 Taskforce, ALA established the AASL/ACRL Interdivisional Committee on Information Literacy in 2003 to

> focus on how to prepare K–20 students to be information literate and [to] provide a channel of communication to the respective divisions. In general, this interdivisional committee will be a forum for sharing ideas on information literacy in K–20 environments and a source of professional development opportunities in this area. (ACRL 2010a)

In addition the Infolit discussion list has been supported by AASL and ACRL since 2005 to facilitate communication between K–12 and academic librarians on information literacy topics. (AASL InfoLit) Amy Duenik initiated this list in response to her own experiences with college freshmen and sophomores who were challenged in using the library catalog, citation styles, and call numbers. Her students also claimed they were taught to copy and paste images from the 'infallible' Internet without attribution. Ms. Duenik further noted

> I just wanted to help make students' transition from high school to college easier. And when I do an introduction to academic research for freshmen, I would like to have a good idea of where to start. (pers. comm.)

Early messages on the listserv discussed concerns among academic librarians on basic search skills. The lack of a common discussion ground for school and academic librarians in the same community was cited as a barrier to communication even at the local level. The challenges Ms. Duenik experienced which led to the beginning the InfoLit discussion list continue to be echoed by others. Boff and Johnson's 2007 analysis reports that students have low levels of satisfaction with information literacy instruction in higher education and claim it "is repetitive and they already know about researching". (Boff and Johnson 2007, 77) Larry Hardesty expands upon this view of students in higher education

> Typically, when asked, most first year students will say they have written library papers in high school or even junior high school and therefore know how to use the library. *This does not mean that they have*

gone beyond compilation of descriptive and unevaluated information, not does it indicate that they know how to use an academic library with its more sophisticated resources. (Hardesty 2007b, 116)

The Library Instruction Round Table of ALA has also devoted considerable effort to bridging the gap between K–12 and higher education by building upon the work of the 1998 Task Force to identify collaborative projects and activities and to foster communication on this vital topic. Their 2009 ALA Annual Conference Brown Bag discussion, "Helping High School Students Become 'College Ready' led to the development of a discussion forum by the ACRL Instruction Section, "Helping Students Transition to College", at the 2010 conference which examined existing collaborations, defined research-related skills students need in higher education, and identified information literacy skills students have and need.

The ACRL Values Report (*Value of Academic Libraries: A Comprehensive Research Review and Report.*), released in December 2010, examines the potential for academic libraries to adapt the experiences and strategies of K–12 libraries in supporting information literacy programs. These experiences include aligning library goals with those of the school community; working with teachers and principals in a continuum of cooperation, coordination, and collaboration; evidence-based practice and action research; and large-scale, statewide studies of the impact of school libraries on student learning. (ACRL 2010b, 58–72)

The Association of Library Service to Children (ALSC) has also begun to play a role in responding to information literacy needs of the children they serve. An online course "Information Literacy from Preschool to High School" has been offered since February 2010. This course is designed to encourage participants to examine their local schools' and state's requirements pertaining to library skills, and to develop methods of using the library to complement those requirements. Participants learn about examples of successful programs, appropriate skills for appropriate ages, creation and presentation of programs as well as marketing of those programs; also, participants will discuss ways that information literacy instruction can be a useful "outreach" tool to increase library and database usage and develop their own information literacy instruction program. (ALSC 2010)

These efforts by ALA and by individual librarians, libraries, and educational institutions have not resulted in a comprehensive information literacy curriculum and environment. The development of information literacy initiatives across the entire educational spectrum continues to face challenges of differing organizational structures in K–12 and higher education, the lack of common expectations across this spectrum, and substantial differences in governmental oversight. Both K–12 and American higher education continue to change and develop, unfortunately in somewhat different directions. The 'standards movement' in K–12 has led to the development of standards from AASL, ISTE, and the P21 partnership which are substantially different in language and in intent from the *Information literacy competency standards for Higher Education Standards* developed by ACRL. Technology, distance learning, and demographics of these two educational systems are also developing in parallel tracks, further complicating the development of a cohesive information literacy curriculum.

Jim Rettig's advocacy of a library ecosystem eloquently speaks to the need for all types of libraries to work together.

> I think of our school, public, academic, and other types of libraries as part of an integrated library ecosystem. If one part of the system suffers, the entire system is threatened and suffers. Libraries offer incredible lifelong learning environments. *No one type of library can deliver learning opportunities from cradle to grave.* But through our library ecosystem we offer these opportunities in abundance. (Rettig 2008)

Rettig's comments point to the interconnectedness of all of the elements that share the same habitat of library services within our society. These interconnected elements include our shared practices in acquiring, organizing, and providing access to materials. Information literacy serves as the shared pathway for understanding these practices as well as for enabling the users we share throughout their lifespan to evaluate, analyze, and apply the information gleaned from these resources. Professional librarians can also learn from a deeper exploration of our ecosystem. The ACRL Values report notes:

> Academic librarians can learn a great deal about assessing library value from their colleagues in school, public, and special libraries. In particular, school libraries and academic libraries share a mandate to help students learn and teachers teach; they have similar missions and, consequently, similar assessment challenges. (ACRL 2010c, 58)

The ACRL Values Report includes a challenge to academic librarians to emulate the ways in which K–12 education uses multiple tools to evaluate the library's impact student learning. These tools include both formal (tests, portfolios) and informal (journals, checklist) assessment tools. (ACRL 2010c, 60–69) The emphasis on economic value and social value studies used by public libraries also demonstrates the differences in how academic, school, and public libraries consider their interrelationship with their users and thus miss the opportunity to consider lifelong learning throughout the entire ecosystem. (ACRL 2010c, 72–82)

The concept of a library ecosystem moves information literacy collaboration activities between K–12 and higher education institutions beyond easing the transition between high school and higher education. Creating this ecosystem, easing the transition, and building lifelong literacy should be the multiple goals of collaboration.

The importance of information literacy in easing the transition between K–12 and higher education is substantiated by a 2005 study conducted by Achieve.org that found that 59% of college instructors are dissatisfied with the ability of high school graduates to do research. (Owen 2010, 20) On February 9, 2010 Tom Reinsfelder reported on the InfoLit Discussion List about the use of Project SAILS to rank the information literacy skills of incoming first year students. His study showed that students did best on documenting and evaluating sources and lowest on selecting finding tools, using finding tool features and retrieving sources. One factor in being able to use finding tools and retrieving sources was identified by a 2006 ETS study that indicated that college students need 'a fairly good knowledge of their field of study before they can develop meaningful refiners'. (Hsin-Liang 2009, 343)

Attempting to develop a comprehensive information literacy curriculum that focuses only on the transition from K–12 to higher education will not meet the need of those students who do not continue their education beyond K–12. High schools often have separate curricula (either defined or de facto) for students who are college bound and those who are not. Does this difference in the future plans of K–12 students also call for the development of differing information literacy curricula in secondary education? If, in fact, there should be two curricula, what is the role of the academic librarian in developing the K–12 curricula for the college bound and what is the role of the public librarian in developing the K–12 curricula for those students who do not pursue higher education (as well as for personal rather than scholarly information literacy)? How should public librarians who work with children be integrated into a seamless information literacy curriculum spanning K–12 school libraries, academic libraries, and public libraries? Addressing the potential needs of both those who continue their education and those who do not will require new symbiotic relationships in the library ecosystem.

CHANGING LANDSCAPES IN K–12 AND HIGHER EDUCATION:

As noted above, scrutiny and public discourse regarding the quality of K–12 education has been intense since the release of *A Nation at Risk*. (United States 1984) For the past 11 years the annual Phi Delta Kappa/ Gallup Poll of the Public's Attitudes Towards the Public Schools has found that Americans feel that education is not as good today as when they were in school. (Bushaw and McNee 2009, 10) Efforts to improve education has led to an atmosphere of standards and standardized testing in K–12 schools. This atmosphere is shifting as part of the "Race to the Top" initiative in which President Obama has pledged on his Education Issues website to

> end the use of ineffective 'off-the-shelf' tests and support new, state-of-the-art assessment and accountability systems that provide timely and useful information about the learning and progress of individual students. (White House 2010)

This change in focus in accountability from high-stakes summative testing to value-added assessment is being accompanied by a change from state standards to the development of common core standards with a focus on college and career readiness. The common core curriculum is based on common core standards that have been adopted by 40 of the 50 states. (Common Core 2010a) The common core standards in English Language Arts have five content areas including writing with an emphasis on research, speaking and listening that requires that "students gain, evaluate, and present increasingly complex information, ideas, and evidence", and the production and critical analysis of media and technology integrated throughout the English Language Arts standards. (Common Core 2010b)

Monica Martinez presented a new vision of K–12 schooling to the Wisconsin State Superintendent's High School Task Force. This movement from a traditional school demonstrates the authoritarian centralized structure of K–12 education as well as a vision that supports an information rich curriculum. Some of the elements (no tracking, multiage placement, flexible scheduling, and organizational structure) also provide a closer parallel to higher education.

FIGURE 7.1
Obsolete High School vs. New Vision High School

Traditional	"New Vision"
Tracking/differentiated curriculum	No tracking/core curriculum.
Grade levels/seat time	Multiage/based on student capability and progress (e.g. VT's Math Emporium)
Standardized assessments	Performance based assessments
Short and fixed time periods	Blocked times and flexible scheduling
Acquisition of information out of context.	Acquisition of information is contextual, builds upon prior knowledge.
Closed classrooms/busy work.	Cooperative learning groups/experiential and authentic work.
Isolation of students	Continuous interaction between students and adults.
Isolation of teachers	Team teaching/teacher collaboration.
Isolation of institution	Institution more closely connected to community.
Very structured-hierarchical and centralized/authoritative	Loosely structured, flat and decentralized, shared responsibility and leadership.

(State Superintendent's Task Force 2006, 13)

Institutions of higher education are also experiencing a shifting landscape in which issues of accountability are prompted by accreditation requirements, the use by some institutions of the ETS ICT Literacy Assessment (ETS 2004) and a greater emphasis on the first year experience. In 2007 Laura Saunders conducted a review of the standards from the six regional accreditation organizations "that revealed that all of them mention information literacy within their standards". (Saunders 2008, 305) This is an increase from three organizations that were found to have this requirement in a 2002 study. (Saunders 2008, 308) Academic librarians with responsibility for information literacy must know the importance that their institutions' accrediting associations give to information literacy as well as know to what extent the administration and faculty of their local institution understand information literacy. These dual levels of knowledge can assist these academic librarians in developing a strategy to leverage the accrediting associations' expectations as part of their collaborations with local administrators and faculty to meet these expectations. This requirement that academic librarians link their outcomes to institutional outcome is being emphasized by ACRL as part of an increasing emphasis on the value of academic libraries. (ACRL 2010c, 12, 16, 55)

First year college student failure rates of 25–50% (Carr 2006, 105) have led to the creation of First Year Experience (FYE) programs at many colleges and universities. The role of the library and information literacy in FYE programs is the focus of a 2007 publication edited by Larry Hardesty and published by the National Resource Center for the First Year Experience and Students in Transition. (Hardesty 2007a) This title looks at the role of academic librarians in the beginning college experience and the "dynamic ongoing reform conversation in American higher education". (Gardner 2007, xv) The impact of prior information literacy experiences on the First Year experience includes a look at the lack of correlation of experiences at the end of high school and the beginning of the first year of college (Oseguera 2007, 43–44) the need to "provide the tools necessary to make a successful academic transition from high school to college" (Rockman 2007, 90), the abilities and expectations that students bring from their high school experiences (Hardesty 2007b, 110 and 116) and the exploration of models for collaboration.

High failure rates for first year students in higher education may also stem from differences in the expectations for high school graduation and college admissions standards. A 2003 survey of 400 college faculty and staff from 20 research institutions asked what students must be able to do to succeed in entry level courses. Habits of mind such as problem solving, critical thinking, and communication skills were assessed as much more important than content knowledge that is the subject of high school competency requirements. (Understanding 2003) The College Board Standards for College Success project has developed model standards for middle and high school students to more closely "reflect 21st-century skills such as problem solving, critical and creative thinking, collaboration, and media and technological literacy." (College Board 2010) However, current high school graduation requirements continue to be focused on course completion rather than on mastery of specific competencies.

ACRL has addressed proficiencies needed for instruction librarians and coordinators in 1998 and 2007 documents. The 2007 document includes twelve proficiency areas: administrative skills; assessment and evaluation skills; communication skills; curriculum knowledge; information literacy integration skills; instructional design skills; leadership skills; planning skills; presentation skills; promotion skills; subject expertise; and teaching skills. (ACRL 2007) These twelve areas cover 41 specific proficiencies, all of which have been ranked by librarians as important, very important, or essential to their jobs. (Westbrook and Fabian 2010, 578) These proficiencies have an emphasis on collaboration, subject knowledge, and presentation of information with less attention to pedagogy and teaching. Item 12.2 addresses the need to "Modif[y] teaching methods and delivery to address different learning styles, language abilities, developmental skills, age groups, and the diverse needs of student learners." (ACRL 2007) However, this standard would be strengthened by a greater emphasis on learning sciences that integrates an understanding of the interrelationships among the cognitive and social aspects of learners with the design of learning environments, instructional methods, and informal learning. Since much of the information seeking and evaluation activities completed by students occur in an informal environment, the understanding of the interplay of these factors should be seen as the basis for all other proficiencies.

As detailed in the 2010 ACRL Values Report, federal government scrutiny of higher education is also increasing. During the George W. Bush administration, the Spellings Commission report furthered this scrutiny. Under the Obama administration, attention on higher education's impact on student learning is being cast as part of national competiveness in an information-based economy. (ACRL 2010c, 6)

A disconnect between the experiences and expectations of students from the millennial generation and that of faculty, teachers, and librarians is a major factor in the landscapes of both K–12 and higher education institutions. A recent study found that 31% of American students were dropping out or failing to graduate from the nations' largest 100 school districts. (Thomas and Date 2006, 364) This dropout rate and the disconnect of many students derives, in part, from the differing life experiences of teachers and faculty and of their students. Many teachers and faculty teach in the way in which they have been taught with pedagogy that is "characterized as serious, methodological, serious, and slow-paced". In contrast today's students multi-task while they get information from multiple sources; work best with multiple rewards and in collaboration; value doing over knowing; and see the consumer and creator as ambiguous roles. (Marks 2009, 364)

The recently released National Educational Technology Plan (NETP) also has the potential to vastly impact the landscapes of both K–12 and higher education institutions. Although the phrase 'information literacy' is only used once in this plan (Transforming 2010, 13), the concept and need for information literacy in a seamless K–20 educational environment is an underlying theme of this report which stresses that learning requires access to information management and communication tools, knowledge building tools, information data and resources, and expert and authoritative sources. (Transforming 2010, 11) The report also states

> students are surrounded with information in a variety of forms, and specific features of information design affect how and whether students build usable knowledge from the information they encounter. (Transforming 2010, 15)

The importance of lifelong learning that is one of the three goals for collaboration for information literacy is also addressed:

> To prepare students to learn throughout their lives and in settings far beyond classrooms, we must change what and how we teach to match what people need to know, how they learn, and where and when they learn and change our perception of who needs to learn." (Transforming 2010, 10)

The importance of collaboration between K–12 and higher education is cited as necessary to removing barriers to higher education, to decrease dropout rates, and to increase student engagement at all levels. (Transforming 2010, xv, xxii)

DIFFERENCES IN LANGUAGE AND VIEWS OF INFORMATION LITERACY

The information literacy standards developed by AASL in 1998 and by ACRL in 2000 were parallel in many ways. (Carr and Rockman 2003) However, the 2007 *AASL Standards for the 21st Century Learner* differ substantially from the higher education standards. The higher education standards focus on skills and performance indicators while the new AASL standards move from skills to dispositions and attributes in an integrated curriculum. At the higher education level, the general standards are supplemented by subject area information literacy standards. Within K12 the AASL standards are one of three information literacy standards developed by national associations.

Information Literacy Competency Standards for Higher Education include five standards:

1. The information literate student determines the nature and extent of the information needed.
2. The information literate student accesses needed information effectively and efficiently.
3. The information literate student evaluates information and its sources critically and incorporates selected information into his or her knowledge base and value system.
4. The information literate student, individually or as a member of a group, uses information effectively to accomplish a specific purpose.
5. The information literate student understands many of the economic, legal, and social issues surrounding the use of information and accesses and uses information ethically and legally. (ACRL 2000)

Reflecting the subject emphasis of higher education that is demonstrated by the section organization in ACRL, some subject areas in higher education have developed their own standards and guidelines with a focus on the specific literatures of the discipline. These include "Information Literacy Standards for Anthropology and Sociology"; "Research Competency Guidelines for Literatures in English"; "Political Science Research

Competency Guidelines"; "Information Literacy Standards for Science and Engineering/Technology"; as well as "Library and Information Resource Instruction for Psychology—Guidelines" (Lloyd Sealy Library 2010) and "Information Retrieval and Evaluation Skills for Education Students" (EBSS 2010). A common feature of these standards and guidelines is reference to specific databases and tools of the subject and a focus on skills. The Education and Behavioral Sciences Section has developed standards that address both the discipline and the role of PK–12 Preservice Teachers. The "Information Literacy Standards for Teacher Education" provide a wholistic view of the information seeking process and the intersection among multiple disciplines; the need to consider developmental appropriateness of information presented to K–12 students; integrates presentation as part of the information seeking process; and recognizes the dual role of information literacy in teacher education in the preservice teachers academic work as well as in the content and curricula they develop for their students. (EBSS IE 2010) The use of these standards and guidelines in first year information literacy classes may be an antidote to students' concern that these instructional sessions are redundant. (Boff and Johnson 2007, 77)

The AASL *Standards for the 21st Century Learner* include four standards that detail skills, dispositions, and assessment strategies. These standards state that learners use skills, resources and tools to:

1. Inquire, think critically, and gain knowledge.
2. Draw conclusions, make informed decisions, apply knowledge to new situations, and create new knowledge.
3. Share knowledge and participate ethically and productively as members of our democratic society.
4. Pursue personal and aesthetic growth. (AASL 2007)

Since information and technology literacy are inextricably linked within K–12 education, the National Educational Technology Standards for Students (NETS-S) issued by the International Society for Technology in Education (ISTE) include information literacy standards. These standards also provide a new vision of education and schooling that is echoed in the 2010 National Educational Technology Plan (NETP). NETS-S aim to advance digital-age learning with standards for creativity and innovation; communication and collaboration; research and information fluency; critical thinking, problem solving and decision making; digital citizenship; and technology operations and concepts. Each of these six standards includes specific skills and outcomes. The two NETS-S standards with the highest relevance to information literacy are research and information fluency and critical thinking, problem solving and decision-making.

The research and information fluency standard is fully articulated as:

Students apply digital tools to gather, evaluate, and use information. Students:
a. Plan strategies to guide inquiry.
b. Locate, organize, analyze, evaluate, synthesize, and ethically use information from a variety of source and media.
c. Evaluate and select information sources and digital tools based on the appropriateness to specific tasks.
d. Process data and report results.

Critical thinking, problem solving and decision making is developed as:

Students use critical thinking skills to plan and conduct research, manage projects, solve problems, and make decisions using appropriate digital tools and resources. Students:
a. Identify and define authentic problems and significant questions for investigation.
b. Plan and manage activities to develop a solution or complete a project.
c. Collect and analyze data to identify solutions and/or make informed decisions.
d. Use multiple processes and diverse perspectives to explore alternative solutions. (ISTE 2007a)

The Partnership for 21st Century Skills (P21) is a national organization of leaders in business and education, including AASL, which was founded to guide schools in meeting the educational needs of the 21st century. Their vision includes six elements for 21st century education:

- Emphasize core subjects.
- Emphasize learning skills.
- Use 21st century tools to develop learning skills.
- Teach and learn in a 21st century context.
- Teach and learn 21st century content.
- Use 21st century assessments that measure 21st century skills.

Learning and innovation skills include information and communication skills; thinking and problem solving skills; and interpersonal and self-directional skills that parallel both the AASL and ISTE standards. P21 defines information skills as: "Analyzing, accessing, managing, integrating, evaluating, and creating information in a variety of forms and media." (Learning 2002, 8-9)

The AASL, ISTE, and P21 standards begin with a focus on student learning rather than on the literature of the discipline. This focus on student learning also looks at the integration of information literacy in the curriculum of specific subjects. AASL's guide to integration, *Standards for the 21st Century Learner in Action*, presents skills ,benchmarks and activities for each grade level. (AASL 2009) ISTE promotes this integration through profiles that identify specific learning activities at four grade levels: PK-2; 3-5; 6-8; and 9-12. (ISTE 2007b) ISTE also developed teaching guides to integrate the standards into the curriculum of specific subject areas. P21 is supporting this integration through the development of ICT (information, communications, and technology) Literacy Maps in Social Studies, English, and Math. (P21 2004-2011)

BARRIERS TO COLLABORATION

Differences in professional identities of librarians and teachers/faculty members; the organizational and authority structures of K–12 and higher education; and the self-identify of the student all present barriers to collaboration between K–12 and higher education. These barriers have contributed to differing expectations for high school graduation and college success that complicate the development of a cohesive K–20 curriculum.

Collaboration among all members of the 'library ecosystem' is complicated by differences in K–12 and higher education at the local, state and national levels as well as by differences in the professional identities of academic and school librarians. The web sites that describe the organization of the Association of College and Research Libraries (ACRL) and the American Association of School Librarians (AASL) illustrate these differing identities. The organization of ACRL is primarily based on collection building and organization with eleven of its seventeen sections focused on a specific academic subject. Only one of the seventeen sections, the Instruction Section, examines the role of the academic librarian as teacher although other sections including Anthropology and Sociology, Distance Learning, Education and Behavioral Sciences, Law and Political Science, Science and Technology, and Women and Gender Studies have committees focused on instruction (ACRL 2010b). In contrast, the members of AASL have a common focus as teacher librarians with their three sections focusing on the specialized roles of some of their members. (AASL 2010)

The role and status of librarian vis-à-vis the classroom-based staff also differs in K–12 and higher education. In K–12 education, the librarian is hired by the same organization as is the classroom teacher, belongs to the same professional category, and is typically located within the same building. In higher education, the hiring of library staff and classroom faculty frequently differs by department and unit, librarians may belong to a different professional category than do the teaching faculty, and librarians and faculty are usually located both organizationally and geographically in different schools, colleges, departments, and administrative units. High school teachers' (including the teacher librarian) loyalty is to their school, students, or profession whereas higher education faculty's (including academic librarians) primary loyalty is to their discipline. (Conley 2005, 6)

David Conley in *College Knowledge* attributes the differing organizational structures of K–12 and higher education to the lack of a true system of education at the national level. (Conley, 2005, 3) Despite an increasing role of the federal government in education since the release of *A Nation at Risk* (United States 1984), most K–12 schools are part of a system within a state or district while higher education is differentiated by funding, by mission, by demographics of their students, and by the political climate of the state or other affiliated institution which sponsors the specific institution.

The substantial differences in the authority structures of K–12 and higher education impact the autonomy of students and faculty resulting in an additional barrier to collaboration among all levels of education. K–12 institutions are largely authoritarian institutions in which attendance is taken, bells ring to indicate the end of class, parents are informed of problems in attendance and behavior, and teachers' curriculum is often dictated by state and local standards and curriculum guides. In contrast, attendance in higher education is often on the honors system (especially in large institutions with introductory courses taught in massive lecture halls), bells are usually absent, parents are prevented by the Federal Educational Rights and Privacy Act (FERPA) from being informed of problems in attendance and behavior, and faculty development of curriculum is a underlying tenet of academic freedom. (Carr 2006, 105) These differing authority structures contribute to a change in students' role identification from high school where they view themselves as community members to college where their self image is as consumers. (Hersh 2005, 28) This change in self-image is driven, in part, by the greater role that choice plays for college students. In contrast to high school, college students are more likely to choose their college, their courses, and, in some cases, their instructors. The requirement that students pay fees to attend college has also been cited as a reason that college students view themselves as consumers. (Maringe 2006)

The difference in authority structure extends to the role that the federal government takes in K–12 and higher education. The federal government has closely scrutinized K–12 education since *A Nation at Risk* was issued in 1984. This scrutiny has continued to the current administration's Race to the Top initiative which is designed in response to President Obama's statement on education issues

> He will foster a race to the top in our nation's schools by promoting world-class academic standards and a curriculum that fosters critical thinking, problem solving, and the innovative use of knowledge to prepare students for college and career. (White House 2010)

The importance of education reform was emphasized by U.S. Education Secretary's Arne Duncan's reaction to the results of the 2009 Programme for International Student Assessment which showed that United States students continue to fail to 'make the grade' among students in 34 countries where the test is administered. "The results are extraordinarily challenging to us and we have to deal with the brutal truth." (Test 2010, A19)

In contrast, the role of the federal government in higher education has, for the most part, been limited to issues of financial aid for students, of gender equity (e.g. Title Nine), and collaboration as a research partner. Only recently has the Obama administration proposed goals for graduation rates for higher education institutions. (ACRL 2010c, 30) This is a far cry from the requirements for specific curricula, standards, and preparation of teaching personnel that the federal government has for K–12 education. These differences mean that the biological community of our shared ecosystem (students, faculty/teachers, and librarians) must adjust to nuances in the physical environment.

PROGRAMS TO BRIDGE THE INSTRUCTIONAL DIVIDE

Many libraries, library and educational organizations, and individuals have developed programs that can serve as models of K–20 collaboration. These programs focus on three areas: resources for librarians, state level collaborative organizations, and resources and programs addressed to incoming students. Although these programs serve to foster collaboration at the national, state, and local levels; none have yet built a comprehensive K–20 information literacy curriculum and environment.

Resources for librarians have been provided in journal articles, by units of ALA, and through funding by IMLS. These resources include research studies, descriptions of individual libraries information literacy programs, programs at ALA, state, and local conferences, and grant proposals submitted to IMLS. Acknowledging that the information from research studies is 'unwieldy' for high school students, Patricia Owen has developed an information literacy checklist that is an inventory tool, a framework for designing information literacy lessons, and an assessment to address student confidence in their research skills. Owen assessed middle and high school info lit curriculum to determine if all these skills were included. (Owen 2010) The EBSS Instruction for Educators Committee has developed a website that introduces information literacy and other education standards in K–12 and higher education and provides examples of collaborative practices. The Network of Illinois Learning Resources in Community Colleges has developed a toolkit "The Toolkit for Success is designed to help teachers/faculty and librarians work together to address the information literacy needs of their at-risk high school and community college students." (NILRC 2010)

The states of Pennsylvania and Illinois have active state level programs to foster information literacy collaboration among all types of libraries. The Central PA K–20 Information Literacy Network has hosted annual workshops since 2004 for librarians from K–12, higher education, and public libraries with a focus on the information literacy needs of students as they transition from high school to college. (Penn State University Libraries 2010) Illinois has sponsored an annual Information Literacy Summit since 2002 with about 140 participants each year from academic, school, and public libraries as well as from library associations. These workshops are held in three locations around the state and hosted by Moraine Valley Community College Library, Logan College Library, and Illinois State University Milner Library for librarians at all educational levels. (MVCC 2011)

Conversations@Belmont is an example of a locally developed program of outreach by an academic library to K–12 librarians. This annual dinner, held since 2005, discusses the Belmont University information literacy program, shares examples of assignments given to first year Belmont students, or invites K–12 librarians to discuss their programs. (Belmont 2010) Most importantly these dinners have are described by Jenny Darshall in an InfoLit posting as having "provided a forum for school librarians, from both public and private schools, to communicate and share ideas".

The Infolit Discussion list provides numerous additional examples of programs directed to K–12 students by academic libraries. Two examples are the Informed Transitions Program at Kent State University and Penn State Mont Alto Library program for dual enrollment students. The Informed Transitions Program, described by Barbara F. Schloman includes a web site www.library.kent.edu/highschool, a high school classroom for hosting visits of high school classes, instructional sessions relating to high school projects, and borrowing privileges at Kent State. As reported by Tom Reinsfelder, the program at Mont Alto Library brings dual enrollment high school students and their school librarian to campus to learn about the university library.

Thomas Kuhn details Redwood High School's information literacy course for college bound seniors that can serve as a beginning model for a K–20 information literacy curriculum. Based upon the Information Literacy Standards for Higher Education, this one-semester independent study course was approved in 2009 and provides each student with the opportunity to

- acquire, manage and use knowledge and skills.
- think critically and creatively.
- practice self-directed learning, decision making and problem solving. (Tampanis 2010)

SUMMARY AND ACTION PLAN FOR COLLABORATION:

Jim Rettig's call for a 'library ecosystem' that can deliver 'learning opportunities from cradle to grave' (Rettig 2008); an understanding of the similarities and differences in K–12 and higher education; and the identification and adaptation of current models of collaboration can all serve as building blocks in the development of a seamless K–20 information literacy curriculum and environment. The development of this environment will require leadership by ALA, its divisions and state chapters as well as action by libraries and librarians in academic, school and public libraries.

ALA should improve the coordination of information literacy efforts by recognizing that information literacy is not just an issue for academic and school libraries and by making information literacy an ALA level priority and a key element of the library ecosystem of academic, school and public libraries. Creation of an Information Literacy Division within ALA might be one approach as ALA's divisions are organized either by type of library or type of library function. However, segregating function from type of library places an economic burden on individual members who must pay dues for multiple divisions as well as creates a artificial communication barrier across all types of libraries and library functions. Perhaps ALA should consider a bifurcated divisional membership in which individuals pay a single fee for membership in a type of library and type of library function division. The creation of a division focused on information literacy (to parallel collections and user services and reference and user services) within this bifurcated membership structure would facilitate the development of a true information literacy curriculum across the library ecosystem. As noted by Thomas Kaun on InfoLit,: "It's no wonder not much gets done when we are being split in so many directions all the time.

The importance of information literacy as an advocacy effort that communicates the critical role of libraries in a democratic society is another compelling reason to raise the association level commitment and coordination. (Carr and Rockman 2003) This coordination and advocacy

should include updating the Blueprint for Collaboration with the involvement of librarians from academic, public, and school libraries including
those who work in children's and youth services.

In addition, ALA should collaborate with ACRL, ALISE and other associations in higher education to articulate the role and professional preparation for teaching librarians in higher education. Professional preparation for teaching librarians in all types of libraries should include instruction
in the learning sciences, pedagogy, the structures of K–12 and higher
education, and information literacy standards for all levels of education.
Collaboration with these other associations should also include the assessment of teacher and faculty knowledge of information literacy standards.
ALA should also consider developing an e-journal with a focus on information literacy and lifelong learning. Divisional publications such as
Knowledge Quest and *College and Research Libraries* often publish articles
or theme issues on information literacy collaboration that may reach a
limited audience because of the schooling level audience for most of their
writings. ALA's state chapters should complement these national efforts
by replicating the models for collaboration in Illinois and Pennsylvania.

Local libraries and librarians should also commit themselves to the development of this seamless information literacy environment and curriculum.
FYE librarians should incorporate partnerships with K–12 librarians into
their work. The necessary skills identified by Boff, Albrecht, and Armstrong
(Boff and Johnson 2007, 77) should be expanded to include collaboration skills with K–12 and knowledge of the K–12 library environment in
the schools from which their FY students graduate. Academic librarians
should know the demographic profile for their students to better understand the geographic and social context of their K–12 experience. This
understanding may involve collaboration with their admissions office
to identify the 'feeder' high schools for their institution and/or the academic profile of these students. At Wellesley College, the librarians work
with the admissions office to identify students who "may be first generation college students, who have not taken advanced placement classes,
who come from less advanced rural or inner city high schools, and/or who
have lower SAT scores than the average incoming Wellesley student."
(Campbell 2007, 249)

School librarians should serve as facilitators for their students by
developing collaborations with local academic and public librarians. The
Redwood High School course for college bound students can serve as a

beginning model for a differentiated information literacy curriculum. School librarians should collaborate with guidance counselors to determine the post school plans for their students in order to determine primary strategic alliances with institutions of higher education. School librarians should also invite academic librarians in their area to address a faculty or parents meeting with tips on effective use of an academic library. An idea that could be a eye-opener for students is to ask a willing college professor to review term papers and have students compare that evaluation with the grade and comments from the K–12 teacher. (Toor and Weisburg 2011, 74)

The creation of a seamless information literacy curriculum and environment will not be an easy task. However it is a challenge that will be bolstered by the commitment to information literacy demonstrated by many ALA units, the underlying theme of the National Information Technology Plan, the efforts of K–12 organizations to develop information literacy standards with a focus on learning and curriculum integration, and the creativity of many academic, school and public librarians. Together we can work together to prepare students and all learners to integrate information, technology, and media literacy within our shared library and learning ecosystem.

References

American Association of School Librarians (AASL) 2007. *Standards for the 21ˢᵗ Century Learner*. Chicago, IL: American Library Association.

———. 2009. *Standards for the 21ˢᵗ Century Learner in Action*. Chicago, IL: American Library Association.

———. Electronic Discussion Lists. 2010a. "INFOLIT" www.ala.org/ala/mgrps/divs/ aasl/aboutaasl/aaslcommunity/ communityinaasl/aasledisclist/INFOLIT.cfm.

———. 2010b. *AASL Sections*. www.ala.org/ala/mgrps/divs/aasl/aboutaasl/aasl-community/aaslsections/aaslsections.cfm.

American Association of School Librarians/Association of College and Research Libraries Task Force on the Educational Role of Libraries. 1998. "Blueprint for collaboration" Chicago: American Library Association. www .ala.org/ala/mgrps/divs/acrl/publications/whitepapers/acrlaaslblueprint.cfm

American Library Association (ALA) Presidential Commission on Information Literacy. 1989. *Final Report* (Chicago: American Library Association)

Association of College and Research Libraries. 2000. *Information Literacy Competency Standards for Higher Education*. Chicago, IL: American Library Association.

———. 2007. "Proficiencies for Instruction Librarians and Coordinators". Accessed at www.ala.org/acrl/standards/profstandards

———. 2010b "About ACRL: Sections." www.ala.org/acrl/aboutacrl/directoryofleadership/sections.

———. 2010c. *Value of Academic Libraries: A Comprehensive Research Review and Report.* Researched by Megan Oakleaf. Chicago: Association of College and Research Libraries.

Association of College and Research Libraries/American Association of School Librarians Interdivisional Committee on Information Literacy. 2010a. www.ala.org/acrl/aboutacrl/directoryofleadership/committees/aas-ilc.

Association of College and Research Libraries Instruction Section "Instruction Section." 2010. www.ala.org/acrl/aboutacrl/directoryofleadership/sections/is/iswebsite

Association for Library Service to Children (ALSC) 2010. "ALA Online Learning. Information Literacy from Preschool to High School." www.ala.org/ala/onlinelearning/servicedelivery/classes/alsc/infolit.cfm

Belmont University Academic Outreach. 2010. "Conversations at Belmont." www.belmont.edu/cas/ao/conversations/index.html.

Boff, Colleen and Kristin Johnson. 2007. "The Library and First Year Seminars: In Depth Analysis of a 2001 National Study." In Hardesty, Larry, ed. (2007) *The Role of the Library in the First College Year.* Monograph no. 45, pages 69–83. Columbia SC: University of South Carolina: National Resource Center for the First Year Experience and Students in Transition.

Bushaw, William J. and John A. McNee. 2009. "Americans Speak Out: Are Educators and Policy Makers Listening? The 41st Annual Phi Delta Kappa/Gallup Poll of the Public's Attitudes Toward the Public Schools" *Phi Delta Kappan, 91* (8) Pages 8–23.

Campbell, Joan. 2007. Case Study 12: Preparing Pathways to Information Literacy: Combining Research, Technology and Core College Competencies for Select First Year Students. In Hardesty, Larry, ed. *The Role of the Library in the First College Year.* Monograph no. 45, pages 249–253. Columbia SC: University of South Carolina: National Resource Center for the First Year Experience and Students in Transition.

Carr, Jo Ann. 2006. "Engaging the Future: Meeting the Needs of Next Gen" in Gibson, Craig, ed. *Student Engagement and Information Literacy* Chicago: Association of College and Research Libraries.

Carr, Jo Ann and Ilene F. Rockman. 2003. "Information-literacy Collaboration: A Shared Responsibility" *American Libraries. 34* (8)

Chen, Hsin-Liang. 2009. "An Analysis of Undergraduate Students' Search Behaviors in an Information Literacy Class" *Journal of Web Librarianship.*

3(4), pp. 333–347.

College Board Standards for College Success. 2009. "About the College Board Standards for College Success." http://professionals.collegeboard.com/k-12/standards.

Common Core State Standards Initiative. 2010a. "In the States." Accessed December 8, 2010 www.corestandards.org/in-the-states.

———. 2010b. "Key Points in English Language Arts." Accessed December 8, 2010 www.corestandards.org/
about-the-standards/key-points-in-english-language-arts

EBSS (Educational and Behavioral Sciences Section) "Publications." 2010. www.ala.org/acrl/aboutacrl/directoryofleadership/sections/ebss/ebssweb-site/ebsspublications/publications.

EBSS IE (Educational and Behavioral Sciences Section Instruction for Educators Committee). 2010. "Information Literacy Standards for Teacher Education." www.ala.org/acrl/standards (publication pending 5-18-2011).

ETS (Educational Testing Service) 2004. " ICT Literacy Assessment: An Issue Paper from ETS". Princeton, NJ: Educational Testing Service.

Gardner, John and Andrew Koch. 2007. "Preface: Drawing on the Past, in the Present to Shape the Future of the First Year Experience in American Higher Education. In Hardesty, Larry, ed. *The Role of the Library in the First College Year.* (Monograph no. 45) Columbia, SC: University of South Carolina. National Resource Center for the First Year Experience and Students in Transition.

Hardesty, Larry, ed. 2007a *The Role of the Library in the First College Year.* (Monograph no. 45) Columbia, SC: University of South Carolina. National Resource Center for the First Year Experience and Students in Transition.

Hardesty, Larry. 2007b. "Strategies for Designing Assignments to Support Information Literacy Activities" In *The Role of the Library in the First College Year* edited by Larry Hardesty. Columbia, SC: University of South Carolina: National Resource Center for the First Year Experience and Students in Transition.

Hersh, Richard. 2005. *Declining by Degrees; Higher Education at Risk.* (New York: Palgrave Macmillan.

International Society for Technology in Education (ISTE). 2007a. *National Educational Technology Standards for Students.* www.iste.org/standards/
nets-for-students/nets-student-standards-2007.aspx.

———. 2007b. *NETS for Students 2007 Profiles.* www.p21.org/index.
php?option=com_content&task=view&id=504&Itemid=185#maps.

Learning for the 21st Century. (2002) Washington, D.C.: Partnership for 21st Century Skills.

Lloyd Sealy Library John Jay College of Criminal Justice. 2010. "Discipline-specific Standards and Guidelines for Information Literacy." www.lib.jjay.cuny.edu/infolit/infolit6.html.

Maringe, Felix. 2006. "University and Course Choice: Implications for Positioning, Recruitment and Marketing" *International Journal of Educational Management 20* (6) 466—479.

Marks, Diane. 2009. "Literacy, Instruction, and Technology: Meeting Millennials on Their Own Turf." *AACEJ 17*(4), 363–377

MVCC (Moraine Valley Community College). 2011. "Information Literacy Summit 2011" www.morainevalley.edu/infolitsummit/about_the_summit.htm

NILRC (Network of Illinois Learning Resources in Community Colleges) 2010. "Information Literacy Toolkit for Success". www.nilrc.org/IMLS/default.asp

Oseguera, Leticia. 2007. "How First Year College Students Use Their Time: Implications for Library and Information Literacy Instruction. In Hardesty, Larry, ed. *The Role of the Library in the First College Year.* (Monograph no. 45) Columbia, SC: University of South Carolina. National Resource Center for the First Year Experience and Students in Transition.

Owen, Patricia. 2010. "Checklist for High School Seniors" *School Library Monthly XXVI* (8), p. 20–23.

Partnership for 21st Century Skills. 2004–2011. "Tools and Resources. Publications." www.p21.org/index.php?option=com_content&task=view&id=504&Itemid=185#maps

Penn State University Libraries. 2010. "Central Pa K–20 Librarians Information Literacy Network." http://libraries.psu.edu/psul/lls/outreach/K–20.html

Rettig, Jim. 2008. "The Library Ecosystem at Work." Accessed at www.ala.org/ala/issuesadvocacy/advleg/advocacyuniversity/additup/about/abt_2.cfm.

Rockman, Ilene F. 2007. "Information literacy and the First Year Experiences in the California State University System." In Hardesty, Larry, ed. *The Role of the Library in the First College Year.* (Monograph no. 45) Columbia, SC: University of South Carolina. National Resource Center for the First Year Experience and Students in Transition.

Saunders, Laura. 2008. "Perspectives on Accreditation and Information Literacy as Reflected in the Literature of Library and Information Science." *The Journal of Academic Librarianship 34*(4) 305–313.

State Superintendent's High School Task Force Report. 2006. Madison, WI: Wisconsin Department of Public Instruction.

Tampalis Union High School District. 2010. *Courses of Study.* http://rhslibrary.org/docs/COS_Advanced_Library_Research.doc.

"Test Reveals 'the Brutal Truth" 2010. Madison, WI: *Wisconsin State Journal,* December 8. A19

Thomas, Pierre. and Jack Date. 2006. Students Dropping Out of School Reaches [sic] Epidemic Levels. http://abcnews.go.com/US/Story?id=2667532&page=1

Toor, Ruth and Hilda K. Weisburg. 2011. *Being Indispensable: A School Librarian's Guide to Becoming an Invaluable Leader.* Chicago: American Library Association.

Transforming American Education: Learning powered by Technology. 2010. National Education Technology Plan 2010. Washington, D.C.: U.S. Department of Education, Office of Educational Technology.

Understanding University Success: A Report from Standards for Success. 2003. Eugene, OR: Center for Educational Policy Research.

United States. National Commission on Excellence in Education. 1984 *A Nation At Risk: The Full Account.* Cambridge, MA: USA Research.

Westbrook, Theresa and Sarah Fabian. 2010. "Proficiencies for instruction librarians: Is There Still a Disconnect Between Professional Education and Professional Responsibilities." *College and Research Libraries 71* (6) 569–590.

White House. President Barack Obama. 2010. "Education Issues Statement". www.whitehouse.gov/issues/education.

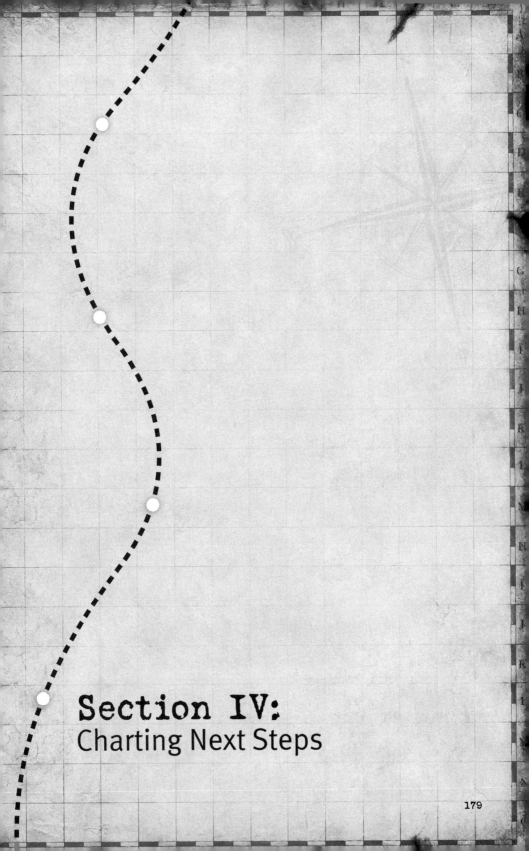

Section IV:
Charting Next Steps

8

Settling Uncharted Territory: Documenting & Rewarding Librarians' Teaching Role in the Academy

April D. Cunningham & Carrie Donovan

INTRODUCTION

Seizing the opportunity to increase the scope and impact of their efforts, librarians across all academic contexts are expanding their role as teachers. Describing, documenting and measuring the effect of librarians as educators have, therefore, become formative challenges for our future. Teaching in libraries has never been limited by the traditional boundaries that typically define learning in higher education (e.g. course credits, classroom time, etc.). This freedom from standardization allows for creative approaches to library instructional initiatives that fit unique academic settings. But a lack of standardization across institutions or as a top-down effort from national professional organizations leaves librarians without a regular and consistent way to describe and assess their teaching. Each institution determines to what extent librarians can engage in teaching and how the committees that decide on tenure, promotion or contract renewals will evaluate and weight librarians' performance as educators. When a librarian contributes to her institution's educational mission with regularity and meaning she should be assured that a recognized mechanism for gauging her impact will make it possible for her to gain access to the institution's established system of rewards. Based on survey data and documented research, this chapter will describe discrepancies among methods of assessment for teaching librarians in different types of institutions of higher education, as well as possibilities for more purposeful and strategic methods of describing and documenting their teaching activities with the goal of rewarding success.

As the authors for this chapter, we represent perspectives and experiences shaped by our work as librarians from a research university and a community college, respectively. In conversations about our unique processes for tenure and the value our libraries place on teaching, we realized that differences abound. Without any justification for these differences, beyond varying institutional missions and organizational cultures, we searched for something in the professional literature to define a connection in our pedagogical practice, in terms of definitions, benchmarks, and standards. Finding nothing definitive, we set out to review the literature and survey our colleagues in order to determine how librarians construct their teacherly roles and what, if any, indicators their organizations use to measure or value these. We are hopeful that our findings and recommendations will create an opportunity for librarians to examine how they document their teaching and what it means for their institutions, their careers, and librarianship.

REVIEW OF LITERATURE
Changes in Higher Education in the United States

Concerns that higher education is out of touch with the needs of students and wider cultural trends are not new. Critics of the ivory tower mentality of professors and academics currently have an easy mark when they attack higher education for failing to produce the economic benefits that are so often promised to students. Instruction librarians must navigate this unsettled environment as the profession strives to make progress toward improved integration with the academy.

The United States does not have a national vision for higher education (in contrast with the European Union's Bologna Declaration, for example) and age-old arguments still smolder and flare because of the friction between workforce development goals and academic idealism (Gaston 2010). Some commentators have even sounded the alarm that we may be in the midst of an education bubble in which the government subsidies and the personal debt dedicated to educational costs prop up a system that no longer fulfills its perceived value (Adamson 2009). Flaws in the assumptions about the macro- and micro-economics of the benefits derived from credentialing and degrees are starting to raise concerns at the same time that the current White House administration is promoting an agenda to significantly increase the number of students completing their college education (Wolf 2009). Large numbers of students are entering college but are not completing it (Bowen 2009). This has long been a problem at community colleges where open access and limited resources combined to leave many students ill-equipped to complete degrees or certificates. More recently, it has become an increasing problem at colleges and universities with entrance requirements as well (Bowen 2009). Among those who see higher education as unresponsive and elitist, this trend is further evidence that colleges and universities have not been accountable enough to the expectations of stakeholders, including students, parents, and tax payers.

Different types of institutions are responding to these pressures in different ways (Oakley 1997). One common theme in the literature about the future of higher education is competition. Ivy League schools and flagship public universities facing unprecedented losses in endowments or cuts in funding have relaxed breadth and depth requirements that could scare off prospective students (Aronowitz 2000). Traditional colleges and universities have reacted to the technological changes driving competition with alarm rather than embracing them pro-actively. At the same time, the fastest growing sector of higher education, the for-profit schools, have leveraged technology to facilitate growth and reach previously untapped markets of students as well as students who probably would have attended traditional schools in the past (Morey 2004). Community colleges in particular are responding to the influence of for-profit colleges and some have looked to the for-profit sector to help ease demand for classes that the community colleges do not currently have the funds to provide (Willen 2010).

Another related issue that many analysts consider a significant pressure in higher education is the accountability movement (Bruininks, Keeney, and Thorp 2010). Much of the momentum for the accountability movement comes from the crisis that many believe awaits the economy if students do not receive the education that our labor market demands (Wolf 2009). The central role that the academy is expected to play in the knowledge economy leads to scrutiny of its processes and outcomes and gives outside forces, including government and corporate bodies, a voice in how higher education is to function. This intensified connection between higher education and the labor market means that the stakes are higher and learning and productivity are seen as having a causal relationship. One commentator remarked that "to be able to learn today is to be able to be productive today" (Do 2008). While some resistance to the managerial trends and the accountability movement is slowing this transition, many universities and colleges are adopting the vision of their role as engines for the economy and producers of productive knowledge-workers (Ohmann 2000).

Part of the inspiration for increased concern about the economic consequences of ineffective education is the perception that the student population has changed. Because the negative economic impact of a large population of underemployed young people is an alarming prospect that could reduce America's power internationally, many analysts are looking to higher education to change our economic outlook by creating more skilled workers (Wolf 2009). This anxiety has created a "de facto 'college for all' strategy" that may be misguided because it ignores the vital role of work-based and career-focused training for underprepared students who are least likely to see a significant return on their investment in college (Lerman 2007, 41–90). Regardless of its limitations, the faith in higher education as a catalyst for economic growth persists. Given this enduring faith, statistics showing that future generations of workers will have lower average education levels than in the past (Kelly 2005) is increasing the pressure to adapt higher education to the needs of adult learners and other non-traditional students (Chao, DeRocco, and Flynn 2007; Levine 1997).

In an effort to respond to the combined pressures of competition, scrutiny of student success, perceived changes in student characteristics, and intensified valuation of workforce development, many colleges and universities have started to emphasize a set of core skills that students will develop (Dunne, Bennett, and Clive Carr 1997). This may be seen as undermining the classical emphasis on developing specialized disciplinary knowledge and is a controversial move away from what many valued as the disinterested pursuit of knowledge that characterized rigor in traditional higher education (Fox 2002). Shifting its resources toward developing students' inquiry skills and raising doubts about the traditional emphasis on content, higher education has adopted a framework of instrumental rationality in response to corporatist demand for flexibility (Aronowitz 2000). This is the primary change in higher education that has affected librarians' roles, often broadening the appeal of the profession's skills and creating a closer match between librarians' pedagogical approaches and the core mission of the academy.

Taken together, these trends in favor of instrumentalist undergraduate general education are increasing tension about how faculty should be evaluated and rewarded and they will have significant effects on the working conditions of most college faculty. They have even led some to question the presumed value of the PhD for the future of higher education (Brien 2009). Faculty who find that their scholarship is no longer valued at colleges and universities where undergraduate enrollment in their disciplines has dwindled and the only classes left to teach are survey courses that fulfill students' breadth requirements are looking for opportunities to pursue their avocation outside the academy (Aronowitz 2000). Administrators are questioning the assumptions underlying the tenure system and critiquing tenure for slowing innovation and responsiveness in higher education (Premeaux 2008). Some commentators question the value of the academic research at the heart of promotion and tenure reward systems because it takes resources away from undergraduate education (Hacker and Dreifus 2010). The long-standing assumption that tenure is necessary for academic freedom is being steadily eroded (Tierney and Bensimon 1996). Tenure always represents a cost to the institution because it reduces budgetary flexibility and the discretion of managers (Kingma and McCombs 1995). According to some critical postmodern critiques, it may also contribute to the stagnation and "entrenched closed-mindedness [that] has eroded public confidence in the academy" (Tierney and Bensimon 1996). Because tenure remains valuable to different types of institutions for different reasons, it is too complex a topic to make broad generalizations about its future prospects. The trend, however, toward a bifurcated system of the dwindling tenured and growing contingent faculty is firmly established. Faculty employed outside of any system of tenure far outnumber tenured faculty and the trend will not be reversed (Gappa 2008). The implications of this systematic inequality also affect librarians because they are marginal insiders with an indirect relationship to the core functions of higher education.

Changing Nature of Librarianship

For a profession so concerned with maintaining its relevance and centrality to the academy, librarians have worked tirelessly to make collections and services networked and available in such a way that the library becomes almost invisible to students and researchers. Without the bulwark of library space or collections to define how librarians' work is perceived and valued, stakeholders and decision-makers may question the necessity of libraries. While the digital information environment requires librarians to be more transparent about their work in facilitating organization and access of information, it also frees librarians to engage in initiatives beyond these. According to Crowley (2001), librarians are right to focus more on developing and maintaining service programs that parallel the values of the institution. In many cases, this involves the librarians' participation in outreach and educational initiatives.

As teachers, librarians can inform and improve upon other areas of their work, based on the understanding that comes from facilitating and observing information seeking and use in authentic contexts, such as the classroom. Librarians teaching information literacy courses have found that direct classroom involvement influences resource selection decisions based on what is practical for students (Donnelly 2000). Barring this instructional role, librarians would be left with only measures of inputs and outputs, rather than student application and learning, to guide their collection management strategies.

Incorporating teaching into a diverse repertoire of professional skills does not happen seamlessly for many librarians. In a survey of 328 public services librarians, Johnson and Lindsay found that instruction was among the top two areas of work that respondents found most satisfying, although it was also identified as the most challenging of all the areas (Johnson and Lindsay 2006). In terms of preparing future professionals for teaching as a core component of librarianship, MLS-granting institutions do not consistently offer coursework in developing pedagogical knowledge and strategies for future libraries. In fact, the University of Washington has been identified as the only institution to make such a course required (Julien 2005).

With the lack of professional preparation and the challenges that accompany teaching, some librarians may struggle to accept this new role as educator; however, it is imperative that they do. Declining reference desk statistics and fewer people in the library indicate a shift in usage behavior that is unlikely to reverse. If librarians' teaching was valued somewhat in the traditional library environment, it should be of primary value now that learners' need for understanding information seeking and use have compounded as a result of the influx of electronic information (Rapple 1997). Additionally, the service-orientation of librarianship is a near-mandate for embracing teaching, as librarians are incumbent to provide the knowledge and abilities necessary to navigate the world of networked information to those who will ultimately become its primary consumers, creators, and curators.

Librarians' Teaching

Most academic librarians still teach in the type of traditional course-integrated one-shots or stand-alone workshops that have characterized library instruction for generations. Many ambitious projects have developed from these efforts and frequently librarians are being asked to participate more fully in students' research, whether as guest instructors who meet with classes multiple times during their research (Gandhi 2005) or as research mentors (Stamatoplos 2009). Studies on the effectiveness of supplemental information literacy and library instruction show mixed results for student outcomes (Cmor, Chan, & Kong 2010; Koufogiannakis & Wiebe 2006; Matthews 2007). At the same time, studies on the impact of this traditional instructional setting on instruction librarians' anxiety and burn-out often raise concerns (Affleck 1996; Becker 1993; Sheesley 2001).

In addition to the supplemental instruction that librarians have long provided as support for the curriculum, many schools are now offering credit instruction on information literacy in classes taught by librarians. Many librarians see this is an essential step toward legitimizing librarianship (Owusu-Ansah 2007). Some of these credit classes are offered as parts of learning communities (Galvin 2006; Lebbin 2005). Student learning assessment remains an important issue for credit instruction on information literacy (Burkhardt 2007; Hufford 2010). Results of these assessment efforts have not been uniformly positive and reveal the complexity of teaching information literacy whether in credit classes or through supplemental instruction (Mokhtar, Majid, & Foo 2008).

Information literacy is now often thought of as a generic skill that students should be able to transfer across diverse learning situations and it has been included in lists of core skills for college students (ICAS, 2000). The current higher education trend that favors generic skills integration throughout the curriculum has been a boon to librarians who are positioned as experts in developing students' research skills and can be a resource for faculty who need to improve their students' academic literacy learning outcomes. Some librarians' research has even measured the effect of information literacy instruction by faculty in other disciplines, suggesting that librarians' interventions with faculty remain a powerful means of promoting the information literacy agenda (Birmingham et al. 2008). In addition to individual courses, librarians are also influencing the development and assessment of core competencies like research skills and information literacy in undergraduate co-curricular programs and activities (Lampert 2005).

As with most other areas of librarianship, technology is also changing the nature of instruction. Whether in credit courses, in tutorials that are analogous to one-shot sessions, or through personalized instruction (Lillard 2003), distance education has become an important mode for librarians to reach students and brings its own challenges and questions. For example, librarians study whether learning is equivalent in face-to-face and online formats (Beile and Boote 2004). They are also involved in collaborations to support cooperative learning online (Bielema et al. 2005).

Overall, librarians' research on teaching and learning follows the same trends that are influencing instruction throughout higher education. Although librarians' role as teachers has met with some controversy, librarian-instructors as a group have embraced student-centered learning and the need to innovate. Just like faculty throughout the academy, librarians have stepped up to demands for evaluation and instructional improvement.

Teaching Role of Librarians: Intra-Professional Perspectives

The question of professional identity, especially as it relates to librarians' role in the academy, has long been debated and lamented by those in the profession as a crisis that contributes to everything from a lack of integration into institutional missions to the inability for effecting change at organizational levels. This internal debate is especially pronounced when librarians' teaching role is the central topic. With the variance in types of higher education institutions and the differing educational cultures they foster, librarians have a spectrum of experiences and views regarding how their teaching can make the greatest impact.

Since Wilson argued in *Library Quarterly* that teaching is an insignificant part of the wide array of characteristics that constitutes the role of librarians to the extent that it is "fiction," (1979) Miller and Tegler described librarians' teaching as "quixotic self-deception," (1987) and Gorman (1991) predicted that technological advances would make libraries so easy to use that instruction should be unnecessary there has been little serious debate about whether or not librarianship should involve an instructional component. Instead, librarians have agonized over the challenges they face in receiving adequate preparation for teaching (Bewick and Corral 2010; Sproles, Johnson, and Farison 2008) and establishing a sense of teacher identity, as it has been clouded by long-standing stereotypes that require justification of librarians' professional worth (Loesch 2010) and teacherly purpose. More recently, librarians have had less of a reason to focus on these questions of identity and are moving toward the more pressing issue of how information literacy instruction should be enacted, assessed, and rewarded, instead of continually justifying it.

Many librarians have achieved success as teachers in the academy through partnerships with disciplinary faculty. As the ultimate proponent for collaborative efforts that facilitate teaching partnerships between librarians and faculty, Evan Farber created a movement that positioned information literacy as an institutional imperative that should be curriculum-integrated and discipline-related (Gansz et al. 2007). Echoes of this approach are apparent in the writing of Ilene Rockman, as well, in her advocacy for the alignment of information literacy standards with the general education curriculum, which resulted in great successes for student learning in the California State University system (2002). Librarians involved in course-integrated information literacy initiatives participate in the design of syllabi and assignments, the development of rubrics, and the assessment of student work as a part of the overall course grade (Auer and Krupar 2005). Involvement in course design and learning assessment situates librarians in a position of consultant and facilitator, in addition to that of instructor.

Beyond participation in existing courses, many librarians encourage the creation and proliferation of new information literacy courses for which librarians would be the sole instructors. While acknowledging some successes have come about through collaborative efforts with faculty, Edward Owusu-Ansah called for librarians to reject their limited instructional function through partnerships with faculty and to engage in the teaching of credit-bearing courses, as these define the parameters for what is taught, learned, and assessed formally in higher education (2007). Echoes of encouragement for librarians to evolve into more strategic instructional roles can be found in the writings of librarians who have taught courses, either information-related or within disciplines beyond libraries. In describing her experience of teaching for the Department of Communications, one librarian labeled the experience as a "renewal" opportunity that allowed her to make a direct contribution to the mission of the college (Partello 2005). Others include self-improvement (Kemp 2006), lasting relationships with students, and insights into the working lives of faculty as additional benefits to teaching credit courses (Donnelly 2000).

While teaching credit courses may seem like the ideal solution for librarians to make a lasting impact on the educational process of their institutions, it is not without its drawbacks. Many of those involve the lack of time librarians have to devote to teaching in light of other various job duties and whether teaching courses should be among librarians' prioritized responsibilities.

Librarians who focus on teaching, rather than other "traditional" professional duties (e.g. reference), may encounter colleagues who do not understand or recognize the value of librarians as teachers (Donnelly 2000), in addition to those colleagues who regard teaching courses outside the library as irrelevant to librarianship (Partello 2005). Because teaching often happens in addition to the other professional functions of reference, management, and collection development, librarians may seek work release for time spent teaching or face the difficulties of being overburdened.

Tenure: Challenges & Opportunities for Librarians

It is likely that the debate regarding tenure for librarians will continue to plague the profession, with both sides steadfast in their justifications and conclusions. For proponents, the benefits are clear: salary, status, and academic freedom. While tenure does serve to leverage librarians' salaries upward (Meyer 1999), it is direct engagement in the primary functions of the institution which brings status equal to faculty that is often more attractive. Librarians who have the opportunity to achieve tenure are well-suited to collaborate with teaching faculty as partners toward integrating information literacy into the curriculum, participate on campus governing bodies, and contribute to the work of committees that shape the strategic planning and evolution of the campus.

Without the same status as teaching faculty, librarians' potential for further isolation from the educational community and its overarching mission is imminent (Slattery 1994). As early as 1972, the Association of College & Research Libraries issued a *Joint Statement on Faculty Status of College & University Librarians*, stating that the "the function of the librarian as participant in the processes of teaching and research is the essential criterion of faculty status." This statement of advocacy was followed by a set of standards from the ACRL on *Faculty Status for College and University Librarians* (2006). The standards demand tenure for librarians, as well as performance and peer review processes aligned with campus requirements. Finally, a 2010 issuance of *Guidelines on the Appointment, Promotion, and Tenure of Academic Librarians* is the ACRL's more recent statement indicating the importance of librarians' criteria for promotion and tenure equaling that of faculty, although the criteria listed mention teaching only as something that "may" be included in the review process.

While the consensus among academic librarians seems to be that librarians' work warrants standing and status on campus equal to that of their faculty colleagues, the path to achieving such status remains amorphous. Throughout the literature, we see references to the awkwardness that comes from librarians' attempts to match their professional competencies to faculty tenure requirements when they do not engage in formal teaching (Cubberley 1996; Hall and Byrd 1990; Hill 1994). Even the faculty who educate future librarians are ambivalent about faculty status in academic libraries because of a perception that the requirements are not a good match for librarians' daily responsibilities (Wyss 2010). Applying the label "teaching" to the variety of activities (e.g., one-shot library instruction sessions, tours, drop-in workshops, credit-bearing courses, e-learning, and teaching in other disciplines) in which librarians engage only serves to further complicates efforts to measure or document student learning in any consistent way for the purposes of professional review. This is compounded by the institutional differences that often result in the use of local criteria and standards for librarians' professional review procedures.

Without a consensus on the professional role of librarians, especially with regard to teaching, the issue of tenure will continue to be problematic. Moreover, if librarians are unable to define their professional identity as including a teaching role, establishing criteria for review and reward of that role will never be widely accepted. In a survey designed to discover the commonalities among criteria for promotion and tenure for academic librarians, Vesper and Kelley (1997) found that teaching was not a tenure requirement for 61% of respondents. Similarly, a survey of librarians from research, doctoral-granting, comprehensive, and liberal arts institutions found that less than half (47.2%) of respondents indicated teaching to be a factor in review for tenure (Park and Riggs 1993). This lack of support and reward structures for teaching could be detrimental to the engagement of librarians in instruction-related activities and even contribute to a sense of "fragmentation" within the profession overall (Slattery 1994).

SURVEY DATA & RESULTS
Methodology

In order to address the perceived effects of evaluation procedures and reward structures on librarians' teaching and the effect of librarians' teaching on their evaluations and rewards, the authors sought the opinions of the instruction librarians themselves. Recent studies and commentaries on the effects of tenure and reward structures on academic librarians' work have not included any explicit evaluation of relationships between status, performance review, and teaching (Gillum 2010; Meyer 1999; Ruess 2004; Welch and Mozenter 2006). The 15-item survey for the current study was designed to measure opinions quantitatively using multiple-choice questions and to collect opinions for qualitative analysis using open-ended questions. The teaching rewards investigated through the survey focus on the institutional contexts that can enhance teaching and learning (Wright et al. 2004). The following data from this survey illuminates the current status of librarians' involvement in teaching in higher education, how this teaching is valued and rewarded, and participants' levels of dedication and satisfaction regarding teaching.

Messages inviting librarians to participate in the survey were posted to professional library listservs, some of which focus on academic libraries and library instruction. The authors decided this was the best way to contact librarians at a variety of institutions, where differing commitments to teaching and various approaches to assigning status to librarians (e.g. staff, faculty, contingent faculty) would result in different types of evaluations and rewards. The survey was distributed over four separate electronic listservs to primarily academic librarians during a span of 3 weeks in October 2010. The population of listserv subscribers resulted in a sample size of approximately 5,000. After removing data from incomplete surveys and from respondents who were not academic librarians with some level of responsibility for instruction, the resulting sample used in this analysis consists of 290 individual responses.

Because there are no other published studies that report instruction librarians' perceptions of the role their teaching plays in their tenure/promotion or other rewards, this study, despite its flaws, is the first step in exploring those relationships. We are careful not to generalize to the population of librarians on the listservs or to the larger population of instruction librarians at academic libraries because of limitations in our methods and the low response rate. However, the themes identified in the survey responses not only provide a foundation for our recommendations for practice, but should also support future investigations into the relationship between librarians' teaching and their professional rewards.

Profile of Respondents

Respondents provided information related to their jobs and institutions. 86% of respondents (N=250) indicate that teaching is one of their primary responsibilities. 37% of respondents (N=106) identified themselves as academic staff, non-faculty. 25% and 28%, respectively, indicated they are tenured (N=73) or currently on the tenure track (N=81). 10% (N=30) were contingent faculty not eligible for tenure. These figures match closely with the proportions of librarians nationally who are academic staff, tenure-eligible faculty, and contingent faculty (Lindquist and Gilman 2008; Lowry 1993).

The majority of respondents (54%) (N=156) hail from teaching-intensive institutions. 23% (N=68) are from research-intensive institutions and 23% (N=66) from comprehensive institutions. These classifications were selected in place of Carnegie Classification because they were considered to represent institutional features related to teaching and learning that are most salient to instruction librarians' work. Comparing these proportions to a national study of librarians by institution type, it is possible that this sample may somewhat over-represent teaching-intensive institutions (most commonly, community colleges and liberal arts colleges) and under-represent research-intensive institutions. Nationally only about

28% of librarians work at community colleges and baccalaureate institutions (corresponding most closely to the teaching-intensive category in this study), while 48% work at doctoral institutions (corresponding with research-intensive) and 24% work at master's institutions (corresponding with comprehensive institutions) (Applegate 2007). Based on our observations, the difference between our sample and the national figures may reflect the fact that librarians who teach make up a smaller proportion of the librarians at doctoral institutions where subject experts and bibliographers who do not regularly teach are more likely to be part of the library staff. At community colleges and baccalaureate institutions, the number of subject specialists in the library is likely to be much lower, and a higher proportion of the librarians on staff are expected to teach.

24% of respondents (N=70) report having a "light" teaching load, 48% (N=139) report having a "moderate" teaching load, 23% (N=66) report having a "high" teaching load, and 5% (N=15) report having an "extremely high" teaching load. The following table presents the median number of non-credit sessions librarians in each category report teaching in a year.

TABLE 8.1
Non-Credit Teaching Load

Reported teaching load	Median number of non-credit sessions/year
Light	16
Moderate	40
High	50
Extremely High	75

Librarian Status

Cross-tabulations suggest that there are significant relationships between librarians' status (i.e., faculty v. non-faculty) and rewards, satisfaction, and perceptions. The majority of academic staff, non-faculty (53%) report that promotion is not a reward that is available to them. In contrast,

85% of faculty librarians, whether tenured, tenure-track, or contingent, report that they have access to promotion. This large, significant difference between faculty and non-faculty librarians' access to promotion ($x2 = 42.788$, N = 275, df = 1, p < .001) may indicate a need in the profession to define appropriate reward structures in environments where non-faculty librarians are not eligible for promotions but still need to be accountable for excellent teaching and, therefore, should be rewarded for their performance.

Respondents were asked how satisfied they were with the emphasis on teaching as part of their performance evaluation. Most librarians are satisfied with how teaching is emphasized in their evaluation process; 26% (N=73) reported feeling very satisfied and 55% (N=152) reported feeling somewhat satisfied. Overall 19% of the respondents (N=53) were not at all satisfied. In order to determine if there is a relationship between satisfaction with evaluations and the librarians' status, a cross tabulation was calculated. A significant relationship exists between status and satisfaction with how important instruction is in the evaluation process ($x2 = 9.991$, N = 278, df = 1, p < .01). Although 19% of the total sample was not satisfied, among academic staff, non-faculty, dissatisfaction rose to 29%. Only 13.5% of faculty librarians were not at all satisfied with the emphasis on teaching in their evaluation process. The effect of this relationship is small, but suggests that the ways non-faculty librarians' teaching is evaluated is often not satisfying.

A small but significant relationship was also found between librarians' status and their perception of their department culture ($x2 = 7.059$, N = 284, df = 2, p < .05). Faculty librarians (79%) were more likely than academic staff (65%) to describe their department as collaborative and transparent. 30% of academic staff described their department culture as "don't ask don't tell" when it comes to teaching, while only 18% of faculty librarians describe their department that way.

Librarians' responses to open-ended questions clarify the relationship between evaluation procedures and satisfaction. Survey respondents reacted positively, overall, to the notion of conducting and using teaching evaluations as an opportunity to improve teaching; however, many indicated that their use beyond that would have minimal impact on performance review or rewards. Evaluations of teaching that are conducted for non-tenure purposes or strictly performance-based reviews are widely seen as ineffectual for mechanisms to recognize or reward teaching. Several responses indicate that teaching evaluations are ignored by supervisors overall, unless they are negative in nature. Even librarians who have formal processes for evaluating teaching as part of tenure review, indicate that it does not "count" as much as research/writing. Although, there is little consensus on this, since criteria for tenure-based teaching evaluations are not well communicated and, as one librarian stated, often considered "a mystery" by those whose teaching they are designed to measure. While an increased dedication among librarians to valuing results of teaching evaluations must happen across hierarchies and organizations, the need for supervisors and administrators to reward teaching as part of formal review processes would help this movement. In addition, these responses suggest that the process by which librarians and their teaching are reviewed must be illuminated in order to engage in assessment and evaluation of teaching as a process for development and improvement, rather than a punitive burden.

Librarians' perceptions of how their evaluation criteria compare with other faculty on their campuses are also significantly related to their status ($x2 = 12.876$, N = 289, df = 2, p < .01). 30% of librarians who have faculty status report that teaching is equally or more important in their evaluations than it is for other faculty on their campus while only 13% of academic staff, non-faculty librarians report the same. More importantly, however, is the lack of awareness among non-faculty regarding evaluation criteria for other faculty on their campuses. A third of academic staff, non-faculty replied that they did not know how the emphasis placed on the evaluation of their teaching compared with evaluation criteria applied to other faculty on their campuses. Only 19% of faculty librarians reported that they did not know how their evaluation compared to the evaluation of other faculty. There is also a significant difference between faculty and non-faculty views on whether the same criteria should be used to evaluate librarians' teaching and other faculty teaching ($x2 = 8.683$, N = 289, df = 2, p < .05): 44% of faculty disagree with the statement that the same standards should be used to evaluate teaching by librarians and other faculty, only 30% of non-faculty disagreed. 8% of faculty librarians did not know if the same standards should be used, while 17% of academic staff librarians did not know. These differences suggest that academic staff may lack awareness of institutional values that are communicated through evaluation procedures and criteria.

Evaluation and Value Placed on Teaching

The most common type of evaluation available to librarians comes from student surveys or assessments that go directly to the librarians. This matches well with the high level of trust that librarians put in their students to evaluate the quality of their teaching. 85% (N=247) of librarians trust their students' evaluations. Reviews of librarians' teaching by their peers are less common; only 31% of respondents (N=89) indicate participating in an informal review process and only 10% (N=30) are formally reviewed by their peers.

TABLE 8.2
Means of Evaluation

Means for evaluating quality of teaching	% of respondents
By student surveys or assessments that go directly to the librarian	45%
As part of the annual performance review	38%
Through informal peer review	31%
By colleagues or supervisor as part of the tenure process	25%
By student surveys or assessments that go directly to the supervisor	17%
Through formal, regular peer review	10%
By external reviewers as part of the tenure process	7%
By no one	25%

25% of respondents (N=71) report that they do not have the quality of their instruction evaluated in any way. While the likelihood that a librarian will not have their instruction evaluated at all increases as the librarian's teaching load decreases, (34% of librarians with light loads report never being evaluated at all), we were surprised to find that 16% of librarians who report high or extremely high teaching loads never have their teaching evaluated either formally or informally. A significant relationship was found between never having your teaching evaluated and not being satisfied with the emphasis on teaching as part of your evaluation ($x2 = 11.442$, $N = 278$, $df = 2$, $p < .01$). 28% of the librarians who do not have their teaching evaluated at all are not satisfied with the emphasis on teaching in their evaluations compared with 16% of librarians who do get their teaching evaluated but are still not satisfied.

Participants were asked how the tenure and promotion processes affected the quality of their teaching. Of the librarians for whom tenure and/or promotion were available rewards, those who had the quality of their teaching evaluated during an annual performance review were more likely than average to say that those processes improved their teaching (tenure: $x2 = 4.609$, $N = 152$, $df = 1$, $p < .05$; promotion: $x2 = 7.301$, $N = 192$, $df = 1$, $p < .01$). Of the librarians who are eligible for tenure or promotion and have the quality of their teaching evaluated during performance review, half say that the processes improve their teaching. Only a third of the librarians who are tenure or promotion eligible but who do not have the quality of their teaching evaluated during performance review reported that the tenure and promotion processes improve their teaching. Reward structures, like tenure and promotion, should be designed to improve performance. The positive relationship found between annual evaluation of teaching quality during performance review and beneficial effects of tenure or promotion on teaching shows that those processes can be designed in ways that improve their effect. Conversely, 75% of librarians who were tenure or promotion eligible but reported that their teaching is not evaluated at all responded that tenure and promotion processes have no effect on the quality of their teaching.

When responding to open ended questions, many respondents cited intrinsic motivators, primarily recognition from students, as the most valued teaching reward. Beyond any formal evaluative or assessment data gathered, teaching librarians who responded to this survey gain important perspectives of the quality of their teaching from students and from interactions with non-library faculty. This feedback is often collected randomly at the request of teaching librarians, in the event that there would be a need to "prove my success as a teacher someday."

Several respondents questioned the implication that teaching rewards would need to come from any other source (the least of those being monetary) than evidence of student learning or student praise. In fact, many responses implied that librarians need not look further than feedback from students and faculty, stating "they are the customers" and "they are the people I'm trying to connect with." Still other respondents lamented the fact that teaching recognition and rewards "are personal, not professional" and that the emphasis of evaluative efforts "is more on quantity, not quality." In addition to the discrepancies among methods for gathering evidence of teaching success, librarians' satisfaction with their departmental and institutional approach to these practices also varies greatly.

If the primary means of measuring librarians' professional contributions are not structured in a way that influences the quality of their teaching then the profession has little hope for large-scale improvement of teaching performance. The survey did show that some rewards are very likely to improve librarians teaching. 80% of librarians with access to participation in teaching initiatives and 83% of librarians with access to compensation for professional development reported that these rewards improve the quality of their instruction. For librarians with access to public recognition of their teaching and compensated prep time, these rewards improved teaching for 66% and 65% of respondents, respectively. However, 51% reported that compensated prep time is not an available reward and 36% reported that public recognition is not available to them. The survey revealed a significant relationship between having your teaching evaluated through informal peer review and having access to public recognition for your teaching ($x2 = 9.242$, $N = 277$, $df = 1$, $p < .01$).

Relationship with the Institution

The rewards that librarians believe improve their performance are part of the institution's structural support for teaching. Respondents were asked to indicate how much their institution valued their teaching compared with how much they valued their own teaching. Most respondents (59%, N=153) reported that they valued their teaching more than their institution valued their teaching. A significant and meaningful relationship was found between librarians' satisfaction with the emphasis on teaching in their evaluation process and their perception that their institution valued their teaching as much as they did ($x2 = 16.345$, $N = 259$, $df = 2$, $p < .001$). A similarly significant and even stronger relationship was found between satisfaction with the emphasis on teaching in the evaluation process and the perception that librarians' values closely matched their departments' values when it came to their teaching ($x2 = 36.470$, N = 261, df = 2, p < .001). Although in the entire sample only 39% of librarians (N=107) felt that there was a close match between their valuation of their teaching and their institution's value of their teaching, only 8% of those who perceived a close match in values still reported being unsatisfied with the emphasis on teaching in their evaluations. 28% of librarians who reported valuing their teaching more than their institution valued their teaching, and 30% who reported valuing their teaching more than their department did, were not satisfied with the emphasis on teaching in their evaluations.

Regardless of how librarians perceive their institution to value their teaching, the overwhelming majority of respondents (76%, N=220) said that they trust faculty outside the library to evaluate the quality of their teaching. In terms of gathering evaluative feedback on librarians' teaching, several respondents indicated in their open-ended responses that non-library faculty bring a valuable perspective due to their knowledge of the success of students' final research output. In addition, these faculty know how well-connected information literacy instruction is to the course goals and curriculum. Many other respondents rely on these outside evaluators simply because they are the ones present during library instruction. Without any internally organized system of review and feedback, this is the only teaching evaluation option for many librarians.

See Table 8.3 for the rewards that were important to survey respondents in influencing their teaching participation.

Relationship with the Department

Regarding departmental culture as it pertains to teaching, the responses were varied. 34% (N=96) indicate they work in a "highly collaborative and transparent environment when it comes to teaching" while 35% (N=98) work in a transparent but not collaborative environment. 23% of respondents (N=64) identified with a "don't ask, don't tell" teaching culture. Department cultures were found to have significant relationships with whether and how librarians' teaching was evaluated. Librarians' attitudes about how their teaching was valued and whom they trusted to evaluate them was also related to the type of department culture where they worked.

TABLE 8.3

The Importance and Availability of Rewards for Teaching

	Highly important	Not available
Connecting with students	91%	‹ 1%
Connecting with faculty	87%	‹ 1%
Changing students' lives	78%	‹ 2%
Getting respect from faculty	74%	‹ 1%
Instructional mission	74%	4%
Increased prestige	46%	5%
Overload pay	11%	62%

A significant relationship was found between department cultures and librarians' teaching evaluations. Overall, 38% of respondents (N=110) reported that a teaching evaluation is part of their annual performance review but only 20% of librarians in don't ask, don't tell cultures are evaluated on their teaching as part of their review. Librarians in collaborative and transparent work environments were much more likely to have their teaching evaluated during performance review (49%). ($x2 = 13.476$, N = 284, df = 4, p < .01). More troubling was the finding that 42% of librarians in don't ask, don't tell cultures were not evaluated at all, compared with 25% of the overall sample who do not get evaluated. Only 14% of librarians who describe their departments as collaborative and transparent report that their teaching is not evaluated at all, suggesting that the overwhelming majority of librarians in collaborative and transparent department cultures do get evaluated. This highlights the relationship of department culture to the policies and procedures for evaluating librarians' teaching ($x2 = 18.211$, N = 284, df = 4, p = .001).

Departments' teaching cultures are also significantly related to librarians' satisfaction and their attitudes about their colleagues. 36% of librarians in don't ask, don't tell department cultures reported that they were not satisfied with the emphasis that their library placed on teaching as part of their promotion and/or tenure process, compared with only 11% librarians in collaborative and transparent environments who said that they were not satisfied ($x2 = 16.361$, $N = 273$, $df = 4$, $p < .01$). 58% of librarians in don't ask, don't tell cultures trust their instruction librarian colleagues to evaluate the quality of their teaching. While this is a strong majority, it raises troubling questions when compared with the 87% of librarians who trust their colleagues to evaluate their teaching in collaborative and transparent departments and suggests that there is a significant relationship between department culture and trust among colleagues ($x2 = 24.581$, $N = 284$, $df = 4$, $p < .001$). Similar effects of department culture on trust were also found to carry over to librarians' attitudes toward their deans or directors. Only 11% of librarians in don't ask, don't tell departments reported trusting their dean or director to evaluate their teaching, compared with 39% of librarians who trust their deans or directors to evaluate them in collaborative and transparent departments ($x2 = 18.511$, $N = 284$, $df = 4$, $p = .001$). Most troubling of all were the six librarians in don't ask, don't tell department cultures who reported that they did not trust anyone to evaluate their teaching.

Respondents' open-ended answers help to give context to the findings about librarians' experiences with peer evaluations. Formalized processes among peers for evaluating teaching are not as common as top-down evaluations related to overall job performance. When systems are formalized among peers, they are cited as "insightful and helpful," due to library colleagues' understanding of challenges in providing information literacy instruction. Survey respondents who did not have opportunities for peer review indicated they would appreciate it more than evaluations from supervisors or administrators. Systems of peer review are not always perfect, however, and several open responses throughout the survey indicated that without guidelines for feedback, colleagues are nearly always positive and problems are rarely identified. One respondent shared that colleagues are "too kind", not offering "useful criticism," but responses indicate that feedback from more experienced library instructors is still valued, overall.

Among librarians surveyed, students were selected as the most trusted evaluators:

TABLE 8.4

Librarians' Trusted Teaching Evaluators

Trusted teaching evaluators	% selected
Students	85%
Faculty outside the library	76%
Instruction colleagues in the library	71%
Instruction librarians from other libraries	36%
Dean or director	27%
Department chair	21%
Non-instruction colleagues in the library	15%
No one	3%

Participants were asked whether their department valued their teaching as much as they did. 53% of respondents (N=155) perceive a close match between how much they value their teaching role and how much their department values it. 40% of respondents (N=117) indicated that they value their teaching more than their departments do. Librarians from transparent and collaborative departmental cultures are more likely to enjoy a close match in values (80%) compared with only 34% of librarians in don't ask, don't tell cultures who reported that their values and their departments' values closely matched. This relationship between department culture and values was significant and strong ($x2 = 40.458$, $N = 268$, df = 4, $p < .001$).

A significant relationship was also found between having the quality of your instruction evaluated during an annual performance review and the perception that your department values your teaching as much as you do ($x2 = 8.747$, $N = 284$, df = 1, $p < .01$). Although only 38% of librarians report that their teaching is evaluated as part of an annual performance review, 46% of librarians who believe that their department values their teaching as much as they do are getting their teaching evaluated during performance reviews. While the effect of this relationship is small, this finding suggests that including an evaluation of teaching as part of performance review shows librarians how much their teaching is valued and that departments where librarians' teaching is valued are more likely to include it as an element of performance review.

Librarians were also asked if their teaching was more, equally, or less important as a factor in their evaluations than it was in evaluations for other instructional faculty at their institutions. After calculating a cross-tabulation between this evaluation factor and librarians' view of the relative value that their department places on their teaching, we found a significant relationship between perceiving that your teaching is less important in your evaluation than it is for other faculty and the feeling that you value your teaching more than your department does ($x2 = 18.349$, N = 271, df = 2, p < .001). 67% of librarians who felt they valued their teaching more than their department also said their teaching was less important in their evaluation than it was for other faculty, which compares with 41% of the librarians who said their departments valued their teaching as much as they did but also said that their teaching was less important in their evaluation than it was for other faculty. No similar relationship was found to exist between librarians' reports of the relative value that their institutions placed on their teaching and their perception of how teaching figured in their evaluation compared with its importance for other faculty evaluations ($x2 = 2.358$, N = 269, df = 2, p = .308).

Survey Limitations & Future Recommendations

Many of the discussions and issues that arose in researching processes by which teaching is evaluated and the ways in which those evaluations are used shed light on the lack of opportunity for librarians to be rewarded for their teaching. Investigations into merit-based benefits that librarians receive as part of their reward for teaching and for documenting teaching excellence were not a focus of our survey, but surfaced as an issue for participants. While intrinsic motivators are certainly encouraging for teachers, librarians must work toward defining librarianship as a teaching profession and joining existing communities of instructional practice, as well as developing our own. To this end, release time for teaching-related activities, the freedom to teach outside library departments, the chance to join faculty teaching organizations, and the support to participate in professional development opportunities related to teaching are of the utmost importance. Not only will this encourage librarians to continue to grow as teachers, but it will also engage librarians in the teaching and assessment continuum similarly to other educators at colleges and universities.

Underlying this discussion of processes for librarian's review and structures for rewarding teaching are issues of organizational culture and trust, specifically as they impact the opportunities for peers to collaborate and participate in symbiotic review processes. Libraries that embrace change and encourage librarians to expand their spheres of influence beyond traditional roles and departmental boundaries are well-suited to adopting teaching evaluative criteria and systems for peer review. Issues of trust can also impact intradepartmental culture that would influence the success or failure of a system of peer review for teaching. While librarians may enjoy the solitary nature of some aspects of their work, teaching is not something that should happen behind closed doors. Instead, it is an activity that should be planned, reviewed, and reflected upon openly and could become, when addressed appropriately, an opportunity to build trust and respect among library colleagues. Additional research in this area would do well to explore librarians' evaluation of teaching and the impact of organizational culture on this endeavor.

PROPOSED BEST PRACTICES

Based on commonalities and discrepancies in these survey data combined with the literature reviewed for this chapter, we were able to identify opportunities for developing best practices for documenting and reviewing librarians' contribution to teaching in higher education, these include: librarian status, librarian involvement in evaluative processes, librarian peer review of teaching, and librarians' criteria for teaching excellence. These best practices are based on the assumption that academic librarians agree that teaching is an important part of librarianship and should be evaluated as something that is valued, both departmentally and institutionally.

Librarian Status

Librarians should have the same status as their campus colleagues involved in teaching. A long debated topic among librarians, tenure and faculty status, is inherent in the problem of librarians' teaching going largely undocumented and unrecognized even as the information literacy movement grows greater all the time. While advocating for librarians' tenure seems a simple solution to many of these issues, it is not a panacea. As an alternative, we advocate for librarians to enjoy the same status, whatever it may be, as faculty on their campus. Findings from the survey suggest that faculty status rather than tenure eligibility make the greater difference in librarians' access to evaluations and rewards for their teaching. Because of variations in structures and policies, different institutions will apply their own labels for the status of the people focused on carrying out the primary mission of colleges and universities, which is teaching. Whatever status institutions bestow upon this work should also be awarded to librarians in order to better align their work with the primary purpose of the organizations in which they work and to support the overall integration of librarians into the institutions' teaching cultures. With status similar to other faculty, librarians will have equality in campus governance, decision-making, and curricular planning in order to ensure the full integration of information literacy education into the curriculum during this current period of renewed dedication to teaching and learning throughout higher education (Bruininks, Keeney, and Thorp 2010).

Librarian Involvement in Evaluative Processes

Librarians should be more aware of and involved with the tenure and promotion process for all faculty. Having an understanding of the criteria by which faculty are evaluated for their teaching will inform librarians' perspective on their role as teachers and what it means for their own promotion and tenure. While librarians at many institutions will undergo a process for tenure or promotion that differs from other faculty, the two processes need not be completely separate. In fact, librarians may benefit from serving on campus committees for promotion and tenure where they will learn the norms that are expected of their colleagues outside the library. An informed perspective on curricular and disciplinary activities will create opportunities for librarians to have an enhanced understanding of campus priorities and goals related to instruction. Similarly, librarians who invite faculty to partake in the review process for their teaching will benefit from disciplinary-focused perspectives on teaching and come to understand their instructional activities on a larger scale.

Peer Review of Teaching

Librarians should be formally peer reviewed in their teaching within an open culture of assessment in their department. Feedback from non-library faculty can be useful in understanding information literacy instruction in a disciplinary context and should be used to guide curricular integration decisions and strategies for improving collaborative efforts. Similarly, student input is invaluable in gauging quality, relevance, and transferability of information literacy instruction. From the research presented here, there is consistent feedback and evaluation offered from students and faculty already. What is missing is a systematic process by which librarians are reviewed by their own colleagues.

The value of peer review among librarians comes from the informed perspective librarians inherently possess regarding the unique challenges and opportunities involved in information literacy education, as well as a shared background in education and professional development. In addition, librarians who participate in peer review are more engaged in the teaching and learning process, from instructional design, to implementation, to assessment and finally reflection. Looking at this process from the outside can allow for self-reflection on the part of the reviewer who achieves a thoughtful approach to critically addressing a colleague's teaching.

Through a formal mechanism involving all librarians at an institution, the movement to understand and advocate for librarians as educators will grow from the ground up and will encourage librarians who may not have been previously involved in teaching to endeavor to understand it, support it, and become involved in it. In addition, formalizing peer review will lessen librarians' tendency toward informal evaluation of teaching; thereby allowing them to feel freer to offer critical and constructive, as well as positive, feedback to colleagues.

Rewards for Librarians' Teaching Excellence

Whether they participate in promotion and tenure or an annual review process, librarians deserve to have formal evaluations of their teaching included as part of these reviews. As a reward for improved performance, as well as an incentive for assessing and documenting teaching, these survey results show that librarians will feel that their teaching is valued more if it is included as part of their review. In addition, libraries and institutions would do well to reward this work through public recognition, invitations to join teaching colloquia, support for professional development, sabbaticals, and release time for teaching in order to help further librarians in their movement toward reinvigorating librarianship as a profession focused on what is most important in higher education: teaching and learning.

Librarians' Criteria for Teaching Evaluation

Librarians' criteria for teaching evaluation should be transparent and consistent. While the faculty model for teaching evaluation is something that librarians should consider as a successful example, teaching for many librarians comes in a variety of forms that may not necessarily correspond with traditional credit-bearing, classroom-based instruction. For this reason, librarians' criteria for measuring teaching quality should be unique to their particular environment with consideration for varying job duties and performance expectations.

The criteria by which librarians are evaluated on their teaching must be well communicated among librarians and across institutions in order to remove the element of mystery surrounding the standards by which librarians' teaching will be evaluated. Librarians should also be made aware of the weight given to the criteria that will influence their performance and tenure reviews (Arreola 2007). These criteria should go beyond articulating expectations for quantity toward addressing outcomes for student learning and acceptable evidence of such learning. Just as information literacy learning outcomes are fundamentally similar across institutions, so should librarians' practice be defined and measured by clearly articulated expectations that could be transferable within and among educational environments.

Consistency & Transparency

Many of the perspectives put forth in the current library literature point toward libraries and librarians in the academy taking on more instructional activities in order to create stronger connections between libraries and the core teaching and learning purpose of their institutions. The question, then, is not whether librarians should be reviewed and rewarded based on their teaching contribution, but how. While it is widely agreed that librarians' teaching contributes to the relevance of libraries and librarians in the academy, there is no clear format for documenting, assessing, or rewarding this activity across institutions. The variance in status of librarians from institution to institution contributes to the discrepancy in teaching reward structures, as does the level of involvement in instructional activities and the type of teaching librarians do which varies greatly by institution and individual. While this is problematic for standardization of practice and assessment, it is imperative for the success of librarians as teachers. The findings from this study suggest that librarians' roles in the academy are dictated more by our profession than by the structure of the institutions in which we work; therefore it is important for each individual librarian to decide how teaching fits into his or her professional life and how it can best contribute to student learning and engagement. What must be consistent is that librarians do continue to contribute to teaching and learning and that the contribution is valued, reviewed, and rewarded, whether monetarily or through other systems of merit or status. Department teaching cultures that are don't ask, don't tell must transition into transparency by examining (and perhaps changing) what they value and finding methods for supporting and evaluating librarians' work as teachers (Wright et al. 2004).

As long as the credit hour and the semester constitute the most widely accepted framework for teaching, learning, and assessment in higher education, much of the instructional activities of librarians will go undocumented and underestimated in official institutional capacities for measurement such as grades, number of classes taught, and number of students reached. Similarly, librarians who teach cannot easily quantify their impact on student learning as they can with the number of hours worked at a reference desk, the amount of time spent on building collections, and by how many individuals those materials were used toward research purposes. To remedy this problem, librarians must begin to establish their own formats for formalization of teaching-related activities in order to create a system of review and rewards. While the criteria for teaching quantity and quality will never be standardized, librarians' teaching at least needs to be documented and reviewed. In an ideal situation, these criteria would then be built into the rewards structure for librarians at each institution. By establishing criteria for measuring and communicating the effect of librarians' teaching, the invisible work of preparing for and improving instruction will become apparent (vanDuinkerken, Coker, and Anderson 2010) and the teaching that is usually done in isolation will instead be the focus of discussion, collaboration, and evaluation (LaCelle-Peterson and Finkelstein 1993). This is the first step toward a clearer understanding of how librarians are being supported by their institutions and will direct attention to the structural deficits that persistently diminish librarians' effectiveness (Wright et al. 2004).

Review criteria should be flexible enough to represent the types of teaching that occurs across positions and institutions, including the following categories:

TABLE 8.5
Criteria for Reviewing Librarians' Teaching

Criteria	Examples
Instructional role	Instructor of record; co-instructor; guest instructor; instructional designer; assessment expert; facilitator; consultant
Instruction type	Credit-bearing course; stand-alone workshop; one-shot session; online learning object; seminar; tour
Instructional impact	# of students directly/indirectly impacted; # of sessions/classes/workshops taught; # of hours spent on teaching-related activities
Instructional assessment	Student work; student feedback; pre- and post-test results; compilations of information literacy data/reports; formal and informal peer review of teaching
Instructional advancement	Evidence of reflective practice; evidence of increased teaching responsibility; evidence of enhanced instructional performance; leadership in creating, developing, or assessing teaching initiatives; continuing education in pedagogy and information literacy instruction
Instructional recognition	Recipient of teaching awards/honors; acknowledgement of teaching excellence; rating of excellent [or equivalent] in performance review for teaching activities

The purpose for establishing criteria is to address the largest current gap in instructional initiatives in academic libraries, i.e. the standards by which we describe and measure the teaching contributions of librarians. It should be up to each institution or library to determine benchmarks for excellence in each area. The quantifiable aspects may be more or less important for certain organizations or positions within those organizations depending upon organizational mission and values, but each librarian should be expected to describe his or her work in terms of its impact on student learning, at a minimum.

Whether these criteria are used for performance or tenure reviews, documentation of librarians' teaching and its impact should be collected, reviewed, and valued with transparency and consistency whenever possible. The symbiotic relationship between performance review and rewards structures also demands that criteria for teaching be agreed upon and used by librarians and administrators. For librarians who spend their career at a singular institution, as well as those who choose to change institutions, this will create consistent methods for setting expectations and measuring excellence as they relate to teaching endeavors. Transparency in documenting and communicating these expectations is important for new hires and seasoned librarians alike. Librarians who are newly hired should understand that teaching or participating in activities that impact teaching and learning is expected. Likewise, librarians whose work has previously been focused on non-instructional activities deserve to have formalized documentation that represents review criteria based on institutional values.

Librarians who are measured by the same or similar criteria as faculty on their campus will already have these teaching criteria built into their review process. For librarians who do not have faculty status or are reviewed inter-organizationally, criteria for measuring teaching will align their work more seamlessly with that of faculty and will create a purposeful connection between librarians and the overall mission of their institution. In addition, similar expectations for teaching excellence among librarians at institutions of varying size and type will allow for enhanced and permanent status of information literacy instruction and librarians as educators in the academy, similar to that which faculty enjoy as members of a discipline, instead of those values being only institution-specific. While standardization among learning outcomes for information literacy makes sense across types of institutions, rigid criteria for defining and measuring teaching excellence is problematic for librarians. A formalized yet flexible approach to review criteria development and implementation will serve to connect librarians to the educational mission common to all institutions of higher education and provide a framework for librarians' improvement and advancement as teachers.

RECOMMENDATIONS & CONCLUSIONS

While it may be argued that librarians' work is to support scholars in their research and teaching and seeking anything more (let alone reward for these activities) goes against the service-oriented professional underpinnings of librarianship and undermines its altruistic motivations, our contention is that the future of the profession depends upon librarians' direct participation and influence on the teaching and learning process. Having progressed from a bibliographic instruction model that situated librarians strictly in the library context, information literacy now provides an opportunity for librarians to expand their sphere of instructional influence beyond the library into the realm of learning across courses, disciplines, and institutions. Through information literacy instruction and programs, librarians are leaders in integrating knowledge discovery and creation into teaching practice with innovative and practical pedagogy.

The Association of College & Research Libraries has provided exceptional support for librarians in their shift toward a more innovative and influential academic library model, especially with regard to the libraries' instructional role. The *Standards for Proficiencies for Instruction Librarians & Coordinators* (2007) has been immeasurably useful in guiding the progress of information literacy programs and the librarians who develop and implement them; however, its limited focus on librarians' whose primary professional duty is instruction makes it irrelevant to librarians who do not manage or oversee information literacy programs. For these librarians, teaching or teaching-related activities should still be articulated and measured. The ACRL would be helpful in drafting and endorsing criteria by which all librarians' teaching could be defined and reviewed, as suggested here.

In order for such criteria to be widely accepted in such a way that they become standard factors for review across a variety of institutions and positions, library deans, directors, and administrators must support librarians in their professional development as teachers and in their teaching activities that may take time away from more traditional library work. Department norms can be altered through the adoption of policies that communicate the expectation that librarians will dedicate time to sharing ideas about teaching, observing each others' classroom teaching, attending professional development activities, sharing lesson plans and syllabi, and introducing new teaching methods (Woods 1999,268-290). In addition, performance standards should be updated to include teaching impact factors for all librarians. The result of implementing criteria to measure teaching activity and quality is not to demand librarians take on additional work or work that does not suit their professional strengths, but instead to align all librarians with the core mission of the institution and to communicate the importance of teaching, in all its forms. Teachers, whether they are librarians or not, feel rewarded when the challenge and intensity of teaching are recognized by their institutions (Wright et al. 2004). Only through evaluation, review, and compensation can the time they spend preparing and improving their teaching be acknowledged. Through such formal review practice, librarians' teaching will be built into the process for merit-based pay, tenure and promotion, and performance review in an appropriate and official way; thereby situating teaching in a place of prominence and purpose in academic librarianship.

As librarians further engage in teaching activities, they will benefit from creating and participating in communities of practice that progress their knowledge of pedagogy and produce opportunities for their unique contribution to conversations on teaching at the institution-level. Librarians who seek to form partnerships with faculty to further their instructional goals or librarians who self-identify as teachers and are therefore singular in their library organizations will enjoy the community and collaboration that comes from joining campus teaching colloquia or participating in the Scholarship of Teaching and Learning (SoTL). In identifying student learning as something that warrants original, evidence-based research, SoTL situates teaching activities in the realm of research, thereby making it potentially more valued by institutions that are research-intensive. While the benefits for librarians who seek support from inter-disciplinary communities of teaching beyond their libraries and professional organizations were not addressed in our survey, we recognize that these opportunities could have great potential for librarians attaining faculty status, furthering teaching partnerships, and re-envisioning teaching as a research-related activity. As librarians continue to increase their sphere of instructional influence, so should they explore such broad communities of practice that may have previously been the province of classroom faculty. Through such investigations, librarians will become familiar with the language, culture, and identity associated with teaching and will be better equipped to offer evidence and justification for the value it holds for librarianship.

Finally, librarians who embrace their teaching role will be the most influential in furthering the progress of review criteria for teaching and advocating for enhanced instructional roles among their colleagues. While the shift in our professional roles is inevitable, we cannot simply sit back and wait for it to happen around us. A more proactive approach to encouraging and inspiring our colleagues to co-teach with us, participate in peer-review of teaching, and document and assess our teaching and its impact on student learning will create a grassroots movement toward the acceptance and eventual celebration of librarians' teaching.

References

Adamson, Morgan. 2009. "The Human Capital Strategy." *Ephemera: Theory & Politics in Organization* 9 (4): 271–284.

Affleck, Mary Ann. 1996. "Burnout Among Bibliographic Instruction Librarians." *Library & Information Science Research* 18 (2): 165–183.

American Library Association. 2006. "Guidelines for the Appointment, Promotion, and Tenure of Academic Librarians." www.ala.org/acrl/standards/promotiontenure.

———. 1972. "Joint Statement on Faculty Status of College and University Librarians". www.ala.org/acrl/standards/jointstatementfaculty.

———. 2006. "Standards for Faculty Status for College and University Librarians." www.ala.org/acrl/standards/standardsfaculty.

———. 2007. "Standards for Proficiencies for Instruction Librarians and Coordinators." www.ala.org/acrl/standards/profstandards.

Applegate, Rachel. 2007. "Charting Academic Library Staffing: Data from National Surveys." *College & Research Libraries* 68 (1): 59–68.

Aronowitz, Stanley. 2000. *The Knowledge Factory: Dismantling the Corporate University and Creating True Higher Learning*. Boston: Beacon Press.

Arreola, Raoul. 2007. *Developing a Comprehensive Faculty Evaluation System: A Guide to Designing, Building, and Operating Large-Scale Faculty Evaluation Systems*. San Francisco: Jossey-Bass.

Auer, Nicole J., and Ellen M. Krupar. 2005. "Librarians Grading: Giving A's, B's, C's, D's, and F's." *The Reference Librarian* 43 (89): 39–61.

Becker, Karen A. 1993. "The Characteristics of Bibliographic Instruction in Relation to the Causes and Symptoms of Burnout." *RQ* 32 (3): 346–357.

Beile, Penny M., and David N. Boote. 2004. "Does the Medium Matter?: A Comparison of a Web-based Tutorial with Face-to-face Library Instruction on Education Students' Self-efficacy Levels and Learning Outcomes." *Research Strategies* 20 (1–2): 57–68.

Beilema, Cheryl, Dan Crocker, Joan Miller, Jennifer Reynolds-Moehrle, and Helen Shaw. 2005. "Faculty and Librarian Collaborations: A Case Study and Proposal for Online Learning Environments." *Research Strategies* 20 (4): 334–345.

Bewick, Laura, and Sheila Corrall. 2010. "Developing Librarians as Teachers: A Study of Their Pedagogical Knowledge." *Journal of Librarianship and Information Science* 42: 97–110.

Birmingham, Elizabeth J., Luc Chinwongs, Molly Flaspohler, Carly Hearn, Danielle Kvanvig, and Ronda Portmann. 2008. "First-year Writing Teachers' Perceptions of Students' Information Literacy Competencies, and a Call for a Collaborative Approach." *Communications in Information Literacy* 2 (1).

Bowen, William G., Matthew M. Chingos, and Michael S. McPherson. 2009. *Crossing the Finish Line: Completing College at America's Public Universities.* Princeton, NJ: Princeton University Press.

Brien, Donna Lee. 2009. "Unplanned Educational Obsolescence: Is the 'Traditional' PhD Becoming Obsolete?" *M/C Journal* 12 (3).

Bruininks, Robert H., Brianne Keeney, and Jim Thorp. 2010. "Transforming America's Universities to Compete in the 'New Normal.'" *Innovative Higher Education* 35 (2): 113–125.

Burkhardt, Joanna M. 2007. "Assessing Library Skills: A First Step to Information Literacy." *Portal* 7 (1): 25–49.

Chao, Elaine L., Emily S. DeRocco, and Maria K. Flynn. 2007. *Adult Learners in Higher Education: Barriers to Success and Strategies to Improve Results.* Washington, D.C.: Department of Labor. http://wdr.doleta.gov.

Cmor, Dianne, Alison Chan, and Teresa Kong. 2010. "Course-Integrated Learning Outcomes for Library Database Searching: Three Assessment Points on the Path of Evidence." *Evidence Based Library and Information Practice* 5 (1): 64–81.

Cronin, Joseph M., and Howard E. Horton. 2009. "Will Higher Education Be the Next Bubble to Burst?" *The Chronicle of Higher Education:* A56.

Crowley, Bill. 2001. "Tacit Knowledge, Tacit Ignorance, and the Future of Academic Librarianship." *College & Research Libraries* 62 (6): 565–584.

Cubberley, Carol W. 1996. *Tenure and Promotion for Academic Librarians: A Guidebook with Advice and Vignettes.* London: McFarland.

Do, Paolo. 2008. "No Future." *Ephemera: Theory & Politics in Organization* 8 (3): 303–311.

Donnelly, Kimberly. 2000. "Reflections on What Happens When Librarians

Become Teachers." *Computers in Libraries* 20 (3): 47–49.

Dunne, Elisabeth, Neville Bennett, and Clive Carr. 1997. "Higher Education: Core Skills in a Learning Society." *Journal of Education Policy* 12 (6): 511–525.

Fox, Claire. 2002. "The Massification of Higher Education." In *The McDonaldization of Higher Education*, 129–142. Westport, CT: Bergin and Garvey.

Galvin, Jeanne. 2006. "Information Literacy and Integrative Learning." *College & Undergraduate Libraries* 13 (3): 25–51.

Gandhi, Smiti. 2005. "Faculty-Librarian Collaboration to Assess the Effectiveness of a Five-Session Library Instruction Model." *Community & Junior College Libraries* 12 (4): 15–48.

Gansz, David, Richard H. Werking, Lynn S. Cochrane, and Pyke Jr. Johnson. 2007. "College Libraries and the Teaching/Learning Process: Selection from the Writings of Evan Ira Farber."

Gappa, Judith M. 2008. "Today's Majority: Faculty Outside the Tenure System." *Change* 40 (4): 50–54.

Gaston, Paul L. 2010. *The Challenge of Bologna: What United States Higher Education Has to Learn from Europe, and Why It Matters That We Learn It.* Sterling, VA: Stylus Publishing.

Gillum, Shalu. 2010. "The True Benefit of Faculty Status for Academic Reference Librarians." *The Reference Librarian* 51 (4): 321–328.

Gorman, Michael. 1991. "Send for a Child of Four! Or Creating the BI-less Academic Library." *Library Trends* 39 (3): 354–362.

Hacker, Andrew, and Claudia Dreifus. 2010. *Higher Education?: How Colleges Are Wasting Our Money and Failing Our Kids and What We Can Do About It.* New York: Henry Holt and Company.

Hall, H. Palmer, and Caroline Byrd. 1990. "The Librarian in the University: Essays on Membership in the Academic Community".

Hill, Janet S. 1994. "Wearing Our Own Clothes: Librarians as Faculty." *The Journal of Academic Librarianship* 20 (2): 71–76.

Hufford, Jon R. 2010. "What are They Learning? Pre- and Post-Assessment Surveys for LIBR 1100, Introduction to Library Research." *College & Research Libraries* 71 (2): 139–158.

Intersegmental Committee of the Academic Senates of the California Community Colleges and the University of California. 2002. *Academic Literacy: A Statement of Competencies Expected of Students Entering California's Public Colleges and Universities.* Sacramento, CA: ICAS. www.universityofcalifornia.edu/senate/reports/acadlit.pdf.

Johnson, Corey M., and Elizabeth B. Lindsay. 2006. "Why we do what we do: exploring priorities within public services librarianship." *Portal: Libraries and the Academy* 6 (3): 347–369.

Julien, Heidi. 2005. "Education for Information Literacy Instruction: A Global

Perspective." *Association for Library and Information Literacy Education* 46 (3): 210–216.

Kelly, Patrick J. 2005. *As America Becomes More Diverse: The Impact of State Higher Education Inequality.* Boulder, CO: National Center for Higher Education Management Systems. www.higheredinfo.org/raceethnicity/InequalityPaperNov2005.pdf.

Kemp, Jane. 2006. "Isn't Being a Librarian Enough?—Librarians as Classroom Teachers." *College & Undergraduate Libraries* 13 (3): 3–23.

Kingma, Bruce, and Gillian M. McCombs. 1995. "The Opportunity Costs of Faculty Status for Academic Librarians." *College & Research Libraries* 56 (3): 258–264.

Koufogiannakis, Denise, and Natasha Wiebe. 2006. "Effective Methods for Teaching Information Literacy Skills to Undergraduate Students: A Systematic Review and Meta-analysis." *Evidence Based Library and Information Practice* 1 (3): 3–43.

Lacelle-Peterson, Mark W., and Martin J. Finkelstein. 1993. "Institutions Matter: Campus Teaching Environments' Impact on Senior Faculty." In *Developing Senior Faculty as Teachers.* San Francisco: Jossey-Bass.

Lampert, Lynn, Katherine Dabbour, and Jacqueline Solis. 2005. "When It's All Greek: The Importance of Collaborative Information Literacy Outreach Programming to Greek Student Organizations." *Research Strategies* 20 (4): 300–310.

Lebbins, Vickery K. 2005. "Students Perceptions on the Long-range Value of Information Literacy Instruction Through a Learning Community." *Research Strategies* 20 (3): 204–218.

Lerman, Robert I. 2007. "Career-focused Education and Training for Youth." In *Reshaping the American Workforce in a Changing Economy*, edited by Harry J. Holzer and Demetra S. Nightingale, 41–90. Washington, D.C.: The Urban Institute Press.

Levine, Arthur. 1997. "How the Academic Profession Is Changing." *Daedalus* 126 (4): 1–20.

Lillard, Linda L. 2003. "Personalized Instruction and Assistance Services for Distance Learners: Cultivating a Research Relationship." *Research Strategies* 19 (3/4): 204–212.

Lindquist, Thea, and Todd Gilman. 2008. "Academic/Research Librarians with Subject Doctorates: Data and Trends 1965–2006." *Portal: Libraries and the Academy* 8 (1): 31–52.

Loesch, Martha. 2010. "Librarian as Professor: A Dynamic New Role Model." *Education Libraries* 33 (1): 31–37.

Lowry, Charles B. 1993. "The Status of Faculty Status for Academic Librarians: A Twenty Year Perspective." *College & Research Libraries* 54 (2): 163–172.

Matthews, Joseph R. 2007. *Library Assessment in Higher Education.* Westport, CT:

Libraries Unlimited.

Meyer, Richard W. 1999. "A Measure of the Impact of Tenure." *College & Research Libraries* 60 (2): 110–119.

Miller, Connie, and Patricia Tegler. 1987. "In Pursuit of Windmills: Librarians and the Determination to Instruct." *The Reference Librarian* 18: 119–134.

Mokhtar, Azura, Schubert Foo, and Shaheen Majid. 2008. "Information Literacy Education: Applications of Mediated Learning and Multiple Intelligences." *Library & Information Science Research* 30 (3): 195–206.

Morey, Ann I. 2004. "Globalization and the Emergence of For-Profit Higher Education." *Higher Education* 48 (1): 131–150.

Oakley, Francis. 1997. "The Elusive Academic Profession: Complexity and Change." *Daedalus* 126 (4): 43–66.

Ohmann, Richard. 2000. "Historical Reflections on Accountability." *Academe* 86 (1).

Owusu-Ansah, Edward K. 2007. "Beyond Collaboration: Seeking Greater Scope and Centrality for Library Instruction." *Portal: Libraries and the Academy* 7 (4): 415–429.

Park, Betsy, and Robert Riggs. 1993. "Tenure and Promotion: A Study of Practices by Institutional Type." *The Journal of Academic Librarianship* 19 (2): 72–77.

Partello, Peggy. 2005. "Librarians in the Classroom." *The Reference Librarian* 43 (89): 107–120.

Premeaux, Shane R. 2008. "Administrative Versus Faculty Perspectives Regarding Academic Tenure." *The Journal of Academic Administration in Higher Education* 4 (1): 47–55.

Rapple, Brendan A. 1997. "The Librarian as Teacher in the Networked Environment." *College and Teaching* 45 (3): 114–116.

Rockman, Ilene F. 2002. "Strengthening Connections between Information Literacy, General Education, and Assessment Efforts." *Library Trends* 51 (2): 185–198.

Ruess, Diane E. 2004. "Faculty and Professional Appointments of Academic Librarians: Expanding the Options for Choice." *Portal: Libraries and the Academy* 41 (1): 75–84.

Sheesley, Deborah F. 2001. "Burnout and the Academic Teaching Librarian: An Examination of the Problem and Suggested Solution." *The Journal of Academic Librarianship* 27 (6): 447–451.

Slattery, Charles E. 1994. "Faculty Status: Another 100 years of Dialogue? Lessons from the Library School Closings." *The Journal of Academic Librarianship* 20 (4): 193–199.

Sproles, Claudene, Anna Marie Johnson, and Leslie Farison. 2008. "What the Teachers Are Teaching: How MLIS Programs Are Preparing Academic Librarians for Instructional Roles." *Journal of Education for Library and*

Information Science 49 (3): 195–209.

Stamatoplos, Anthony. 2009. "The Role of Academic Libraries in Mentored Undergraduate Research: a Model of Engagement in the Academic Community." *College & Research Libraries* 70 (3): 235–249.

Tierney, William G., and Estela M. Bensimon. 1996. *Promotion and Tenure: Community and Socialization in Academe.* Albany, NY: SUNY Press.

VanDuinkerken, Wyoma, Catherine Coker, and Margaret Anderson. 2010. "Looking Like Everyone Else: Academic Portfolios for Librarians." *The Journal of Academic Librarianship* 36 (2): 166–172.

Vesper, Virginia, and Gloria Kelley. 1997. *Criteria for Promotion and Tenure for Academic Librarians: CLIP Note #26.* Chicago: Association of College & Research Libraries.

Welch, Jeanie M., and Frada L. Mozenter. 2006. "Loosening the Ties that Bind: Academic Librarians and Tenure." *College & Research Libraries* 67 (2): 164–176.

Willen, Liz. 2010. "Amid Budget Cuts and Overcrowding at Community Colleges, For-Profit Institutions Seek a Niche." *The Hechinger Report.* http://hechingerreport.org/content/amid-budget-cuts-and-overcrowding-at-community-colleges-for-profit-institutions-seek-a-niche_4493.

Wilson, Pauline. 1979. "Librarians as Teachers: The Study of an Organization Fiction." *The Library Quarterly* 49 (2): 146-162.

Wolf, Alison. 2009. "Misunderstanding Education." *Change* 41 (4): 10–17.

Woods, Jennifer Q. 1999. "Establishing a Teaching Development Culture." In *Faculty in New Jobs: A Guide to Settling In, Becoming Established, and Building Institutional Support,* 268–290. San Francisco: Jossey-Bass.

Wright, Mary C., Nandini Assar, Edward L. Kain, Laura Kramer, Carla B. Howery, Kathleen McKinney, Becky Glass, and Maxine Atkinson. 2004. "Greedy Institutions: The Importance of Institutional Context for Teaching in Higher Education." *Teaching Sociology* 32 (2): 144–159.

Wyss, Paul A. 2010. "Library School Faculty Member Perceptions Regarding Faculty Status for Academic Librarians." *College & Research Libraries* 71 (4): 375–388.

9

Information Literacy Reality Check

Nancy H. Seamans

INTRODUCTION

Twenty years of information literacy in libraries provides an opportunity for reflection on both what we've accomplished and what faces us as we look ahead. Having had a small role in the information literacy movement at several institutions and in several different positions for many of those twenty years, I am offering my perceptions of where we are and where we're headed.

I can't pinpoint it exactly, but my awareness of information literacy as a formal concept first came in the mid-1990s. I was working as a generalist librarian at a small private college, doing a variety of things, one of which was teaching. As I worked at becoming a better library teacher, I started looking for like-minded librarians and in the process discovered information literacy concepts. I was delighted to find the structure that was provided by ALA's explanation of information literacy (American Library Association 1989) and by ACRL's Information Literacy Competency Standards (Association of College and Research Libraries 2000) and enthusiastically embraced what they meant for my library teaching. They also provided me with the structure for my dissertation research (Seamans 2001), which further strengthened my enthusiasm.

Moving from my more generalist role, I then had the opportunity to try to make information literacy a cornerstone of a university library instruction program. This is where some of my early doubts started to form. The information literacy message seemed to be difficult to sell—

not only to university administrators but also, far too often, to librarians. The changes in library teaching that I felt had to occur for librarians to succeed as the flag-bearers for the information literacy message seemed too often to be met with lack of interest by my library colleagues. With the passage of time, and with increasing administrative responsibilities, I have become less and less sanguine about how we are doing in terms of making information literacy a keystone program for academic libraries.

I know I am generalizing. I know that many people, many institutions, many organizations are doing incredible work with implementing the information literacy standards, with creating discipline-specific standards, with helping librarians become superb library teachers. But I am not convinced that we have made a compelling case for libraries to be the ones providing leadership in information literacy implementation on our campuses. Additionally, in an environment where there are conflicting agendas within the library, and competition for resources on our campuses, I'm not sure that we can or should tie the future of our libraries to information literacy programs. I will agree that information literacy programs may be a component of our future, but I think we must shift away from seeing them as one of the primary methods for demonstrating our relevance and importance to our user communities. So with this as background, I would like to talk about some of my disappointments and frustrations with the first two decades of information literacy. But I will also attempt to balance those disappointments against what I perceive of as remarkable successes. I have discussed information literacy issues with several library leaders via face-to-face conversations, email, phone conversations and with an electronic survey that asked them to reflect on the current state of information literacy, and I will present some of their views of where the information literacy movement is now and where it is headed. I will also offer opinions, mine as well as others, on what I think is the future role of information literacy in the academic library.

As I discussed information literacy with a number of library leaders, the majority were reluctant to be quoted. I quickly realized that I would have discussions with a greater level of candor if I offered anonymity to these deans and directors and university librarians. To that end, I will be reflecting this when providing their comments about the state of information literacy in academic libraries. All quotes without attribution are from these library leaders who, during the past few months, were willing to talk with me, respond to email, and participate in telephone conversations. I do appreciate the willingness of a few respondents to be quoted by name, and though I have not identified them in the body of the chapter, they are acknowledged at the end of the chapter.

I am well aware that the information literacy movement is international in scope, but what I know best is very US-centric, and very focused on 4-year and research institutions. I am making no pretense of being comprehensive in my comments but instead am offering food for thought—an information literacy reality check from one library administrator.

Framing my discussion be the successes of the information literacy program at Purdue University. In 2007, James Mullins wrote a chapter entitled *An Administrative Perspective* for a book entitled *Proven Strategies for Building an Information Literacy Program* (Curzon 2007). Mullins, who is the Dean of Libraries at Purdue University, discussed the importance of information literacy to the academic library, concluding with, "The competition that an administrator must always contend with when allocating resources, is balanced by the perceived impact and benefit to students and faculty. Information literacy is obviously at the top of the priority list." I used that statement about information literacy being at the top of the priority list for academic libraries as the starting point for my discussions with library leaders. Additionally, Mullins also graciously responded to questions (Mullins 2010) thus providing me with the opportunity to update the Purdue story and to use its successes as a counterpoint to some of the disappointments I'll be noting.

DEFINING INFORMATION LITERACY

As I look at how we have used the information literacy standards during the first two decades, I'm struck by a couple of things. The first is the challenges we created for ourselves when we from the beginning used the word *literacy*. It has its own meaning and is generally understood to be the ability to read, or perhaps even the ability to read and write. It can be modified, as in *information literacy*. But does that then mean that information literacy is the ability to read and write information? Or should we go to a broader comprehension of literacy and define it as *understanding?* That means that information literacy is the ability to understand information. From a non-library perspective, *literacy* modified by *information* is a muddy concept, creating for librarians a frequent need to explain what we mean by *information literacy*. Though most librarians have the traditional definition down pat, our constituents have not necessarily embraced the concepts though they actually have quite often embraced the phrase.

To further complicate things, we in the library community have also modified literacy by a number of other words and concepts. So libraries also have initiatives that focus on things like Family Literacy (Alire 2010), Visual Literacy (ACRL/IRIG 2010), and Consumer Health Literacy (Zionts et al. 2010), and outside of the library community we encounter Media Literacy (Consortium for Media Literacy 2010) and New Media Literacy (New Media Literacies Research Group 2010),and this list is by no means exhaustive. We librarians may have done ourselves a great disservice by how we've diffused our focus on basic literacy and thus on all of the other very important initiatives that we've undertaken. Naming is important, and in the case of information literacy I am not convinced that we have done it well.

On the other hand, the phrase *information literacy* has become embedded in the contemporary lexicon. On a number of campuses the phrase is included in strategic plans, and frequently comes up when faculty talk about the library. I'm not convinced that our campus administrators or our faculty really understand what the phrase means, or what kind of changes it suggests for teaching and learning and for the library and librarians, but at least they say it and if we are lucky they sometimes even link it with the library.

The phrase also turns up in a number of non-library settings. A good and recent example is in the March/April 2010 issue of *EDUCAUSE Review*. An article entitled *Faculty and IT: Conversations and Collaboration* (Hager and Clemmons 2010) discusses the need to work with classroom faculty in "planning, delivering, and assessing the use of academic technology in higher education...." The second of three steps that IT people should take is all about information literacy: "Step 2: Encourage conversations about student learning outcomes and information literacies that prepare students to succeed in higher education and beyond." Nowhere in Step 2 does the word library appear, but the fact that the authors use the phrase is a significant accomplishment. Recent publications are rife with articles about students not being as Web-savvy as they think they are or how students use Google (but not particularly well), and go on to talk about the need for students to acquire information literacy skills even if libraries are not identified as the place where these skills are most often taught. Jimmy Wales, Wikipedia's founder, spoke recently (Wales

2010) about the need for better information literacy skills, though in the interview he never mentioned libraries. So on one hand I am encouraged by how often I see information literacy referenced in non-library higher education writing. We librarians can take great pride in the fact that people have heard us. However, I am frustrated that even as others use the phrase libraries are not necessarily given *ownership* of some of the information literacy solutions.

And where I see problems and frustrations, others see opportunity. One library leader reported conversations with faculty "about how new media projects fit within a broad view of information literacy, new styles of communicating"—thus an embracing of an expanded definition that accommodated a different kind of interaction with faculty members. Another noted that "information literacy is a concept that...needs a more cohesive bond to computer, writing, and research literacy...." Mullins notes that at Purdue data literacy is being added to the traditional definition of information literacy.

Several library leaders pointed to the critical thinking skills that are an integral component of information literacy and suggested that it is in teaching these skills that the library can have an impact. However, it was also noted by several of these library leaders that faculty and administrators do not necessarily think of the library as a place where these skills are taught. In this vein, one library leader noted that what faculty and administrators *do* embrace is the teaching of research skills and the concepts of lifelong learning, both of which can be components of an information literacy program. This is affirmed by Mullins who notes, "Often times we find that faculty don't understand or know the term information literacy, but once we begin to describe its concepts and principles they recognize it immediately. They may tend to call it critical thinking, research skills, etc., and we don't mind that. Our goal is to insure that the students become knowledgeable about how to locate and evaluate information that they need now in their work at Purdue and in the future in their work and their lives generally." (Mullins 2010)

One thoughtful response noted different ways by which librarians, faculty and students understand information literacy: "I think librarians have at times mistaken operational skills for true information literacy, which is closely related to critical thinking and analysis. I think the faculty has mistakenly thought their assignments assured information literacy when, in fact, students were not required to make critical choices about what information to use and how to use it. Students often confuse skill with manipulating web browsers and search engines with information literacy." However, this library leader then went on to note a sense that the concept is "understood better now than in the past, and is being seen as an essential learning outcome on many campuses."

During the past few months as I have discussed information literacy with library leaders, it has seemed increasingly obvious that the definition may be in need of an adjustment. The term as initially presented now seems oddly outdated and limiting. The most successful definitions have often proven to be the ones specific to an individual campus, thus allowing those involved to define information literacy in the way that best meets the needs of the administrators, faculty, librarians and students at that institution. One library leader has gone so far as to suggest that librarians should be promoting a cluster of literacies that all students need to be successful at our institutions and beyond, as informed citizens. It is in this context that the concept of the Blended Librarian (Bell and Shank 2004) might take on even greater importance, with the idea that "library practitioners would help each other to improve their knowledge of and ability to apply the theory and practice of instructional design and technology to improve our ability to connect with faculty for the purpose of achieving student learning outcomes." But regardless of how we proceed, there is benefit to a shared understanding of what information literacy does mean or could mean to us as a profession. Perhaps the beginning of the third decade is the appropriate time to make sure that at least the broad concepts of information literacy are shared by the majority of us.

IMPLEMENTING INFORMATION LITERACY PROGRAMS

Beyond definitions, how information literacy programs have been implemented has caused me some small degree of anxiety. Of particular concern is how often we have invested responsibility for an information literacy plan or program in one person—an instruction coordinator or an information literacy coordinator. With some notable exceptions, this seems to isolate information literacy into a stand-alone unit rather than integrating it into all aspects of the life of the library and, ultimately, the campus. The challenges inherent in a successful program often mean that success is built upon the largest possible number of librarians in an institution understanding the importance of information literacy instruction and buying into it. Though a coordinator *can* make this work, it is often only because of top level support and often only because of the personality of the coordinator—someone who is a champion for the information literacy endeavor. And if this is too invested in one person, that person's departure from an institution may signal the end of the information literacy program—though of course it may also signal the beginning of a program at another institution!

It is appropriate here to draw the distinction between the implementation of a successful information literacy *program* and significant successes that individual librarians are realizing with innovations in instruction. A programmatic success means that there is broad campus buy-in and involvement by both library personnel and campus faculty members and administrators. It is possible for library teachers to be extremely creative and effective in the classroom with no information literacy program in place. It is possible to have excellent library instruction or even information literacy instruction because of the efforts of individuals. However, I think it is less likely that an information literacy *program* will be effective, successful or sustained without significant commitment from library administrators.

In addition to administrative commitment, there are several other aspects to consider in terms of long-term sustainability of a successful information literacy program. One is certainly the need to ensure that more than one librarian is engaged in the information literacy endeavor so that the departure of an individual doesn't end up sinking the entire program. Another is to invest in the success of the program by providing the appropriate levels of support and training to both the librarians involved and to support staff members who may be developing instructional modules or serving in the library in new or different ways in order to free up time for teaching librarians. Being attuned to changes on campus in academic or administrative thinking and then taking advantage of what those changes signal for the library can help ensure that the information literacy program both has a place in the planning for the institution and may help the program be nimble and responsive to changes taking place on campus.

However, perhaps one of the most important components of sustaining an information literacy initiative is also one that we find most difficult, and that is the willingness to give primary responsibility to others if that's what will ensure the program's success. Should a faculty member embrace the information literacy concepts and want to take ownership of them, we must ultimately be willing to take a secondary role in how these skills are taught to students. This will be difficult to do since we tend think of information literacy as a library initiative, but, when appropriate, we must be willing to do so.

The Perfect Storm

I am particularly struck by two things that Mullins reports from Purdue. The first is that he describes the *"perfect storm* for gaining support for information literacy....."* At Purdue this was the arrival on campus of Dr. Sharon Weiner as the new Wayne W. Booker Endowed Chair in Information Literacy at the same time as a task force of the University Senate was working on core curriculum issues, and "a decision [was made] by the University Library Committee to focus its agenda on information literacy for the 2009-2010 academic year." (Mullins 2010) This resulted in information literacy being recommended as a core competency for the university. As a parallel to this, library leaders discussed the need to "sell" information literacy to campus administrators and faculty, to educate them and market to them the benefits of an information literacy program. In my view, Mullins' *perfect storm* is often what makes the difference between a program that has the potential to enjoy broad success as opposed to one that may languish regardless of efforts to market a program to the campus community. Having the confluence of all of the right pieces— people, library initiatives, campus initiatives—can be what makes or breaks a broad-based endeavor of this nature.

Another striking point made by Mullins is how much of a commitment is required for an information literacy program to succeed. He notes that at Purdue "...we also removed all librarians from public service points, to provide them more time to commit to instruction. The management and supervision of day to day functions within the Libraries have been delegated to the professional staff (non-librarian) and clerical staff." (Mullins 2010) This is a sea change for libraries and demonstrates the depth of institutional commitment required for libraries as they take responsibility for a successful information literacy program. It also demonstrates the need for library administrators to clearly articulate expectations and be prepared to address resistance. In the Purdue situation, Mullins comments on this, noting, "The increased demand for information literacy instruction required that we increase the number of librarians involved in instruction, and in order to meet that need, the last fully librarian-staffed reference desk in the Humanities, Social Sciences and Education Library was eliminated in 2009. A single point service desk was created. Although this was met with some dismay by the librarians, they soon adjusted and worked to increase their interaction with students and faculty in new and more dynamic ways." (Mullins 2010)

Another point to consider is whether information literacy can succeed on a campus without a formal program. For at least one library leader, it cannot: "In my opinion, information literacy requires or at least implies a formal program, which in the ideal world would be understood and endorsed by university administrators and teaching faculty." And even having a formal program is no guarantee of success. I would speculate that there are a number of institutions that actually have formal information literacy programs but are seeing spotty implementations and limited successes.

In Person vs. Tutorials

Scalability is perhaps one of the biggest challenges to successful implementation. Something that works on a small campus or in a few classes at a larger campus may be difficult to implement when there are 3,000 first-year students or 40,000 undergraduates involved. Though technology has provided us with some ways of addressing questions of scale, including tutorials like the highly-regarded and much-used and –adapted TILT—Texas Information Literacy Tutorial, technology cannot provide all of the answers. And even if technology does provide some answers, we still have "librarians who will not think outside the box in terms of how to deliver IL [information literacy.]"

Many institutions have created modules, tutorials, videos, and assorted other methods of offer the opportunity of delivering information literacy instruction without having to place a librarian in front of a class. These are of varying quality and have been used with varying degrees of success. One library leader suggested that "we look beyond educating massive groups and focus on virtual delivery and personalized delivery" while also acknowledging that staffing and resources are perhaps our biggest obstacles to implementing successful programs.

But as we look at electronic means for delivering instruction, we are often too willing to ignore one that may be the most successful. As noted previously, we are generally reluctant to give up ownership of information literacy to the faculty members on our campuses. Mullins has recognized this challenge and has identified and is acting to implement the obvious solution: "We are clear in understanding that librarians will not do all of the information literacy [instruction], that our goal is to teach the fundamentals of information literacy and to help faculty incorporate the principles in their courses, not requiring that a librarian instruct in each class." (Mullins 2010) I worry that too often we have invested so heavily in information literacy as a library initiative that even when it is not feasible for library personnel to teach all students we have been reluctant to share the responsibility.

One library leader captured this question of technology usage quite succinctly when noting: "I believe we would achieve our desired goal if we relied far more heavily on the type of online tutorials that JISC [United Kingdom's Joint Information Systems Committee] has offered for more than ten years." And another noted that while we must not diminish the role of instruction at our institutions, we will need to "move away from all of the instructional customization that is currently taking place."

PROFESSIONAL DEVELOPMENT
Teaching Librarians

If nothing else, twenty years of focus on information literacy instruction has resulted in librarians becoming much better teachers. Though it has often been an effort, we have taken very seriously our role as library teachers and have developed teaching skills that are often among the best on campus. This may be because we know we have to engage our audiences quickly and efficiently, so we know that we must pay more attention to pedagogy than do faculty members on our campuses who have the entire semester in which to make their points.

But it seems to have been difficult for us to understand information literacy as a new concept that requires us to think very differently about our library instruction. At some point early in my information literacy engagement period, I ran across Dane Ward's table (Ward 1997) [Figure 9.1] that compared and contrasted bibliographic instruction to information literacy. It was revelatory for me and encapsulated into one place what had been troubling me about what I was often seeing among librarians: a tendency to take traditional bibliographic instruction, wave a wand over it, and designate it as information literacy instruction. Indeed, I clearly recall a librarian sighing and saying that this was just the newest name for what she had always been doing; that we could call it anything we wanted to call it but she would continue to teach what she had always taught, and what she had always taught was bibliographic instruction. Regardless of what she and many other librarians say, information literacy instruction requires us to fundamentally rethink the way we teach.

Library instruction is the broad category and within it reside bibliographic instruction, information literacy instruction, technology instruction and tool-based instruction. All are important components of a good library instruction program, but they are really not interchangeable kinds of instruction.

From Ward (Ward 2010): "Information literacy instruction is definitely a shift in our thinking towards which we are still growing. I believe many of our colleagues have difficulty making this shift because what's required

FIGURE 9.1
How is Information Literacy Different from Bibliographic Instruction?

Bibliographic Instruction	Information Literacy
1. One-shot instruction	Integrated into the curriculum
2. Focuses on learning to use library resources	Focuses on information management
3. Often not linked to classroom assignments	Integral to course and assignments
4. Session often focus on passive learning	Active learning
5. May lack clearly defined goals & objectives	Goals & objectives are carefully linked to course
6. Librarian lectures, demonstrates	Librarian & faculty facilitate learning
7. Librarian provides instruction asked for	Librarian & faculty design and implement instruction

remains outside of their experience providing one-shot instruction. Librarians are frequently not well-positioned in the academy to participate meaningfully in the deep learning that information literacy requires."

Mullins also points out the shift in thinking that needs to take place and reports how that shift happened at Purdue: "The Purdue Librarians had an epiphany during a workshop... and that was, we should not be instructing only on how to find the right information using Libraries' resources to meet course requirements; rather the goal should be to prepare students to be able to address and approach a question or problem, define the question or problem, and determine the information resources needed, critique what they have found and integrate what they have located into their class work. The goal is not only to teach them about information resources, but to help them understand a process or methodology that can be applied time and time again, while at the University or later when they are working in their career or, more generally, in life." (Mullins 2010)

Several library leaders pointed out another challenge inherent in developing an information literacy program: Many librarians do not want to teach. One library leader noted "lackluster performance by those involved in teaching information literacy." Others noted the need to have a retirement or a move by a librarian to another position in order to be able to hire or promote those who wanted to teach and were interested in becoming good teachers. Mullins acknowledges both aspects of this problem: "Librarians are not trained as teachers, so they need help in developing lesson plans and classroom skills. We have done some of this but we need to do more." Mullins also reports a conversation with a librarian who said, "if I had wanted to be in the classroom I would have chosen teaching as a field, I chose librarianship so I wouldn't have to be in the classroom...." He then goes on to comment, "that may have been possible in the past, but that is not likely or desirable today." (Mullins 2010)

Assuming New Roles

Given that librarians have not always been provided with learning opportunities to become good teachers, and that there is perhaps even some resistance to assuming that role, it is incumbent upon library leaders to provide some degree of teacher training plus time for librarians to become comfortable in the classroom setting. One library leader commented that "[l]ibrarians must be seen as faculty with instructional goals just as classroom faculty are seen." Another noted the "inability of some librarians to adapt their instruction to new modes of delivery..." and went on to point out that "...[d]eveloping new courses or new ways to instruct takes time and it can be challenging for many to find that time." Identifying the resources to support library teachers can also be problematic. Though many campuses provide teaching centers or support for pedagogical development, if librarians are not perceived of as teachers it is often difficult to obtain that support. Additionally, as noted by one library leader, "library constituents just don't think of us as educators...." So, both identifying ways to acquire teaching skills and being seen as campus teachers are two sides of the same issue.

But it goes even further. Referring again to Dane Ward's table of the differences between bibliographic instruction and information literacy instruction, there are additional challenges for the teaching librarian. Ward notes that "Librarian & faculty design and implement instruction" (Ward 1997) in information literacy instruction; I believe such collaboration is often alien to us as librarians. There is also implicit the notion that ultimately we librarians may not "own" the instruction that is taking place but have instead served as consultants to a faculty member and have then turned over the actual instruction to that faculty member. Mullins goes so far as to point out that it wouldn't be feasible to expect librarians to provide all information literacy instruction: "We are clear in understanding that librarians will not do all of the information literacy, that our goal is to teach the fundamentals of information literacy and to help faculty incorporate the principles in their courses, not requiring that a librarian instruct in each class (it wouldn't be feasible)." He further notes that "... the only way a strong information literacy program can survive and be totally integrated into the curriculum is by faculty acceptance, adoption, and integration into the courses. Libraries faculty/librarians will be the advocates, the experts in new methodologies and resources for the integration of information into assignments and projects." (Mullins 2010) This may mean not only giving up our instructional opportunities to others, but also confronting our campus faculty members about the inadequacies of assignments that theoretically demonstrate student information literacy. One library leader points out, "Faculty assignments are the drivers of information literacy and engagement in the literature of specific disciplines." We may be placed in the awkward position of having to confront a faculty colleague about an assignment that does NOT appropriately demonstrate student understanding of information literacy concepts. And though a challenging role for many librarians, Mullins also notes that the positive is "a greater recognition of the librarians as faculty colleagues through the work they are doing in information literacy." (Mullins 2010) But though we may be very excited to be viewed as a partner in the teaching enterprise, there can be some uneasiness with this role.

ASSESSMENT

As librarians have implemented information literacy programs on our campuses, we have been faced with the challenges of assessing the success of those programs. Both the ETS iCritical Thinking™ Certification examination (ETS 2010) and Project SAILS ® (Standardized Assessment of Information Literacy Skills) (Project SAILS 2010) provide standardized tests for assessing student information literacy skills. [Disclosure: I worked briefly with the Project SAILS ® people at Kent State University as the instrument was developed and tested.] Both instruments have been adopted at a number of institutions throughout the United States and mechanisms for assessing information literacy skills in student populations. Both instruments have been tested extensively and can serve to inform a campus about programmatic successes. Both instruments have also served as models for new assessment tools that have been developed and implemented at individual campuses.

Where we have been less successful, in my view, is in assessing student learning outcomes in courses that have information literacy components integrated into them. We still struggle with how we will know that our instruction has been effective and has resulted in student learning or changed behaviors. Too often, librarians rely on what one library leader characterized as the "we get invited back" method of assessment: We really don't know whether students learned anything but we keep getting asked to repeat the instruction so we must be doing something right. Instead of relying on invitations as a method of assessment, we instead "need to focus on improving student outcomes (freshman to sophomore persistence, graduation, improved grades)...." Demonstrating cause and effect will be challenging, but without the attempt to do so we will have difficulty persuading campus administrators of the need for or value of our programs.

One library leader discussed a proposed assessment program where First Year Seminars might be used as a mechanism for establishing baseline understanding of student information literacy skills. This would be followed by assessment within senior seminars, thus providing a way to determine whether information literacy skills have been accumulated throughout a student's academic career.

Mullins points to a possible assessment project at Purdue that would focus on at-risk students, to test "the impact that information literacy could have (and this is what we will be testing) in leveling the playing field for students who attended rural or inner city schools and may have a decent GPA but didn't have access to the kind of information resources that students in more affluent communities might have had, and are, therefore, at a disadvantage in locating resources in support of papers and other projects they may be working in during their first year at Purdue, and consequently may be more likely to drop out of Purdue." (Mullins 2010) This is the kind of assessment program that could provide many of us with ways of approaching campus administrators with a tool that would not only demonstrate the library's value to the institution but also might help a group of students that are in need of additional assistance.

There are instruments available to us, and there are programmatic assessments that are being used or implemented that will provide us with ways of knowing how successful we are with information literacy instruction. But we must always be looking for ways to not only be involved with courses but to also influence the learning objectives of those courses, and to contribute to the design of assignments that contain information literacy components. One library leader pointed out that "there is also a reluctance at many institutions on the part of faculty to collaborate with librarians in designing courses and assignments." As we work to change that mindset, we must also look for all possible ways to demonstrate that information literacy skills are a key component of student success and that we can contribute to student learning by being involved with teaching those skills.

As library administrators, we are increasingly being asked to demonstrate to our campuses that we add value to the academic enterprise. We are no longer able to count things—acquisitions, door counts, questions answered, classes taught, etc.—and the point to these things as reasons why the library adds value. Instead we need to recognize that impact on teaching, on learning, on research, on funding are measures that are valued. Demonstrating the value of information literacy is challenging and will continue to be challenging, but it is something we must do if we are to see broad campus support for this initiative.

BROAD SUPPORT FOR INFORMATION LITERACY

In my conversations with library leaders about information literacy on their campuses, I was pleased but also surprised to hear how many find this initiative to be compelling and important for their institutions. Approximately half of those with whom I talked indicated that information literacy is definitely the number one priority for their library, and the remainder recognized it has having a significant place in the programs and services they were offering. My surprise was that even half of them considered this to be the primary priority! I had expected more of them to reflect the reality of one library leader who noted that information literacy was but one of many important initiatives, and that the primary challenge to it being higher on the list is a lack of clear understanding of how important it is to our campuses. But for many information literacy is unequivocally the highest possible priority, and it is definitely on the list for the rest and seems destined to stay there for the foreseeable future.

In addition to the commitment by librarians, it is important to acknowledge the support of a variety of organizations and individuals that individually and collectively have supported libraries and librarians in developing new information literacy initiatives and have provided an astonishing array of materials, people and programs that explain and advocate for information literacy programs. The list of organizations focused on information literacy efforts, and of individuals who have made information literacy their life work, is extensive and has resulted in new ways for librarians to understand both broad programmatic issues and more narrowly focused discipline-specific implementations. Support for discipline-specific guidelines has been notable and the guidelines developed have been embraced formally and informally by a variety of professional organizations. It is the support and advocacy of these organizations and people that has made information literacy what it currently is. Though I do have concerns and frustrations about how things have evolved and are evolving, I also feel that the broad support for this initiative has been key component to its growth and evolution and will be critical as we look forward to the next decade of information literacy.

LOOKING AHEAD—THREATS AND OPPORTUNITIES

Information literacy is now entering its third decade, and I see opportunities available to us that outweigh the threats that we must overcome. One campus leader suggested that we are perhaps even entering into the golden era of information literacy, where a broad understanding of the skills needed to be successful as a student or a teacher or a researcher are recognized as a component of library services and programs and are valued by campus administrators as a way to help ensure the success of a variety of initiatives across our institutions.

There is some evidence that the rather narrow definition of information literacy is being changed at the institutional level and that those changes will perhaps result in adjustments to the official definitions. There are indications that new definitions might include not only information literacy but also technology fluency, writing skills, familiarity with a variety of new media tools, and other skills beyond the somewhat narrowly-defined information literacy component. And with new definitions come new opportunities to collaborate with others on our campuses and expand our reach and our influence even further.

Increasingly, there is a sense of the information literacy initiative taking hold on campuses, with the implementation of programs spanning a broad continuum from early development to full-fledged integration into the curriculum. There is also a sense that the technology will increasingly serve us well as we look to scale programs and make them available to all students on our campuses, regardless of size.

As a profession we have done a remarkable job in embracing pedagogy and becoming very effective teachers. Today, librarians not only provide support for learning on our campus but in some cases provide leadership for learning how to be good teachers. Our skills as teachers will be critical as we become more integrated into courses and curricula at our campuses. We are increasingly comfortable with new and different roles that take us beyond our traditions and into new areas on campus and within disciplines. And we are broadly looking for ways to provide our campus leaders with ways to understand our value to the academic community that will result in increased assessment of all areas of our operations, including information literacy instruction and programs.

(There is one critical area where I believe we should either recognize failure and move on, or acknowledge that it should never have been part of the discourse of information literacy, and that is in promoting the aspect of information literacy that results in an informed citizenry. We have generally acknowledged that the need to promote information literacy goes well beyond teaching our constituents how to use library resources, and when we discuss information literacy we include references to helping to develop an informed citizenry. Whether there is a valid theoretical underpinning to that aspect of information literacy remains a question (O'Connor 2009) and whether we have had any successes in including this in our information literacy instruction or programs is suspect. Even if we can find a rationale for thinking that creating an informed citizenry, the existing mechanisms for doing this seem to be no different from those we use to teach database access, so too often focused on immediate skills acquisition and less on the transference aspects of information literacy skills. I tend to take personally the inability of my fellow citizens—particularly those young enough to have likely received some kind of information literacy instruction—to be analytical and discerning in, for example, discussions of the current economic situation. Based on the how uninformed our citizenry seems to be I have to think that we as librarians have been less than successful in helping to create an informed citizenry and should perhaps admit that it is outside of both our purview and our ability to accomplish and to remove this component from our discussions and definitions. But this is a certainly more of a personal quibble and not one that has been reflected in my conversations with other library administrators.)

Looking ahead specifically at the role of library administrators, and using the words from conversations, discussions and interviews with library leaders, we will continue to need to "sell" our services to our campuses and make campus leaders understand "that our students need to graduate with effective information literacy skills if they are to be effective in their careers and as informed citizens. Librarians are the best professionals on campus to help students develop this expertise." We will continue to need to help our institutions develop ways to assess information literacy skills, and if and when a deficiency is identified, we must be prepared to provide solutions. We will need to recognize even more the mandate to provide a variety of ways for students to acquire needed skills and to create "a dynamic suite of library and related academic services that students can access at point and time of need." We will need to be "visionaries and advocates for information literacy, seeking every opportunity to make it more central on our campuses. We also need to make it central in our libraries and devote the necessary resources to it." We need to "keep this on the agenda and allocate resources." We will need to "educate and market, and not just to faculty but to students and to the administration." At some institutions we will also need to educate and market information literacy *within* the library and "make sure all working there are on board and understand it." This may require a culture change and if so, as library leaders we will need to make sure that this culture change happens. We must provide the mechanism for library personnel to acquire new skills. We must communicate our commitment to change and to new roles for the library in the life of the campus. We must look for ways to be innovative in how we interact with our colleagues. But most importantly, we must look for our own "perfect storms" and take advantage of the events on our campuses that allow us to put forward the library as a leader in providing student support.

As noted, one library leader posited that the information literacy movement is just now coming into its own. If that is the case, and I agree that it may be, perhaps a call to action is warranted. What is it that library administrators must do now to make sure that our information literacy initiatives continue to survive and thrive? What can we draw from the Purdue experience that will have relevance for our own institutions? Based on my conversations, my experiences, let me suggest the following. This is a personal list, surely not comprehensive, but one that I hope will generate additional discussion and more ideas of how library administrators can support information literacy initiatives. It is a two-part list with the first part being a reflection of what I feel that we, the library community, can and must address—so actions that are internal to the library. The second part consists of my thoughts of what we must hope that others in our communities will be recognize as their responsibilities—so actions that are external to the library.

We, the broad library community, must:

- Provide appropriate levels of leadership, serving as visible and persuasive advocates for our campus information literacy initiatives.
- Recognize that as collections budgets are increasingly stretched and we are no longer able to be valued primarily because of our spending power and collections sizes we should shift some of the focus to what we can do to support student learning.
- Provide appropriate levels of support, tools, resources and training to ensure the success of our information literacy programs.
- Shift emphasis away from providing building-based services to providing classroom-based services.

- Shift the cultures of our libraries toward teaching and outreach to our campuses.
- Experiment, recognize successes, be willing to fail, but always look for ways to innovate in how we support the instructional mission of our campus communities.
- Accept the notion that good information literacy instruction may have nothing to do with knowing how to use library resources, but may instead focus on skills needed to find a job in a new city, buy a car, or plan a spring break trip.
- Value all aspects of excellent customer service, creating an environment in which our users value all of the services that we provide for them.
- Recognize which aspects of student learning the library "owns" and which are "owned" by faculty members, but be willing to recognize when it is time to give up some of our ownership or to blur the dividing lines.
- Reassure librarians that sharing information literacy responsibilities with faculty members is a positive (and perhaps necessary) aspect of a program and something that will return numerous benefits both in terms of improved student learning and better instruction.

What we cannot be completely responsible for, and what we must look for in the broader academic community, includes:

- Graduate students, their role as future faculty, and recognition of how critical they will be to future successes of our information literacy programs.
- Campus administrators' interest in the library's impact on student learning rather than in our ability to make students feel welcome on our campuses, though we must still strive to maintain our personal connections with our constituents.
- Different ways that learners learn and the increasingly-important role of instructional design principles.
- Partnerships with those who are preparing students for our colleges and universities, and instilling good information habits in younger students, before they have established bad and/or traditional library habits.

- Senior faculty members who often have more flexibility and less to lose than junior faculty and may be better information literacy partners for us.
- Expectations of the library differ from campus to campus, and understanding how faculty members and administrators view our libraries is critical to developing a successful information literacy initiative.
- Schools of library and information science that will prepare graduates for their roles as teaching librarians or a "blended" librarians, with an accompanying expectation that our librarians will have teaching excellence (not just teaching, but excellent teaching) as a component of their professional portfolios.
- Campus champions from outside the library who will help us to differently articulate the need for campus information literacy initiatives.
- Collaborations with anyone on our campuses who is willing to collaborate, and using the varied skills of our campus partners to enhance our initiatives.

And though we can hope for support from the broader campus community it is ultimately us as library leaders, who are responsible for the success of information literacy initiatives on our campuses.

We must also look to the research being conducted by our colleagues, and both learn from that research and act on suggested ideas for additional research. Using but one example of such research, Gilchrist's 2007 dissertation, *Academic Libraries at the Center of Instructional Change: Faculty and Librarian Experience of Library Leadership in the Transformation of Teaching and Learning* (Gilchrist 2007) provides both insights into some of the challenges we face as we implement information literacy programs and affirmations of what we are doing well and where we can look to improve, but also offers some of the opportunities for further investigation. Gilchrist's work is by no means unique, but does provide a recent example of the quality of information literacy research that is being conducted and the additional questions that need to be asked as we proceed with this initiative.

As I think about my concerns and reflect on the role of information literacy in academic libraries today, on where the movement has come from and where it seems to be going, I think that may be correct. As I think about my disappointments and frustrations they seem to be rooted in impatience. I am convinced that we do have a critical role to play in supporting the students at our institutions but am concerned that we have not been as effective as we need to be either in claiming that role or in making our campus leaders understand and recognize that role. The amount of information available to students, faculty and researchers will continue to grow exponentially, and the role that we must play in helping our users find, evaluate, manage and use that information, regardless of format, will be increasingly important. So perhaps the third decade will be the decade when libraries and information literacy initiatives become synonymous and there will be a widespread recognition that we are "not only preparing students for their classes but for their future place in society."

ACKNOWLEDGEMENTS

The remarks from library leaders came from twenty nine colleagues who are University Librarians or Deans or Directors of college or university libraries. During the past year I had structured conversations about information literacy issues with a number of them. In addition, I used an electronic survey to generate additional discussion. The majority of those who talked with me agreed to the discussions and to greater candor on the condition of anonymity. However, several library leaders did agree to my using their names. Though I have anonymized all of the comments, I would like to acknowledge the following library leaders for their participation:

- Nancy Baker, University of Iowa, Iowa City, IA
- Sylverna Ford, University of Memphis, Memphis, TN
- Jill Gremmels, Davidson College, Davidson, NC
- Bonnie MacEwan, Auburn University, Auburn, AL
- Michelle L. Young, Clarkson University, Potsdam, NY

I would also like to thank the others who spent time talking, emailing and discussing, and for their honesty in sharing both the successes and failures they have seen with the information literacy programs at their institutions.

Special thanks are due to James Mullins, Purdue University, West Lafayette, IN. Jim has been exceedingly generous with his time and his viewpoints, and I appreciate having the opportunity to learn more about an information literacy program that must be considered one of the most successful in the United States.

References

ACRL/IRIG. 2010. Working definition of visual literacy—ACRL/IRIG Visual Literacy Standards. http://acrlvislitstandards.wordpress.com/2010/08/06/working-definition-of-visual-literacy.

Alire, Camila. 2010. ALA | ALA, President Dr. Camila Alire launch Family Literacy Focus. www.ala.org/ala/newspresscenter/news/pressreleases2010/january2010/alire_ols.cfm.

American Library Association. 1989. Presidential Committee on Information Literacy. www.ala.org/ala/mgrps/divs/acrl/publications/whitepapers/presidential.cfm.

Association of College and Research Libraries. 2000. ACRL | Information Literacy Competency Standards for Higher Education. www.ala.org/acrl/standards/informationliteracycompetency.

Bell, Steven, and John Shank. 2004. The Blended Librarian. http://blendedlibrarian.org/index.html.

Consortium for Media Literacy. 2010. Center for Media Literacy. www.medialit.org.

Curzon, Susan. 2007. *Proven strategies for building an information literacy program.* New York: Neal-Schuman Publishers.

ETS. 2010. iCritical Thinking: About the Product. www.ets.org/icriticalthinking/about.

Gilchrist, Deborah. 2007. *Academic Libraries at the Center of Instructional Change: Faculty and Librarian Experience of Library Leadership in the Transformation of Teaching and Learning.*

Hager, Mark J., and Raechelle Clemmons. 2010. "Faculty and IT: Conversations and Collaboration." *EDUCAUSE Review* 45 (2) (April): 58-59.

Mullins, James. 2010. Information Literacy—3d decade—questions. September 22, 2010.

New Media Literacies Research Group. 2010. New Media Literacies. www.newmedialiteracies.org/the-literacies.php.

O'Connor, Lisa. 2009. "Information Literacy as Professional Legitimation: A Critical Analysis." *Journal of Education for Library and Information Science* 50 (2): 79-89.

Project SAILS. 2010. Project SAILS—Standardized Assessment of Information Literacy Skills. https://www.projectsails.org/index.php?page=home.

Seamans, Nancy. 2001. Information literacy: a study of freshman students' perceptions, with recommendations. Blacksburg, VA: Virginia Tech.

http://scholar.lib.vt.edu/theses/available/etd-05142001-104550.

Wales, Jimmy. 2010. "Tech therapy—Episode 72: Wikipedia's Co-Founder Calls for Better Information Literacy." *The Chronicle of Higher Education,* June 9. http://chronicle.com/article/Audio-Wikipedias-Co-Founder/65841.

Ward, Dane. 1997. "How is Information Literacy Different from Bibliographic Instruction?" *LOEX News* 24 (4 (Winter 1997)): 9.

———. 2010. Personal communication. August 3.

Zionts, Nancy, Jan Apter, Julianna Kuchta, and Pamela Greenhouse. 2010. "Promoting Consumer Health Literacy: Creation of a Health Information Librarian Fellowship." *Reference & User Services Quarterly* 49 (4): 35-359.

About the Authors

Courtney Bruch is a Reference/Instruction Librarian at Front Range Community College where she currently works with students, faculty and library staff to build a comprehensive library instruction program. She is a graduate of both ACRL's Immersion Tracks for Program and Assessment.

Jo Ann Carr is Director Emerita from the University of Wisconsin Madison School of Education Media, Education Resources, and Information Technology (MERIT). Her areas of research and study include curriculum libraries, integration of library and information technology services, and information literacy throughout the PK-lifetime.

April D. Cunningham has been the Library Instruction Coordinator at Saddleback College in Southern California since 2005. In pursuit of her Ed.D. in Educational Leadership, she is currently researching the constraints and supports that influence the contributions community college librarians can make to student learning.

Carrie Donovan is Head of Teaching & Learning for the Indiana University Libraries, where she works with students, faculty, and instructors to connect the Libraries to student learning. With more than ten years of experience providing information literacy instruction to a diverse university community, Carrie is committed to ensuring the relevance of libraries and librarians through educational initiatives and teaching partnerships.

James Elmborg is associate professor in the School of Library and Information Science at The University of Iowa where he has been since 2000. Before joining the faculty at Iowa, he was an academic librarian specializing in information literacy and information technology, first at Washington State University, Pullman and then in South Carolina at Furman University and Wofford College. He has a Ph.D. in English from the University of Kansas, where he taught for ten years before becoming a librarian.

Noël Kopriva is the Agriculture, Natural Resources, and Design Librarian and Instruction Coordinator for Evansdale Library at West Virginia University.

Michelle Millet is the Head of Research Services at the University of Texas at San Antonio where she leads a department of instruction librarians, building an information literacy program at a emerging research institution. She previous directed a campus wide information literacy program at Trinity University and is currently a member of the ACRL Institute for Information Literacy Immersion faculty.

Robert Schroeder is a reference and instruction librarian at Portland State University. He liaisons to both the Edcuation and University Studies departments, and coordinates the library's general education program. He is also an instructor in the School of Library and Information Management at Emporia State University, where he teaches a Reference and User Services class to their Portland cohort. His current areas of research include the role of affect in library instruction and new models of scholarly publishing. He can be reached at schroedr@pdx.edu.

Nancy H. Seamans is a former instruction librarian who is currently Dean of Libraries at Georgia State University.

Celene Seymour is director of Marshall University's South Charleston Library and coordinator of the university's school library media program to prepare K-12 librarians. She sees the need for and challenges of providing information literacy instruction as a common concern for librarians from elementary through graduate school. Dr. Seymour has an MLS and Ph.D. in English, focused on rhetoric and linguistics, and has been an academic librarian for 24 years.

Carroll Wetzel Wilkinson has been the Director of Instruction and Information Literacy at West Virginia University Libraries and has directed a university-wide information literacy course enhancement project for three years. She is a graduate of Wells College in Aurora, New York; the Rutgers University MLS program; and ACRL's Immersion Tracks for Program and Assessment.

Anne E. Zald is Head of the Instruction Department, University of Nevada Las Vegas Libraries and previously held positions in the libraries at the University of Washington, Oberlin College, and Wayne State University. Since 1999 Anne has served as a faculty member for ACRL's Immersion programs which provide professional development for academic librarians in the areas of instruction and managing instruction programs. Anne attended Oberlin College and the University of Michigan (AMLS).

Index